SUSPENDED
APOCALYPSE

Also by Dylan Rodríguez

Forced Passages:
Imprisoned Radical Intellectuals
and the U.S. Prison Regime

SUSPENDED APOCALYPSE

White Supremacy, Genocide,
and the Filipino Condition

DYLAN RODRÍGUEZ

University of Minnesota Press
Minneapolis • London

An early version of chapter 3 was published as " 'A Million Deaths?': Genocide and the Subject of Filipino American Studies," in *Positively No Filipinos Allowed: Building Communities and Discourse*, ed. Antonio T. Tiongson Jr., Edgardo V. Gutierrez, and Ricardo V. Gutierrez (Philadelphia: Temple University Press, 2006), 145–61.

Published by the University of Minnesota Press
111 Third Avenue South, Suite 290
Minneapolis, MN 55401-2520
http://www.upress.umn.edu

Library of Congress Cataloging-in-Publication Data

Rodriguez, Dylan.
    Suspended apocalypse : white supremacy, genocide, and the Filipino condition / Dylan Rodriguez.
        p. cm.
    Includes bibliographical references and index.
    ISBN 978-0-8166-5349-2 (hc : alk. paper) – ISBN 978-0-8166-5350-8 (pb : alk. paper)
        1. United States – Relations – Philippines. 2. Philippines – Relations – United States. 3. Genocide – Philippines. 4. Racism – United States. 5. Filipinos – Social conditions. I. Title.
    E183.8.P5R64 2010
    305.800973 – dc22

                                                                            2009033093

Printed in the United States of America on acid-free paper

The University of Minnesota is an equal-opportunity educator and employer.

16   15   14   13   12   11   10   10   9   8   7   6   5   4   3   2   1

Contents

Acknowledgments

This book has been shaped by multiple political influences and interventions, the most important of which have been the people who have challenged, nourished, and productively disrupted my thinking on the historical present of white supremacist genocide and its layered production of the Filipino (and thus my own) condition. Of course, these influences and interventions are unquantifiable and are as often accidental and unexpected as they are deliberate and intentional. I am humbled by the simple fact that an immediate and extended family, as well as a cherished political–intellectual community, has unconditionally backed me in my effort to participate in a knowledge production that engages the historical state of emergency in which we are collectively located. The work of identifying and radically confronting the political structures that compose us as people subjected to — and who are thus also the troubled subjects of — the ongoing U.S. nation-building project is not an individual labor, and so I hope that anything decent and useful in these pages will be taken as a reflection of everything beautiful and inspired about the people I list here.

There are people whose impact on this book has been fundamental. Rick Bonus, Oscar Campomanes, Jodi Kim, Martin Manalansan, Jared Sexton, Andy Smith, and Tony (Kuya Ton) Tiongson Jr. provided substantive critique, insight, and encouragement of different aspects of the project; they have imprinted my thinking in crucial ways. I am especially indebted to Kuya Ton (and his coeditors Ed Gutierrez and Rick Gutierrez) for soliciting and publishing an early version of chapter 3 in the landmark anthology *Positively No Filipinos Allowed: Building Communities and Discourse,* published by Temple University Press in 2006. Vorris Nunley, Michelle Raheja, Amalia Cabezas, Tammy Ho, Keith Harris, Traise Yamamoto, Erica Edwards, Mariam Lam, Jonathan Walton, Alessandro Fornazzari, Freya Schiwy, and others, friends with whom I share a day job at the University of California, Riverside, have formed an intellectual and political community that has kept me alive and, in important moments, thriving. My departmental colleagues Victoria Bomberry, Jayna Brown, Anthony Macias, Jennifer Najera, and Robert Perez, along with the aforementioned Jodi Kim, directly and indirectly facilitated my progress and are often the people on whom I rely for the most immediate and urgent institutional support. I am thankful for their presence in the Department of Ethnic Studies.

I often claim certain friends and scholars as a kind of extended political, intellectual, and affective family, and my central hope is that the "familial" bonds we form are radical, liberationist, and creative rather than conventional or parochial. Keith Camacho, Ruthie Gilmore, Jolie Chea, João Costa Vargas, Martha Escobar, Roberto Labrada, Gabby Ocon, Adrienne Hurley, Dio Mendoza (the brilliant artist), Viet Mike Ngo (who, after spending two decades in prison, must be released from his California cage), Raman Prasad, Vianey Ramirez, Sormeh Ayari, Randall Williams, Craig Gilmore, and others have shared many a meal, laughed at too many jokes, and provided me the backbone to move around in the world as I do. David Martinez, Amar Raheja, and Alfredo Cruz have been great interlocutors and fishing partners, and the mental clarity I attain in my time with them has been essential to the completion of this book.

I am grateful to Richard Morrison and Adam Brunner at the University of Minnesota Press for their patience, attention, and obvious commitment to this book. I cannot imagine a better publishing and editorial experience than the one I have had with them, and it is no accident that my first two books have been published through the University of Minnesota Press.

I would not have had either the courage or the capacity to complete this book without the guidance, unflinching support, and mentorship of Angela Davis, Arif Dirlik, Avery Gordon, Joy James, Lisa Lowe, Gary Okihiro, David Pellow, Laura Pulido, Beth Richie, David Roediger, Phil Scraton, Neferti Tadiar, and Ruthie Gilmore. James Turner's influence on my thinking is permanent, as is the model of intellectual seriousness embodied by Shelley Wong. Steve Cullenberg, the late Emory Elliott, Katherine Kinney, and Toby Miller have literally kept me at U.C. Riverside. Lucy Burns, Jody Blanco, Lisa Yoneyama, Tak Fujitani, Denise Ferreira da Silva, Lisa Park, David Leonard, and Jim Lee generously listened to my ideas, and each convinced me that my labor is part of something larger, collective, and historical.

I must give special thanks to the organizers of and participants in two unmatched political–intellectual and scholar activist events during the spring of 2008: "Philippine Palimpsests: Filipino Studies in the Twenty-first Century" at the University of Illinois and "From the Plantation to the Prison: Imprisonment and U.S. Culture" at Yale University. Augusto Espiritu, Lisa Cacho, and Martin Manalansan organized "Philippine Palimpsests," which was a historically unprecedented gathering of U.S.-based Filipino scholars. Reynaldo Ileto, Kimberly Alidio, Richard Chu, Julian Go, Linda Maram, Nerissa Balce, Victor Bascara, Francisco (Kiko) Benitez, Jody Blanco, Lucy Burns, Denise Cruz, Kale Fajardo, Theo Gonzalves, Victor Mendoza, Martin Joseph Ponce, Jeffrey Santa Ana, Sarita See, Alan Isaac, Rick Baldoz, Anna Guevarra, Emily Ignacio, Dina Maramba, Robyn Rodriguez, Neferti Tadiar, Benito (Sunny) Vergara, Rick Bonus, Genevieve Clutario, and Constancio Arnaldo produced a rich, dense, and catalyzing body of dialogue. The work of David Stein, Sarah Haley, Naomi Paik, and others involved with Yale's Marxist and Cultural Theory Working Group resulted in my invitation to "From the Plantation to the Prison," and their thoughtful responses to chapter 5 of this book were both affirming and enlightening. Fellow panelists Ruthie Gilmore and Colin Dayan, along with roundtable participants Hazel Carby, Michael Denning, Lisa Lowe, and Caleb Smith, formed a community of thinkers of which I was utterly humbled to be a part. Their critical affirmations helped assure me that this project was worthwhile, and I hope the contents of this book do not disappoint them. A visit to the Philippines in December 2006 was fundamental to my revision and conceptual rethinking of this book during a formative time of writing and political work. I am deeply indebted to Oscar Campomanes and the following colleagues, each of whom played a distinct role in ensuring that my visits to Ateneo de Manila University, University of Santo Tomas, and University of the Philippines were rich with critical conversation, debate, and dense theoretical labor. Gary Devilles at Ateneo, Floro Quibuyen at UP, Ferdie Lopez of the UST Filipino American Writers and Scholars Lecture Series, Lito Zulueta of the *Philippine Daily Inquirer* and the *UST Varsitarian,* Jack Wigley of UST Press, and Delan Robillos and Jae Jalandoni Robillos of Artery Manila are gracious and generous people to whom I am thankful.

Certain graduate students helped me think through aspects of this book, in the form of intensive conversations, organized campus lectures and colloquia, and knowledge shared over a good meal. Michael (Miget) Bevacqua, Alfred Flores, Tami Nopper, Tasneem Siddiqui, Dean Saranillo, Damien Schnyder, Jewels Smith, and Gina Velasco, along with Jolie Chea and Martha Escobar, set a standard for critical acumen and intellectual integrity. I eagerly anticipate the completion and publication of their projects, which are both vital and original. Maita Sayo and R. C. Cruz, under the leadership of Oscar Campomanes, facilitated my December 2006 visits to the University of Santo Tomas and Ateneo de Manila University in the Philippines. Maita's incisive responses to my public lectures, along with R.C.'s effective organization of multiple events, helped make the visit extraordinary. The critical exchanges and spirited debates that took place during and after these campus events helped hone the theoretical framework of this book.

Working with undergraduate students at U.C. Riverside often breathes life, joy, and productive rage into a place that can be stifling, reactionary, and provincial. I mention here only a few of the students (many of whom are now graduate students) who kept me alive during my seven years at the campus: Damon Cagnolatti, Arlene Cano, Juan Correa, Diana Flores, Alex Garcia, Min-Ling Li, Holly Lim, Jose Lopez, Lorena Macias, Julio Paz, Jocelyn Romero, Senna Servati, Carla Villanueva, Kenneth Lebleu, Jocelyn Wong, and Azi Zohrabi. They enlivened me intellectually and emotionally, while David Vu and Lanna Chau helped keep my (physical) spine as strong as possible.

"Personal" political genealogies, as mapped by such book acknowledgments, are inevitably constituted by familial and biological genealogies. Elenita Culla, Amalia Bantigue, Anthony (Oni) Rodriguez (brother), Realista Rodriguez (mom), Edgardo Rodriguez (dad), Yumi Belanga (sister), Tita Chay Rodriguez, Tito Raul Rodriguez, Tita Mila Tubice, Carlo Tubice, Chari Arespacochaga, Derick Garcia, and Ninong Walden Bello are part of this work (whether they like it or not!). Oni, in particular, provides both a nuanced intellect and a sharp wit that command the best of my writing and thinking.

Finally, my lovely wife and best friend, Setsu Shigematsu, is the most generous, loving, and supportive person I know. She has to deal with me every day, so aside from her scholarly brilliance and political courage, she just might be an earthly deity. My son, Viet Taer Rodríguez Shigematsu, and daughter, Sayaka Encarnación Rodríguez Shigematsu, inspire me to write with urgency, conviction, and loving rage. I hope they will be proud of me for the right reasons.

Filipino American Communion

Cultural Alienation and the Conditions of Community

> There are many persons in this struggle of the colonies
> against colonialism who up till now are still struggling
> merely for unity. Because, as they are unable to wage
> the struggle, they confuse unity with struggle.
>
> — Amilcar Cabral, *Unity and Struggle*

The Racial Analytics of the Filipino Condition

White supremacy and racist genocide are the mobilized global
logics of U.S. nation building and have irrevocably constituted
the Filipino condition in excess of localized or temporally discrete military and state practices. *Suspended Apocalypse* is a
reflection on the genealogy of the Filipino condition in relation
to the durable global structures of American white supremacist
statecraft and regimes of U.S.-mediated racist state violence more
generally, within and beyond the political and cultural geographies of warfare, colonialist conquest, and genocide. In the
following pages, I offer a conceptual and theoretical accounting
of the historical architectures of the Filipino condition — including that of its resident community and identity formations — that
rethinks the technologies of race and its corresponding statecraft

1

of violence as the essential assemblages of an unrecognized genealogy.

In proximity to the multiculturalist formation of "Filipino American" discourse, including its academic variants, I initiate this project from a perhaps peculiar, and significantly polemical position that for some will be entirely acceptable and reasonable: that there is not, and there really cannot exist a Filipino or "Filipino American" subject, or collective identity, in even the most temporarily coherent — much less momentarily stable or authenticated — sense of community and identity. By way of clarification, I am not suggesting that self-identified Filipino Americans have somehow "failed" to convene and materialize a social presence on which everyday galvanizations of biographical experience, rationalized or contrived political interest, and geographic affinity rest.[1] In such organizational and cultural mobilizations, Filipino Americans have been successful to such an extent that the 1990s yielded a veritable renaissance of Filipino Americanisms across professions, discursive fields, and cultural forms. (I will more closely examine the significance of this period of discursive–political production in chapter 2.) While *Suspended Apocalypse* explicitly addresses — and thus relies on — an archive of popular cultural, scholarly, and journalistic production anchored in the "Filipino American" rubric as its central point of conceptual and methodological departure, this book also attempts a conceptual disarticulation of Filipino Americanism through a theoretical centering of its vexed conditions of possibility. I argue that the historically particular and absolutely unique common sense on which Filipino American social identity rests, and thus the commonly accessed philosophical structures, popular cultural productions, and political assumptions on which Filipino American existence — and "community" — relies, fundamentally cannot survive a critical scrutiny that takes seriously the ongoing symbiosis of two epochal historical developments: (1) the elaboration of militarized white supremacy as the central social formation and political logic of "race" in the U.S. national formation, and (2) the constitution of an American liberal sensibility, governmentality, and contemporary multiculturalist social intercourse in and through the material historical arrangements — and indelible traces — of genocidal state violence (a political–theoretical problem that I will more rigorously elaborate in chapters 3 and 4).

Thus, rather than remaining thematically or conceptually anchored to a coherent notion of "Filipino" or "Filipino American" identity, community, or subjectivity, this book involves a critical theoretical engagement with the historical and political conditions through which Filipinos are subsumed by, relate to, and materially convene in the ongoing global projects of U.S. national formation. I am especially concerned with the fundamental and determining function of "race" as a structure of dominance[2] in the production of the Filipino global condition, in the contemporary and long historical sense. An interdisciplinary, critical race studies approach to this Filipino "race" problematic, I contend, requires a sustained conceptualization and theorization of the lineage of the Filipino relation to U.S. (global) white supremacist statecraft, and to regimes of U.S.-mediated racist state violence generally, including and beyond the political and cultural geographies of American racial genocides (chapter 5 will extrapolate this argument as the book's final point of departure). By extension, this book meditates on the troubled articulation between Filipino community and identity formations (including "diasporic" renditions) and this genealogy of racial/racist discourse and violence. Polemically, *Suspended Apocalypse* challenges the received wisdom (the "Filipino American common sense" I discuss in the next chapter) that there is nothing organically "racial" (or "racist") about Philippine social formation and Filipino/Filipino American subjectivity. Analytically, this book also challenges the common understanding that the political identities, cultural productions, and violences enacted by Filipinos under the rubric of race generally derive from the external influences of U.S. cultural and political hegemony in the Philippines. The following pages are therefore engaged in a critical displacement and productive disarticulation of a Filipino racial common sense that misconceives race, racism, and raciality as fundamentally "American" (or even Spanish) productions or political artifacts, and that theoretically locates race outside the primary social forms and fundamental axes of sociohistorical determination that materially produce the Filipino condition, including in moments of relative "national" autonomy.

Suspended Apocalypse argues that the ontological condition of possibility for contemporary Filipino and Filipino American subjectivities — including projects of community and cultural integrity — is formed by the historical technologies and institutional architectures of global white supremacy, and that these technologies and architectures inscribe Filipino social materialities across the historical moments, cultural geographies, and political projects of U.S. nation building. My argument is enabled in this trajectory by Denise Ferreira da Silva's charting of the "analytics of raciality" in her landmark text *Toward a Global Idea of Race*. Specifically, her examination of the "first moment" of the analytics of raciality — instituted by post-Enlightenment Europe's epistemological turn toward scientific reason — coincides with the critical project I am initiating here. According to Silva, the episteme of race decisively transformed in and through the hegemony (and violent domination) of Eurocentric scientific rationality, which shifted the discursive regimes of race and "the racial" to produce "bodies and social configurations as signifiers — expressions and actualizations, respectively — of two kinds of minds."[3] It is my contention that Filipinos, no less than other racially formed collectivities impacted by the practices of conquest, colonization, and global dominance, sit squarely within the structuring anxiety that continues to be produced through the juxtaposition of these "two kinds of minds." Hence, the ongoing dilemma of Filipino subjectivity — arguably most acute in the cultural productions and identity projects of Filipino Americanism — is the assumptive (global) social requirement of an adequate civil subjectivity: that is, one that simultaneously redeems the Filipino from the accompanying pathologies and inadequacies of a particular legacy of subjection to others, and exhibits (performs, proves) competence to assume the alleged responsibilities of self-governance. Silva concisely outlines the dichotomy of minds generated in this first moment in the analytics of raciality in a manner that helps to make sense of the Filipino ontological condition that I am beginning to outline:

> Through the deployment of strategies of engulfment that always already assume that post-Enlightenment European (white) bodies and (civilized) social configurations are not submitted to the regulative and productive force of the universe, the science of mind produces . . . two kinds of minds, namely, (*a*) the *transparent I,* which emerged in post-enlightenment Europe, the kind of mind that is able to know, emulate, and control powers of universal reason, and (*b*) the *affectable "I,"* the one that emerged in other global regions, the kind of mind subjected to both the exterior determination of the "laws of nature" and the superior force of European minds.[4]

Filipino subjectivity, and Filipino Americanist articulations of the Filipino condition most especially, are deeply committed to proving the Filipino's immunity (and active, self-correcting resistance) to Silva's racial "affectability." This commitment, in turn, forms a guiding tension within the realms of cultural production, political mobilization, and collective identity construction in which Filipinos act out the complex desires of self-determination: in fact, for Filipinos, self-determination can *only be* an abstracted (and entirely unpragmatic) desire that is already overdetermined by massive cultural and material evidence of the external determinations of Filipino racial subjectivity. There is no "prior to" or "outside of" colonial dominance, genocidal conquest, and neocolonial rule for the putative Filipino subject, since its very moment of articulation reinscribes the coercions and massive fatalities underlying the historical processes of Philippine nation making.

This genealogy also suggests that the epistemological condition of Filipino and Filipino American subjectivities is articulated through a grammar of rationality, institutionality, and desire that is "nonracial" in most of its formal enunciations (e.g., rhetorics of Philippine independence, Filipino or Filipino American citizenship, nationalism, cultural identity, collective pride) but which is entirely constitutive of a modern racial analytic in which Filipinos are structurally expelled from the domains of Silva's "transparency" (the rational, autonomous, and self-determining "I" that the Filipino subject aspires to embody, but always cannot quite attain). This racial analytic constitutes and reproduces the disrupted self-articulation of racial and protoracial historicity that characterizes the most common self-narrations of the Filipino condition. Thus, the identifiable presence of racial significations in Filipino discourse and historical articulation are simultaneously sanitized and collapsed by a common (though no less strategic) critical *illiteracy* that radically undertheorizes, and generally misconceives, the overdetermination of the Filipino condition by the long symbiosis of overlapping technologies of race, violence, and global white supremacy.

It is within this discursive architecture of Filipino arrested raciality that we might prevail on a differently generative reading of Sen. Albert Beveridge's famous 1900 articulation of the white supremacist premises of American empire:

> The Philippines are ours forever, "territory belonging to the United States," as the Constitution calls them. . . . We will not repudiate our duty in the archipelago. . . . We will not renounce our part in the mission of our race, trustee, under God, of the civilization of the world. . . . He has marked us as His chosen people, henceforth to lead in the regeneration of the world. . . .
>
> [The Filipinos] are not capable of self-government. How could they be? They are not of a self-governing race. They are Orientals, Malays, instructed by Spaniards in the latter's worst estate.
>
> They know nothing of practical government except as they have witnessed the weak, corrupt, cruel, and capricious rule of Spain.

What magic will anyone employ to dissolve in their minds and characters those impressions of governors and governed which three centuries of misrule has created? What alchemy will change the Oriental quality of their blood and set the self-governing currents of the American pouring through their Malay veins? How shall they, in the twinkling of an eye, be exalted to the heights of self-governing peoples which required a thousand years for us to reach, Anglo-Saxon though we are?

Let men beware how they employ the term "self-government." It is a sacred term. It is the watchword at the door of the inner temple of liberty, for liberty does not always mean self-government. Self-government is a method of liberty — the highest, simplest, best — and it is acquired only after centuries of study and struggle and experiment and instruction and all the elements of the progress of man. Self-government is no base and common thing to be bestowed on the merely audacious. It is the degree which crowns the graduate of liberty, not the name of liberty's infant class, who have not yet mastered the alphabet of freedom. Savage blood, Oriental blood, Malay blood, Spanish example — are these the elements of self-government?[5]

While portions of Beveridge's speech are by now quite well known to both casual and professional students of the Filipino historical experience, the oration has generally been read as a discursive artifact of a demeaning racial past that has since been distanced from the contemporary formation of Filipino subjectivities. Beveridge's pronouncements are thus most frequently invoked in Filipino American discourses as the provocative opening shot in a telos of civil subjectivity that culminates with Filipinos vindicating themselves from the dehumanizing and insulting narratives of a racist U.S. state. The pedagogical punch line follows: Filipinos are *now* capable of self-rule, rational calculation, and functional (civilized) sociality, having decisively refuted Beveridge's evaluation that, "as a race, their general ability is not excellent. Educators, both men and women, to whom I have talked in Cebu and Luzon, were unanimous in the opinion that in all solid and useful education they are, as a people, dull and stupid."[6]

I would suggest, however, that Beveridge's discourse of Anglo-Saxon civilization — which invokes and extends the classical cultural geographies and political tropes of genocidal Manifest Destiny[7] — read alongside his myriad references to Filipino affectability (their subjection to "blood," "Spanish example," and "infancy") reflects the central tenets of a fundamental and structuring epistemological condition in which Filipinos continue to produce collective knowledges, identities, and political desires. (I will revisit these concerns through extended meditations in chapters 4 and 5.) This is also to argue that the Filipino condition generally, and the genealogy of Filipino Americanism especially, is persistently formed by the analytic of racial affectability, and that Filipino community and subject formations have never ceased responding to the notion that "the common people in their stupidity are like their caribou bulls.... They are incurably indolent.... They are like children playing at men's work."[8]

Aside from inhabiting a vexed space of affectability that is itself consumed with the desire to morph into the (self-)knowing, reasoning "transparent I" of this first moment in the analytics of raciality, Filipinos also disarticulate clean theoretical narrations of "Asian" and "Asian American" racialization and racial subjection within U.S. national formation. Silva writes that the production of "Asian difference" in the U.S. "national text" relies significantly on the construction of early twentieth-century Chinese and Japanese immigrants through mutually reinforcing discourses of (*a*) the "Orient" as a site of "civilization" difference (in which ostensible Orientals are *affected by* their stationary, obsolete, and decadent sociocultural forms) and (*b*) the Asian labor migrant as *exterior to* the "national I" of U.S. prosperity (although whose laboring "coolie" body was essential to the American nation's making). Thus, according to Silva, Asian Americans inhabit an "ambiguous placing" within the U.S. racial nation-building project, which "has allowed them to move in and out of the boundaries of cultural difference as either 'yellow

peril' or 'model minority,' without ever leaving the place raciality has assigned them."⁹ Her examination further suggests that
the vacillation of the U.S. racial analytic in relation to Asian subjects is most concretely characterized by a somewhat pragmatic
swaying of political and economic expediency:

> For every time the U.S. [political economy] has required Asian labor,
> the borders of Asian difference have been open to whichever favored
> nationality would be retained, as well as to whichever disfavored
> nationality would be placed outside.... Such a magnificent under-
> taking belongs in globality, for it enables the writing of the Asian
> subaltern subject both as a threat to and as an excessive signifier
> of that which only whiteness properly signifies, the subject able to
> actualize the economic and juridical ends of reason.¹⁰

While Silva's characterization does resonate with the historical
racialization of the Chinese and Japanese presence in the United
States, it also catalyzes a theoretical elaboration of the peculiarity of the Filipino condition in relation to the American racial
nation-building project.

Filipinos do not easily constitute a "nationality" in relation
to the historical nuances of U.S. jurisprudence: first, in the
aftermath of a genocidal conquest, they obtained the status of
formal colonial subjects of the United States for the first half
of the twentieth century (a status accompanied by the "virtually unprecedented manner [in which] the U.S. government
established colonial rule in the Philippines with the declared
purpose of self-liquidation of that rule, and enlisted the collaboration of the Philippine elite to this end").¹¹ Second, the
colonial nomenclature for the legal relation between Filipinos
and the U.S. nation-state during this period — the ambiguous
juridical positioning of the Filipino as "U.S. national" — was
also a de jure distinction that classified Filipino labor migrants
apart from their other "Asian" immigration cohorts, and in
fact facilitated an accelerated influx of Filipinos to the United
States during the first three decades of the twentieth century,
largely as labor recruits of U.S. agricultural, fishing, and other

industries in Hawaii and on the West Coast.[12] (The passage of the 1934 Tydings-McDuffie Act ceased classifying Filipinos as U.S. "nationals" and thus restricted "alien" Filipino immigration to fifty persons per year, while outlining the protocols for the initiation of formal Philippine independence in 1946.) This is to say that Filipinos cannot be adequately situated within the racial logics of Asian American difference and affectability.

As such, I would elaborate Silva's schema by suggesting that the Filipino condition within the historical flux and political geographies of the early twentieth century is more accurately characterized as the production of (and experimentation with) a structurally contingent "affectable" racial figure — that is, the characterization and logic of Filipino affectability is essentially experimental and unfixed. This is unlike the processes through which other racially subjected figures are violently reified and fixed in their affectability — for example, for Silva, Native American difference is fixed through racial obliteration and this becomes the "embodiment of the wilderness upon which U.S. American subjects would inscribe their 'civilization.'"[13] In multiple ways, Filipinos have formed the primary material on which the U.S. racial analytic inaugurates and shifts the social and racial projects[14] in which affectability assumes historically specific meanings (pivoting, in part, on economic and political expediencies); in turn, these changing productions of racial affectability — conceptually and experientially manifesting on the vexed Filipino body and subjectivity — have been essential to the U.S. national text and racial-cultural telos. Finally, it is worth emphasizing that Filipino affectability and racial difference breaks decisively from Asian American rubrics when its condition of possibility is conceptualized as the experimental postscripting of American racial genocide. This suggests a framing of the Filipino condition, and a critique of Filipino Americanism, that exceeds the analytical strictures of "empire" and in fact enriches the global theory of race that Silva offers.

The overarching argument of this book is that the production of the "Filipino American" is defined — essentially and fundamentally — by a complex, largely disavowed, and almost entirely undertheorized relation to a nexus of profound racial and white supremacist violence. Prior to and during the material articulation of those embryonic forms of empire and colonialism that are inscribed on the Philippine local and Filipino global conditions, techniques of social liquidation (including and exceeding biological and physical extermination) condensed on the bodies of Filipinos within and across a diversity of cultural geographies (from the incipient metropol to indigenous territories). The ongoing consequence of this historical encounter is a relation of violent alienation with modernity, the colonial state, and the nation-state form itself. Yet the coherence of Filipino American subjectivity relies on the persistent rearticulation and dispersal of this alienation, such that white supremacist colonization and genocidal conquest constitute laboriously distanced points of radical disruption and disintegration for the telos of Filipino and Filipino American identity.

The historical undeniability of the U.S. white supremacist state's militarized detonation of Filipino life (during and beyond the turn of the twentieth century), as well as its generative and socially formative domination over the Philippine nation-state and Filipino diaspora, is the past and present with which Filipinos cannot come to terms: this is why the allegation of Filipino American community and the ongoing project of Filipino American subjectivity, in the context of these historical processes of dominance, can only cohere through ultimate gestures of allegiance to the violence of the American nation-building project. An exemplary illustration of this constitutive alienation marks an appropriate point of departure for the remainder of the book.

Disturbing Origins: The Practices and Vicinities of Filipino American Communion

Suspended Apocalypse finds one of its scenes of political origin in April 2000, at the University of California at Berkeley: a well-organized core of antiracist student activists initiated an audacious, nonviolent occupation of Barrows Hall, provoking a clumsy police response and reawakening ambitions of a reconstituted movement for the invigoration and transformation of Ethnic Studies. No less a principled disruption of business-as-usual for the post–affirmative action white supremacist university, the organizing tactic and spatial poetics of this building occupation offered a jarring demystification of the technocratic professionalist schooling / bureaucratic culture of the U.C. system. In a rather stunning juxtaposition to the political ambition and antiauthoritarian animus of this direct action mobilization, however, a sizeable group of Filipino American undergraduates communed just outside Barrows Hall's eastside doors, utterly ignoring the accumulating theater of political crisis that surrounded their rehearsal for the annual campus gala known as Pilipino Cultural Night, or PCN. This particular PCN practice encompassed a typically hackneyed repertoire of dancing, marching, and melodrama — a mosaic of bodily activity that would have gone unnoticed if it was not so obviously pleading ignorance of its own historical moment. It is toward the historical condition of possibility for the (non)meeting of these two, proximate mobilizations of racial communion — one antiracist, insurgent, and counterhegemonic, the other multiculturalist, narcissistic, and ahistorically "culturalist" — that the theoretical trajectory of this text turns.

The historical contexts and social significance of Pilipino Cultural Night have been well addressed (though at times somewhat uncritically celebrated) by numerous writers, critics, and scholars.[15] Enacting a hallowed if contrived Filipino American performative commodity, the process of making the PCN prepares a stage spectacle that channels the creative energies and political pretensions of upwardly mobile Filipino American professionals whose premises of ethnic unity rest on their capacity to articulate a telos of membership within the modernist narratives of American nation building. A rigorous overview of the PCN as a changing, multivalent, and innovative cultural form, however, is not my intent here. Instead, I am interested in the cultural and political geography of the PCN as a Filipino Americanist community-building maneuver that is neither (*a*) autonomous of the political–cultural antagonisms that its participants might disavow or defer in the present time of their multiply sited performances nor (*b*) isolatable from its most direct conditions of possibility as a state-sanctioned multiculturalist performance form. ✔

As musician and cultural critic Theo Gonzalves has aptly surmised, PCNs "may not intend to self-consciously speak to the signs of the times, but the PCN genre poses for us invitations to interpret the work of culture under the shadow of late capital."[16] I would add that the protracted political labor of the PCN invariably sustains a troubled relation to the racist and white supremacist institutionalities of U.S. universities and colleges, thus amounting to a vexed collective endeavor that makes use of the institutional forms of hegemonic multiculturalism while generally withdrawing from a present-tense critique of white supremacy, within and beyond the discrete sites of higher education. Thus, the attention I am paying to this specific historical moment in the life of the PCN is conducive to the overarching engagement with the political materiality of Filipino Americanism that this book encompasses.

Puzzled observers and witnesses — many of whom (including the author) would become active in the brief and intense antiracist movement catalyzed by the Barrows Hall occupation — surrounded the dancing-acting Filipino Americans of Barrows Hall, watching them move to mock history, destiny, and the fleeting moment *now*. The doors behind their breeze-way rehearsal had been quickly and efficiently locked from the inside (thanks to activists' creative use of Kryptonite bike locks), as chants and handmade protest banners emanated from Barrows Hall windows. Still, stunningly, the Filipino American performers continued their filing, shuffling minstrelsy just outside of violence and danger, self-distanced from the time and moment of emergency, asserting their obligation to indulge in comfortable political indifference even as they acted the part of virtuous Philippine "indigenous" warriors on their makeshift rehearsal stage (replete with invisible spears and masculine aboriginal grunting on cue). Bamboo clapped together as dancers hopped between, while stage left were awkward renditions of hip-hop moves emblematic of a culturalist negrophilia that was, and had long been, central to the discursive apparatuses of a U.S. antiblack racism that Filipino Americans had somewhat recently discovered.

The PCN rehearsal scene had become bizarre, an abrasive melding of the ludic worlds of MTV and *National Geographic* — the student-performers were simultaneously inventing, rehearsing, and assimilating an eager (if stridently amateurish) production of the Filipino American real. Personal independence and bourgeois ethnic pride, intertwined and complex preoccupations of Filipino Americanist desire, had begotten a choreography that, in this moment, trivialized a danger so present that the aesthetic of the rehearsal was drowned in an arrogant defiance borne of presumptive American entitlements. The students' movements mocked the very historical moment in which their rabid fabrications of Filipino American "history" and "community," and their sincere though no less flimsy counterfeiting of a native homeland, had become a collective gesture of allegiance to a repressive, deeply racist university apparatus: California had passed the paradigmatic Proposition 209 less than three years earlier, rendering affirmative action illegal and immediately reopening classical pathways toward institutionalized white supremacy. (The juridical move also promised to inhibit Filipino American admissions to the University of California, after a decade of moderate increases deriving from the U.C. system's recognition of Filipinos as an underrepresented minority group.)[17]

This 2000 scene at Barrows Hall was, in retrospect, a veritable clinic in Filipino Americanism, a laboratory of cultural production that exceeded signification of the contingent and collective, remaking memory and moment as one performative artifact of a fleeting, though no less elite, institutional presence. It was an enunciation of Filipino American existence, a performative coming of age and rigorously scripted embrace of a banal, post–civil rights multiculturalist liberalism. Of course, the internal drama of such scenes of collective identity construction (rehearsal) amplifies the disarticulation, fragility, and constitutive failure of Filipino American subjectivity, the space in which the performance of community and contrivance of a collective Filipino Americanist bond defers the dread, terror, and guilt reserved for those who experience and embrace what is just beyond this time and place. ✓

While the PCN's circulation is relatively contained to college and university campuses across the United States, its transparent affinity to the structuring rhetorics, historical narratives, and modernist rationalities composing Filipino Americanist discourse situates it as a primary and productive — rather than ancillary or reflective — practice of Filipino American community building. For many participants, the PCN is the first (and only) context in which they will sustain a collective project with a group of self-defined "Filipino Americans." The organizers and performers of the shows consistently and self-consciously project an eclectic imaginary of their collective "selves" across ✓ historical time and cultural geography. In this context, the self-referential structure of the PCN narrative inscribes, revises, and reproduces a rather durable discursive structure for the meeting and interchange of Filipino American (and putatively Filipino)

Male participant in Pilipino Cultural Night rehearses as several University of California police prepare to enter Barrows Hall.

subjectivities. As importantly, the PCN organizing process lasts almost the entire school year, often dominating students' intellectual and emotional energies, and thus ritualizes and materially convenes a modality of Filipino American social intercourse. This theater of subjectivity is thus, for our purposes, entirely appropriate as a point of departure for this critical project.

By early evening, the shrugging indifference of the Barrows Hall PCN rehearsal was punctuated by the looming presence of five armed police officers positioned outside the breezeway. Strange spectators to the choreography of these model Filipino American subjects, the cops ate PowerBars as they anticipated orders to quell the disturbance inside.

The rehearsal did not break a step, even as acquaintances of the directors and performers suggested in passing that a change of venue might be appropriate. Weeks later, edified by incessant practices and meticulously edited scripts, these Filipino

Americans would initiate the PCN festivities by placing reverent hand over heart and singing the national anthem of the United States of America, punctuated by a wistfully foreign song of the Philippine nation, these strangely joined routines forwarding a gala of nativist costume, song, and amateurish overacting, a quaint celebration of survival and resistance, assimilation and upward mobility. But in this opening scene at Barrows Hall, the performers were simply rehearsing outside, in the spring-time dusk, bodies overflowing the breezeway of the rust-colored office building named after the man who established his academic career by subjecting these very same performers' ancestral figures to the gaze of the iconic colonial anthropologist.[18]

The figures were dancing hard, following directors' orders, channeling imagined ancestors, blocking the building's east exit, where they would follow their obstinate choreography even as the police declared the building a liberated territory eight hours later, open for business-as-usual. UCPD's exaggerated mobilization of riot control tactics occurred in concert with the early evening drum beats of the PCN's rehearsal of a traditional Filipino dance, while the collective of black, brown, and a few white and Asian American student activists — mostly undergraduates majoring in Ethnic Studies, none of them self-identified "Filipinos" or "Filipino Americans" — defied the lurking punitive threats of the university administration and awaited the inevitable storming of the building by the campus police.

The April 2000 revival of the Third World Liberation Front (twLF), arriving near the thirtieth anniversaries of the "original" incarnations of the TWLF — U.C. Berkeley's (1969) and San Francisco State University's (1968) conjoined legacies of student-led, radical antiracist and anti-imperialist social movements — was an expression of insurgent democratic desire, productively audacious in its claiming of the university as "ours," over and against the white supremacist fortification that U.C. Berkeley had become in the aftermath of the white nationalist and neo-conservative multiculturalist anti–affirmative action Proposition 209 debacle.[19] In just a few weeks, this incipient 2000 student insurrection — one that, in its earliest moments, held potential for a massive and politically principled disruption of an increasingly reactionary and openly racist campus — would be quelled, reorganized, and politically disciplined by a smug crew of older Bay Area activists tied to the local liberal and progressive left establishments (fittingly, a few of these interveners were veterans of the "original" Third World Liberation Fronts of three decades prior). The possibility of a sustained, creative, and collective cultural modality was rather quickly absorbed into the myopic pragmatism and transparent pseudoradicalism of a few Bay Area nonprofit progressives and liberal "revolutionaries," who tamed the budding twLF by orchestrating the construction of a "negotiating team" and then proctoring (infiltrating) it. In no time at all, there would begin a charade of meetings between "our" negotiators and the administrative business suits glazed with bureaucracy and armed with legal pads and plausible denials. There would begin, at those conference tables, the stunning sell-out of the six student activists who faced trumped-up felony charges from the Barrows Hall occupation. (Almost all of our older Establishment Left proctors seemed to disappear from the scene once the legal proceedings against the "Barrows Hall 6" started, embittering many and arousing suspicion in a few.)

But this part of the political drama was incidental, nothing more than a narrative indulgence for the dancing acting figures who rehearsed to know nothing, the apparition of fools in their willful ignorance, yet at once the emblems, heroes, and role models of this Filipino American communion, inhabiting all we were meant to become. Their obedient institutional presence — an allegory of cosmopolitan civic personhood — resonates with the lofty idealization spilled forth five years later by the regional chair of one prominent national Filipino American organization:

[The Filipino American youth] has the ability to combine the *best of both worlds*: the best in the Filipino — a sense of family, faith in God, a sense of community, with the best in American society — entrepreneurship, a sense of independence, all the opportunities open to him, and the determination to succeed. All that the young Filipino-American has to do is to seize the moment and move on with pride, with intelligence, and with confidence. If he keeps his goal in front of him, he will succeed.[20] [emphasis added]

Reinscribing the strictures of this immigrant American moral telos, the Barrows Hall breezeway choreography pledged indifference to the mounting drama in which it had become involuntarily entangled, committed instead to an affective praxis that fortified the PCN rehearsal as an urgent enactment of this Filipino American "best of both worlds." Here, then, was an attempt to fix and stabilize the constitutive ruptures embedded within the contemporary "global" cosmopolitanism that the Filipino American civil imaginary so actively rearticulates (a symptom of the Filipino condition that I will examine with detail in chapter 4).

The rehearsing figures were again approached by several of us and urgently informed of developments in the building behind them. We asked, pleaded, that they show some form of solidarity with their politically courageous classmates inside (and if not, that they at least move their rehearsal to another building in deference to the emergent crisis at hand). The directors of the communion responded: PCN was only a few weeks away, and this was an important rehearsal. They needed to look good for their parents and grandparents, and plus, didn't we realize that Robert Berdahl, the U.C. Berkeley chancellor, would be in attendance? (Berdahl would repeatedly sic the UCPD on their classmates during the hunger strike that followed the building occupation, resulting in one mass arrest and a number of minor incidents of police harassment and violence.)

Included in the pronouncements of the twLF, issued at the outset of the Barrows Hall takeover, was a call for a permanent (tenured or tenure-track) faculty hire in "Filipino American Studies," an incidental element of the twLF platform that flew under the radar, but that nonetheless recalled the central — and unfulfilled — objective of two decades of ineffective haggling by Bay Area Filipino American students, community members, and (often self-appointed) spokespeople. Although not a single one of the Barrows Hall occupiers was a self-identified "Filipino American," this new twLF was nonetheless engaged in arguably the most militant and self-endangering action ever to be taken in support of "Filipino American Studies" at the U.C. system's flagship campus. In the shadow of this demand — and even after some were told that the twLF was *fighting for them* — the figures continued their rehearsal-communion as if at an innocent distance from the political moment that had already, generously, attempted to embrace them: *they* were the self-declared Filipino Americans of this opening scene, counting steps to a choreography that they, despite all evidence to the contrary, believed was some kind of Philippine "tribal" dance. Barbara Gaerlan's genealogy of the Pilipino Cultural Night traces this performative auto-anthropology to students' appropriations of the Bayanihan Dance Company's cultural fabrication of a Philippine nationalist modernity. Bayanihan, founded in 1957, offers a transpacific (and transhistorical) touchstone for a uniquely Filipino American multiculturalist modernism:

> In my interviews with Filipino American students about the source of their interest in learning such dances for the PCN, invariably they cited a desire to learn about indigenous cultures of the Philippines of which they were previously unaware. They perceived the dances as an anthropological window on Philippine culture. At the same time, without observing a contradiction, they appreciated the modern theatricality of the Bayanihan genre, saying that it gave them a venue for expressing Filipino culture in the United States of which they could be proud. *They seemed unaware that, in addition to theatricality, the Bayanihan included another "modern" feature, Orientalism.*[21] [emphasis added]

Gaerlan's characterization is perceptive, rich, and deeply informed by anthropological and historical archives. In the case of the political–cultural moment I am visiting here, however, I would contest the notion that the students were *ignorantly* engaged in an exotic, culturally reifying Orientalist creative practice; rather, I would suggest that these Filipino American subjects — cultural producers no less — were absolutely self-conscious in their auto-ethnographic scripting of cultural artifacts that were, at once, (1) substantively Other to their modalities of social intercourse, biographical trajectories, and political–cultural identifications, and (2) materially present and generative to a structure of Filipino American *communion* (the ritualized and often programmatic activity of fabricating, gathering, and identifying a moment of ideological and affective unity) and *community* (the PCN's scripts, artifacts, and rehearsals that imagine and culturally produce the ambitions and abstractions of shared identity).

Thus, the PCN rehearsal at Barrows Hall was a relatively intentional (if theoretically underarticulated) performance of cultural reification and political identity. The labors of ignorance and performances of Orientalist desire therein — from the profound refusals to engage (and to thus actively disavow) the twLF action and the state violence it confronted, to the blithe reconstructions of a Philippine indigeneity entirely at odds with the context and content of its cultural appropriations — were foundational, not accidental or incidental, to this geography of Filipino Americanism. Thus, for the Barrows Hall PCN rehearsal to articulate (even momentary) solidarity with the counterinstitutional activist maneuvers of the twLF was unthinkable: the twLF's praxis, which in its opening frame was animated by a radical critique of the constitutive violence, dehumanization, and racist statecraft of the U.S. nation-building project, was heresy in the presence of this Filipino American communion, which could not accommodate a disarticulation of its own banal,

University of California police arrest Third World Liberation Front student activists at Barrows Hall, using a variety of pain holds to force physical compliance.

multiculturalist patriotism and devout loyalty to white institutionality. No less grave and self-important in its trappings of sacrosanct unity than the Catholic ceremony of communion, the Barrows Hall PCN rehearsal signified a protoreligious internal allegiance, a ritual repetition that (not accidentally) refracted the protective sanctity of eating and drinking the body and blood of Christ. Yet such exercises of fixing and stabilization always and necessarily fail to obtain closure, and as such constantly require extensive labors of orchestration. Filipino Americanism is commonly, precisely such a modality of communion, resonating with (and at times more clearly appropriating) the particular Catholic practice of disciplinary consumption and behavioral regulation (ingesting Christ while engaging in rigorous modalities of collective assembly that make spatial sense of the holy eating act itself). By evening, the twLF building occupation had attracted a crowd of two hundred or so students on the west side of the building, many of whom would not have supported or paid much attention to the issues articulated by the twLF were it not for the emergent political spectacle of low-intensity police violence. This crowd had begun loudly chiding and scolding the UCPD for their overeager physicality and "pain-hold" arrests of twLF activists. Meanwhile, PCN scriptwriters and directors were reprimanding dancers and complementary actors for flubbing lines and not sticking their steps, while keeping backs turned to the east side Barrows Hall vestibule.

What are we to make of such scenes of communion, to the extent that they so conspicuously defer the emergency of the moment by signifying, embodying, performing, and ritualizing a community *outside of, apart from, and disidentified with*, the political crisis in its midst? How can the subjects of communion so seamlessly proceed as putative neutral parties — literal sideshows — to sites of political confrontation that explicitly delineate the punitive limits of institutionalized multicultural discourse?

"Cultural Alienation": Toward a Critical Conceptualization of the Filipino Condition

Several hours later, the building occupation effectively ended. A couple of hundred people remained outside the west end of Barrows Hall and shouted at the cops as they arrested each of the demonstrators in a prolonged choreography of a different sort, the police handcuffing and dragging individual twLF'ers out of their nonviolent sit-in circle and punching a few here and there. The students were arrested, served their papers, and released from police custody at the east end vestibule: appropriately, the activists were bodily "freed" onto center stage of the still ongoing PCN rehearsal. As it approached midnight, the Filipino Americans danced and acted their way around the somewhat disoriented twLF arrestees, in a cumbersome rendition of their communion's condition of possibility.

This opening scene allegorizes and materially inscribes a political–cultural tension that is constitutive of Filipino American communal formations generally. The opening drama recalls Fanon's meditation on the existential and geographic dislocation of the postcolonial petite bourgeoisie from the culturalist ordering of the colony, stranding the "native middle class" away from the semblance of civic space and material privilege that it was accorded under the colonizer's watch. Here we can reenvision the political drama of Barrows Hall by embedding its scenes in the historical circuits of a colonial white supremacist Pacific:

> When we consider the resources deployed to achieve the cultural alienation so typical of the colonial period, we realize that nothing was left to chance and that the final aim of colonization was to convince the indigenous population it would save them from darkness. The result was to hammer into the heads of the indigenous population that if the colonist were to leave they would regress into barbarism, degradation, and bestiality.[22]

In resonance with Fanon, poet Luis H. Francia writes:

> [W]herever we may have been born and wherever we choose to live, America can never be a neutral subject for Filipinos. Dealing with Filipino-ness is to deal with this condition, with a fall from grace, when the twin-headed snake of Spain and America seduced us with the promise of boundless knowledge — we too could be white gods! — even as we reposed in an unimaginably beautiful garden.[23]

While I would contest Francia's depiction of the Filipino condition as a "fall from" any kind of existential "grace," the thrust of his statement is no less compelling: there is a historical rupture, a cultural trauma that accompanies the acknowledgment that Filipinos are in — and of — the body of the American "snake." Francia's declaration echoes the insidious agendas of early twentieth-century U.S.-sponsored missionary schools in the Philippines, which massaged the minds of the "natives" into a classical colonial resonance with Fanon's cultural alienation. Schirmer writes:

> In developing neocolonial techniques for the treatment of their Philippine colony, U.S. imperialists did not rely on economic power alone to buttress their rule. They quickly turned to ideological influence as another base from which to secure political control by indirect means. Popular education, the organization of a public school system in the Philippines, became the chief focus of this effort....
>
> Since the U.S. imperialists' outlook was marked by racism, their sponsorship of public education in the Philippines meant exposing the mass of the Filipino people to white supremacist attitudes in an organized way.[24]

Nationalist Philippine historian Renato Constantino extends this critique in his famous essay "The Miseducation of the Filipino," arguing polemically:

> [F]rom its inception, the educational system of the Philippines was a means of pacifying a people who were defending their newly-won freedom from an invader who had posed as an ally. The education of the Filipino under American sovereignty was an instrument of colonial policy. The Filipino had to be educated as a good colonial. Young minds had to be shaped to conform to American ideas....
>
> The educational system established by the Americans could not have been for the sole purpose of saving the Filipinos from illiteracy and ignorance. Given the economic and political purposes of American occupation, education had to be consistent with these broad purposes of American colonial policy. *The Filipinos had to be trained as citizens of an American colony.*[25] [emphasis added]

I invoke these passages at length in order to instantiate a theorization of Filipino *and Filipino American* cultural alienation within the epoch-shaping project of U.S. nation building and its white supremacist colonialist animus. That is, I am interested in foregrounding the indeterminacy and political ambivalence that "Filipino American" discourse attempts to foreclose in its frequent allegations of separability from "Filipinoness" proper, and I am similarly invested in displacing the assumptive assertion of the "Filipino American" as ontologically congruent with an "American" political–historical telos. Put differently, I understand the Filipino condition as a lived structure of inescapability from multiple epochal violences — white supremacist colonization, genocide, and modernist nation building — that persistently coheres its self-comprehension through a system of historically alienated pronouncements: this is the political–discursive labor of rendering the Filipino as compatible with the "transparent I" of Silva's racial analytic, an extended monologue of rationalizations that produce the Filipino as a subject somehow unaffected and undisturbed by an epoch of death, terror, and conquest. (Echoing Fanon, Constantino recalls that "the Filipino mind has come to regard centuries of colonial status as a grace from above rather than as a scourge.")[26] It is this discursive and political coherence that I wish to radically challenge in *Suspended Apocalypse*.

Generative in this opening scene of manifest cultural estrangement is a historical tension that resonates through the production of Filipino Americanism and its embodied sites of rehearsal. One side of the tension involves a totality defined by cultural and historical loss — a structured erasure and distortion of indigenous identities and identifications under the regimes of Spanish and American colonialism, which encompass accelerated and irreparable physical and ecological obliteration as the historical premises for the cultural and political forms of the colonizer's incipient "civil society." This settler conquest, occupation, and national reformation, formed through the institutions and racial analytics of white bourgeois subjectivity and embodiment (bourgeois liberal democracy, nominal public schooling, missionary Catholicism), imprints the multicultural drama of the Filipino American communion at Barrows Hall and elsewhere: Filipino Americanism as a discursive communal possibility and instigation of identity is unthinkable absent its sturdy allegiance to the American civil society form, and as such must articulate through a generalized (if only sometimes "critical") allegiance to the political integrity and essentialized moral legitimacy of the United States of America in its localized institutionalizations (in this scene, U.C. Berkeley) and as a putative "national" hegemony writ global. Cultural alienation, then, is both the flexible medium of the Filipino American rehearsal across its geographies of production, as well as the vernacular through which its figurations become pedantic political melodrama.

The second, more readily available dimension of Fanon's cultural alienation is embedded in the scene of the PCN rehearsal itself. Amid a localized political insurgency and mobilized police violence, this was, after all, a Filipino American communion busy with the work of remaking an Other culture, profoundly *not* at odds with the site and dominion of its busy embodiment. Filipino American self-love, cultivated in this communal moment, recalls Benedict Anderson's well-known contention that

> [t]he cultural products of nationalism — poetry, prose fiction, music, plastic arts — show this love very clearly in thousands of different forms and styles. On the other hand, how truly rare it is to find *analogous* nationalist products expressing fear and loathing. Even in the case of colonized peoples, who have every reason to feel hatred for their imperialist rulers, it is astonishing how insignificant the element of hatred is in these expressions of national feeling.[27]

(Appropriately, Anderson follows this passage with an extended quotation of *Mi último adiós,* the poem penned by Philippine nationalist hero José Rizal on the eve of his execution under the Spanish colonialist state.) Contrivances of a romantic, lush national/Philippine culture and history are consistently inscribed through the bodily movements and spatial organization of the PCN scene, matching and mirroring the omnipresent American Bildungsroman of national–ethnic evolution through mimetic mystifications of "Philippine" roots, mythologies, and cultural/biological lineages. To echo Gonzalves, "the tacit assertion being made [in the PCN narrative form] is that the Philippines is a sturdy repository of 'knowledge,' a repository of authentic representations of Philippine life that can be accessed and brought back."²⁸ The rehearsal and repetitive performance of this contrived, essentialized Philippine national culture — whether theatrical renditions of the Manila slave galleons, hackneyed variations of *tinikling*, or pseudo-ethnographic representations of tribal rituals — acts out the tension of cultural estrangement, a nexus of endangerment and cultural (mis)identification that Lisa Lowe maps eloquently:

> Culture is the medium of the *present* — the imagined equivalences and identifications through which the individual invents lived relationship with the national collective — but it is simultaneously the site that mediates the *past*, through which history is grasped as difference, as fragments, shocks, and flashes of disjunction. It is through culture that the subject becomes, acts, and speaks itself as "American."²⁹

The Filipino American performance/production offers relief, on the one hand, from a colonial and imperial political unconscious of suspended apocalypse: this choreography responds to the everlasting interrogative "What is my (Philippine/Filipino American) 'national' history?" through a decisive disavowal of cultural and historical loss.

I am suggesting that the currency of Filipino American enactments — across their various textual and discursive forms — invokes a guiding ambivalence, as well as a strategic assimilation, to the historical trajectory of the U.S. national/civil form. There is a hegemonic Filipino Americanism that insists on the postponement of a (potentially) radical antagonism with U.S. sovereignty as a white supremacist, colonialist, warfare apparatus, Filipino Americanism often articulates as a discourse of self-valorizing heroism, a "rescuing" of national culture from the violent silences wrought by U.S. and Spanish imperialism, as well as a discursive "liberation" of the Filipino from domestic and localized varieties of white supremacy. Finally, as dramatized by this opening scene at Barrows Hall, the most powerful resolution enacted by the Filipino American communion is the recuperation of an objectively conservative, and often aggressively insular sense of coherence, wholeness, unity, and identity over and against the manifest conflict, tension, and contradiction that surround on all sides and that represent threats of destabilization to already fragile and parochial performances of Filipino American community. ↙

The Filipino American is a constitutive figure in the post-1965 reconstruction of American civil society through the descriptively multiracial, multiethnic, and multicultural nationalist narratives of the "post–civil rights" moment. The coherence and integrity of this social and discursive formation, also rendered in this opening scene, is edified by the capacity of the state (under generalized civilian sanction) to exert militarized dominion in strategic localities, across putatively sovereign or "private" territories. As such, this Filipino American communion signifies a relation of performative distance to that which poses a putative threat to the sanctity of (American) state dominion — the insistent procession of the PCN rehearsal *just outside* of the twLF's bodily confrontation with the UCPD, in other words, must be understood as a *political* articulation and embodied scheming of the affective limits of community in this instance.

Conclusion: Unpacking the Scene

I begin with this "thick description" of a specific (archival?) moment of Filipino American communion as a prelude to the next chapter's examination of the material ideological projects that assemble a "Filipino American common sense." One of the overarching arguments of this book is that the production of Filipino American common sense is animated by a peculiar relation of allegiance to a transpacific, archipelago-to-continent projection of "America," which is manifest in new and amplified ways as self-authorized Filipino *American* spaces are constituted and institutionalized. Chapter 2 is thus framed by Gramscian-influenced conceptions of social formation and proceeds by focusing on the political and historical conditions of possibility for the political–cultural integrity of the Filipino

American subject. The Gramscian formulation of hegemonic common sense illuminates the articulation and inscription of a field of assumptive principles, political positions, hierarchies of value, and articles of faith that cohere and reproduce particular "historical blocs" and, ultimately, "hegemonic blocs" in given historical moments. It is in part through this conceptual rubric that I describe, define, and critically theorize the field of Filipino American discourse (Filipino Americanism).

My attempt in this introductory chapter to address the under-theorization of the Filipino global relation to white supremacist "racial" regimes (including and exceeding the colonial and neocolonial moments) anticipates the presentation of another central theoretical problematic in chapter 3. Focusing on the embryonic moments of U.S. racist state violence and genocidal conquest in the Philippines, and revisiting the racial/racist institutional and social projects organic to the historical processes of Philippine national formation and Filipino American identity construction, the chapter argues for a spatial and historical reconceptualization of the Filipino–American relation that incites conversation with a genealogy of radical antiracist and liberationist praxis, as well as with the scholarly work of critical race studies, Native American and indigenous/aboriginal studies, African American/Africana studies, and the emerging subfield of critical genocide studies. I contend that enunciations of "Filipino American" social existence, and narrative rationalizations of the Filipino condition more broadly, are overdetermined by an originating and structuring relation of death that extends the material historical processes and cultural mechanics of a white supremacist social logic, resulting in the ongoing inscription of racist genocide as the condition of possibility for the Filipino's sustained presence in (and proximity to) the United States.

The spatial and affective juxtaposition between the overlapping (and conflicting) sites of the twLF's counterinstitutional, antiracist protest action on the one hand, and the carefree rehearsals of a PCN performance on the other, are directly related to the Fanonist genealogy of the Philippine "national bourgeoisie" that I substantively engage in chapter 4. There I examine the notion of Filipino American communion as something more than just another variation of liberal assimilationism, banal multiculturalism, or even multiculturalist neoconservatism. Rather, I consider this ritualized modality of community formation as the rendition of a particular "American colonial/neocolonial" ontology.

Departing from the structuring tensions of the Barrows Hall scene, *Suspended Apocalypse* is in critical dialog with Allan Isaac's notion of the "Filipino American" as "but a set of traces, masks, and misrecognitions in American law, borders, and drama" marked by "the construction of a colonial space rendered invisible to the American polity: the unincorporated territory."[30] Enabled by Isaac's framing, I am concerned with this condition of obscuring — and of being obscured — as the social dilemma to which Filipino Americanism responds. In fact, the ritualized communions of desire that form the localized geographies of Filipino American identity and community (such as in the Barrows Hall PCN rehearsal) seem precisely to constitute collective rebuttals to the "misrecognition" and "invisibility" of which Isaac writes. Here the extended labor of fabricating the social materiality of the "Filipino American" is a stubbornly modernist response *within* (and not simply against or outside) a genealogy of U.S. conquest, genocide, colonization, and imperialism, and imprints the Philippines and Filipinos in a putatively "postmodern" moment.

In sustaining a critique of Filipino Americanism, then, *Suspended Apocalypse* seeks to do more than allege or imply what Isaac calls a "language connecting" communities of color. I am attempting to show how, in multiple cultural productions, scholarly and popular archives, and political projects, the historical possibility and, in fact, the flesh-and-bone materiality of such "solidarities" is already available. Engaging a different kind of political critique and praxis, I meditate in the book's final chapter on the radical potentials of another trajectory of Filipino subject formation and historical (racial) identification, particularly as situated against the racial and white supremacist social formation of the United States in the current moment. Politicizing the rubrics, political orchestrations, and statecraft of "disaster" in the planned atrocity of Hurricane Katrina and the precedent (and, I argue, materially connected) environmental event of Mt. Pinatubo's explosion near Metro Manila, I gesture toward a productive confrontation with the white supremacist racial analytic of Filipino subjectivity.

Deformed Nationalism and Arrested Raciality

The Grammar and Problematic of a "Filipino American" Common Sense

> The question is this: of what historical type is the conformism, the mass humanity to which one belongs?
> — Antonio Gramsci, *The Study of Philosophy*

The Outlines of a Problematic: "Filipino American" Common Sense

Post-1965 Filipino Americanism is, from its moment of articulation, a material discourse and self-consciously popular cultural formation that intends a communion of desires, historical identifications, and political allegiances. In its most contemporary forms — that is, once it is conceptualized as an architecture of collective identity that may incessantly reference, but does not organically descend from, the social and cultural formations embodied by early twentieth-century Filipino plantation laborers, farm workers, fishing and cannery migrants, *ilustrados,* and/or other alleged Filipino American "pioneers" — Filipino Americanism can and must be understood as an essentially deformed nation-building project. I invoke the terms of deformation here not as an accusation of insufficiency, ineptitude, or (nationalist) unfaithfulness, but rather as a conceptual shorthand for the peculiarity and historical specificity of Filipino

Americanism as an expression of allegiance✓with the local and global political logics of the contemporary U.S. nation-building project within which the Filipino American communion is a minor component. As a deformed nation-building project, Filipino Americanism is neither a "nationalist" material discourse within the traditional spectrum of insurgent, hegemonic, and reactionary nationalisms, nor does it qualify as a political and ideological inventory for incipient "nationhood," in the context of political self-determination, independence, or land rights. Rather, the material discourse and popular cultural circulation of Filipino Americanism encompasses a broadly pitched desire for (1) *civil recognition* as a viable and self-contained collective subject of the U.S. polity (including and beyond nomination as "citizens" of the nation), and (2) *cultural valorization* as cooperative with and richly contributing to the historical telos of American nation building in the post–civil rights, multiculturalist moment.✓The first desire has especially facilitated the articulation of an authentic, late twentieth-century Filipino American civil society that purports a decisive abandonment of colonial and neocolonial Filipino subjectivities (pathologized and dismissed as "the colonial mentality" in Filipino American circles) in exchange for a figuration of composed, collective social intercourse compatible with the rubrics of empowerment that structure the U.S. social formation. A logical production of this civil intercourse has been the renaissance of Filipino American cultural production and public communion since the 1990s, which includes an acceleration in the scale and sweep of organizational activity, creative artistic work, scholarly publication, and academic pedagogy explicitly housed within the discursive field of Filipino Americanism, and fulfilling the common notion of a cultural renaissance as "any revival, or period of marked improvement and new life, in art, literature, etc."[1] The second desire further elaborates Filipino Americanism as a deformed "national" cultural production, in which the abstract figure of the Filipino American as a viable civil subject of the United States reanimates as a willing, postmodern *nationalist* subject–patriot whose praxis of contribution to the outfits and institutionalities of U.S. global dominance are complexly and sometimes contradictorily conditioned by the self-recognitions of civil marginality (including those rendered by the complications of citizenship or visa status, neocolonial governmental politics, and the social products of putative racial difference).

❡ Here I am most concerned with the proclamations, assumptions, and political (non)demands that enable the circulation of a common sense that claims and coheres a social space within the "multicultural" institutionalities and discursive systems of the "post–civil rights" U.S. social formation. I am also interested in how Filipino Americanism articulates a peculiar American "civilian" (nationalist) ontology that is inseparable from — and profoundly productive of — a liberal (that is, arbitrarily inclusionist and ideologically pluralist) American multiculturalism that inaugurates new modalities of American hegemony, across scales and historical moments⟦How, in other words, does Filipino Americanism enrich and enable the relations of dominance integral to U.S. social formation even as elements of Filipino American discourse periodically allege to confront, critique, displace, or correct perceived historical injustices against "Filipino Americans" (and even other "people of color")? Framed more broadly, what are the shared ideas, narratives, political assumptions, and belief/faith structures that render Filipino Americanism ideologically coherent and culturally viable as the conceptual space within which putative "Filipino Americans" convene and self-identify? ⟧

This chapter initiates a symptomatic reading of Filipino Americanism by identifying some of the common terms and rhetorical modalities through which it articulates allegiance to the structuring rhetorics, political and governmental institutionalities, and cultural apparatuses of the U.S. racist state②and the racial formation to which it is central. Theoretically, the chapter attempts to sketch, elaborate, and critically engage the outlines of a problematic: I am arguing that Filipino Americanism cannot be adequately understood as a material discourse and social project unless the (generally unspoken and taken for granted) ideological and assumptive frameworks within which it is invented, engaged, and culturally projected are constantly subjected to critical scrutiny. Here I am appropriating the theoretical gesture of Louis Althusser's well-known critique of humanism, particularly his incisive analysis of humanist thought's repetitive construction of "epistemological obstructions" that preempt, displace, or render illegible a historical materialist method of social analysis. For Althusser, the humanist problematic is characterized by its persistent assertions of ideological positions that masquerade as *the* objective, "scientific," and/or "theoretical" frameworks within which philosophical and political questions may be articulated in a given historical context:

> It should be recalled that the ideological function of these notions with theoretical pretensions does not consist in *posing* real *problems,* and thus in opening up the theoretical field. . . . It consists, rather, in *imposing in advance* — masked by fictitious problems devoid of scientific content — ready-made *solutions* that are not *theoretical* solutions, but merely theoretical *statements* of "practical" solutions. . . .
>
> To put it schematically, the ideological notions in question here are merely transcriptions, with theoretical pretensions, of *existing states of affairs.* . . .
>
> Therefore, far from *opening up* the theoretical field in which it would be possible to pose real problems scientifically, these ideological notions, which are basically nothing but theoretical transcriptions of actually existing social *solutions,* have the function of preventively *closing off* the field they pretend to open up, thus making it impossible to pose any real problems.[3] [emphasis in original]

Crucial to the longer work of forming a critical inventory of the Filipino condition, then, is a reading of the problems, concepts, and social antagonisms that are both implied in and absent from the empirical surfaces of Filipino American discourse, and of how those points of potential discursive rupture — those moments and sites that might enable a radical *disarticulation* of the conceptual coherence of Filipino Americanism — are postponed, absorbed, and expelled from the lexicon (words, expressions, meanings) and grammar (rules governing the language) of "Filipino American common sense."

This chapter thus examines both the select expressions and constitutive logics of an academic and popular discourse that emerged with particular prominence during the 1990s, staking specific claims in relation to the substance, content, and historical significance of a publicly articulated Filipino American subjectivity and identity. A surge of civic and nonprofit organizations, performance art, high school, college, and university student groups, print media, academic programs, and other cultural and institutional forms precipitated a veritable "Filipino American renaissance," meshing with an acceleration of scholarly production that increasingly located the academic "Filipino Americanist" within hegemonic sites of knowledge production and institutional formation. It is not my intention to offer a sufficient summary of this cultural and intellectual movement here. Rather, the chapter proceeds by briefly revisiting a few texts that reflect some of the central political, conceptual, and ideological foundations for the social ambitions of an "authentic" Filipino American subjectivity. Following Neferti Tadiar, my purpose in addressing these few texts is to suggest the outlines of a critical framework that can facilitate theoretical elaboration of the premises of connectedness between the otherwise dispersed surfaces of Filipino American discourse across its many contexts and material sites, while also stressing the need for perpetual sociohistorical contextualization of the ideological threads and core political convictions that compose particular, crystallized moments of Filipino American discursive enunciation and their complementary fantasies[4] of identity and community formation.

Speaking to the larger analytical scheme of the book, I am offering a symptomatic reading of several formative moments in the recent elaboration of Filipino Americanism, with particular attention to the points of identification on which the discourse anchors its claims to public subjectivity (or "community"), and special attention to the ways in which these claims shape a trajectory and modality of institutionalization that forecloses engagement with the constitutive contradictions, complexities, and political antagonisms that vex the Filipino American figuration. In part, I am attempting to outline the rudimentary belief structures of Filipino American common sense while meditating on how these belief structures — which are often convoluted, internally contradictory, and complex — become intelligible and accessible.

How does this body of common sense establish the relatively durable and identifiable ideological premises through which moments of Filipino American identity formation, collective action, and political formulation become possible? Finally, my critical engagement in this chapter is guided by a particular attention to the overarching concerns of this book, which concern the constitutive tensions between the normally violent machinations and movements of the twentieth-century U.S. racist state, the particular genealogy of conquest and colonialism forming the historical Filipino relation with the U.S. nation-building project, and the specific formulations of rational subjectivity and collective civil ontology that uncomfortably locate Filipino Americanism within the rubrics of a white supremacist racial analytic.

The Political Labor of Filipino American Common Sense

Benedict Anderson has written that "communities are to be distinguished, not by their falsity/genuineness, but by the style in which they are imagined."[5] To refract this framing, it is the labor underwriting the style that forms my terrain of critical engagement. In this theoretical context — which privileges examination of the common conceptual premises that enable and encourage the ongoing activity and work of a collective self-imagination — the production of a Filipino American common sense is a rather extraordinary labor, in many ways produced by its moments of inarticulateness and lack of closure. It is structurally fragile and implosive despite its appearances of simplicity and charades of transparency.

It is precisely because this method of symptomatic reading‿ attends to the illustration and elaboration of the contours of a problematic that its analytical process is rather different from that of a conventional "close reading" or ethnographic "thick description" of specific literatures, archives, or cultural artifacts. Instead, by visiting multiple, seemingly dispersed and relatively disconnected articulations of Filipino American discourse and examining the historical context and discursive logics through which these articulations are expressed, dynamically elaborated, and internally reproduced, this critical approach offers a strategy of productive demolition for its object of analysis: that is, an outline of how Filipino Americanism constitutively generates the grounds of its own disarticulation, as well as an activist critique of Filipino American common sense that attempts disruption of the openly affirmed and tacitly gestured bonds of allegiance and solidarity between Filipino American subjects and the national project to which they declare and/or embody political commitment and historical identification.

The scope of this elementary critical reading departs from the work of other writers, activists, and scholars who since the early 1990s have generated a corpus of work that assesses the emergence of explicitly activist, progressive, or otherwise counterhegemonic Filipino American, Filipino diasporic, and U.S. Filipino communities and political formations, including social movement histories of Filipino labor organizers, LGBT activists, immigrant rights advocates, feminist solidarity groups, and the

U.S.-based anti–martial law and antiglobalization movements.[6] These activist formations of political and cultural community generate multiple, contested trajectories for engaging social transformation and offer moments of identification that at times may critically intervene on the common, parochial Filipino Americanism that I am engaging in this chapter.

Martin Manalansan IV, in his groundbreaking ethnography of *bakla* (gay and queer) Filipino immigrant men in New York City, offers a stunning critique of Filipino American discursive conventions when he argues:

> The processes of globalization and transnationalism have complicated, if not transformed, the ways subjects create a sense of belonging and identity. Notions of being Filipino, American, or gay cannot be easily apprehended in static, essential terms alone.... In the face of these realities, queer diasporic subjects, particularly those from the Third World, who are confronted with multiple displacements, are faced with the monumental tasks of creating and refiguring home....
>
> Filipino gay men are not typical immigrants who "move" from tradition to modernity; rather, they rewrite the static notions of tradition as modern or as strategies with which to negotiate American culture. Immigration, therefore, does not always end in an assimilative process but rather in contestation and reforming of identities.[7]

Manalansan, among others, depicts how lived queer subjectivities consistently reform, transform, and/or multiply the socially embodied identities of Filipinos in the United States, including and exceeding the narrower categorical projections of the "Filipino American." The purpose of this chapter, then, is to further enable such a critical approach by paying sustained theoretical (rather than descriptive) attention to the allegations of communal coherence and civil unity that both precede and accompany the critical departures offered by scholars like Manalansan: here, the primary analytical focus is on enactments of Filipino Americanism that project a retroactive recuperation into the multicultural nationalist political telos and narrative

Bildungsroman of the United States in the late twentieth and early twenty-first centuries, which in significant part imagine the pluralist "empowerment" of Filipino Americans within the U.S. civil fabric as a primary social labor and political desire.[8] Thus, the political intercourse of counterhegemonic Filipino communal formations and the emergence of putatively subaltern Filipino diasporic/migrant communities are shadowed, contradicted, and constituted — in ways that remain somewhat underanalyzed — by an ensemble of articulations that commune Filipino Americanism as a viable public *of and for* the hegemonic political, moral, and cultural structures and strictures of the U.S. social formation.

The overtly political enactments of Filipino American common sense are not discretely and narrowly "liberal" in form or outcome, although they do generally work through the institutional and discursive logics of what E. San Juan Jr. has called a "ludic multiculturalism."[9] There are, as well, readily available neoconservative, classically conservative, and reactionary appropriations of the multiculturalist social mandate that position Filipino American formations across the hegemonic political spectrum of U.S. popular discourse. In this context, Filipino American common sense encompasses an ongoing popular project that, on the one hand, politically confronts and displaces both U.S.-based and diasporic Filipino progressive, insurgent, and counterhegemonic praxis, while, on the other hand, formally articulating with the vernaculars of progressive and critical work engaged by Filipino scholars, activists, artists, and other political–intellectual workers. To clarify: it is precisely the accessibility and ideological eclecticism of common sense that renders it an unavoidable field of political engagement for people involved in the labors of social transformation and incisive scholarly critique. Sustained theoretical attention to the construction and discursive circulation of this Filipino American "real," then, aggravates the common cultural–ideological and densely theoretical antagonisms between (1) the project of a common sense–making that persistently portrays a stability and coherence of Filipino American existence that is in relative harmony with U.S. *national* existence, and (2) the indelible materialities of a Filipino historical condition that has formed at the conjunctures of distinctly "American" crises of white supremacist colonial violence and (national) meaning across the late nineteenth, twentieth, and early twenty-first centuries.

My symptomatic reading in this chapter similarly departs from the insightful ethnographic work of Rick Bonus, whose text *Locating Filipino Americans* responds to a generalized "lament that Filipinos are largely invisible in most accounts of U.S. history and in contemporary scholarship...comprising a 'silent minority' frequently lumped together with Chinese, Japanese, Korean, Indian, Vietnamese, and Cambodian peoples under the rubric Asian American."[10] Bonus's study, which focuses on the construction of Filipino American social geographies in Southern California, pays rigorous attention to the nuances of collective identity formation and the social and civil consolidation/institutionalization of "Filipino Americanness." As such, the text encompasses a thick analytical description of community formation that clearly delineates the condition and dynamic articulation of Filipino American sociocultural spaces. In attempting "to unravel what it means to be Filipino and American at the same time," Bonus is responding to some classical concerns in the fields of Asian American and comparative ethnic studies. He proposes that

> [T]he particular practices of community and ethnic identity formation I uncover represent a need to respond to and resist invisibility, exploitation, silencing, and racial constructing, by history and by institutions, as well as a desire to claim a "space" within the rubric "American" on their own terms.[11]

Following Bonus, this chapter reads formulations of community, identity, and sociocultural (spatial) construction against the grain. I am, in other words, reassessing the "particular practices" so deftly illustrated in Bonus's ethnography by questioning the foundational terms of discursive struggle on which they are based, the disciplinary and sometimes punitive conditions on which these practices are rendered operative as "community" endeavors, and thus the constitutive incommensurability of an alleged Filipino American figurative coherence with the densely crisis-ridden — and hence imminently disarticulating — social context that enmeshes the dynamic and multiple pronouncements of the allegation itself. To the extent that it sustains a sociocultural existence (or constructs sociocultural space) by cohering as a sign of collective identity and identification, community, and social movement, I contend that the labor of *making* the Filipino American also forms a moment of radical diagnosis for the current formation of the United States of America as a multiculturalist national project.

The Schema of Filipino Americanism: Gramsci's Common Sense and Hall's Gramsci

While historically oppressed and subaltern groups often construct worldviews and ethical systems that radically contest — or at minimum substantively resist — the conditions of their subjection, the condition of the contemporary U.S. social formation (in its globally localized variations) rests on the fulcrum of a hegemonic national culture that is flexible, expansive, and interpellating, rather than rigid, discrete, or externalizing. Such is the epochal context of an emergent Filipino American common sense, an ongoing knowledge production that revisits Antonio Gramsci's conceptualization of the ensemble of cultural–ideological assumptions that constitute and periodically transform the processes of "social relations" in modern social formations. Gramsci, in his conceptualization of "common sense," references the changing and internally contested body of popular knowledge, shared assumption, and faith-beliefs that shape the structuring of and relations within civil society, or what are more commonly apprehended as the sets of presumptive truths that tacitly form the parameters and discursive spheres of everyday social intercourse, from individual conversation to mass-framed political debate.

In Gramsci's formulation, the dynamic and flexible architecture of a popular common sense is essential to the sustenance of relative social equilibrium in complex modern industrialized societies. This common sense is fundamentally produced, transformed, and dominated by (1) the emergence, reproduction, and constant reconstitution of a given society's hegemonic bloc (a formation cohered through a dynamic coordination of interest, desire, and affect within and between classes, governing blocs, and self-identifying social groups or movements), (2) identifiable (though often overlapping and politically discontinuous) social organisms and institutions (themselves produced through the changing interactions between "state" and "civil society"), and (3) the momentary historical and political imperatives of social (national) reproduction (e.g., the need to respond to economic, state, or projected moral crises, and hence to restore the relative equilibrium of "hegemony").⑫ The theoretical primacy that Gramsci gives to the cultural, ideological, and subjective dimensions of everyday social life — and the emphasis he places on the socially and materially formative aspects of these dimensions — is what, in part, distinguishes his conception of hegemony and social formation from more reductive, economistic models of Marxist social and political thought. This analytic also enables multiple appropriations and revisions of the Gramscian schematic for critical studies of race, identity, and community formation. Stuart Hall thus stipulates:

> [Gramsci] shows how the so-called "self" which underpins [subordinate] ideological formations is not a unified but a contradictory subject and a social construction. He thus helps us to understand

one of the most common, least explained features of "racism": the "subjection" of the victims of racism to the mystifications of the very racist ideologies that imprison and define them.[13]

It is the latter strain in Hall's elaboration of Gramsci's theoretical usefulness — the notion that the assumptive objects or victims of racial and racist social technologies also, unavoidably, live and work within the very racial/racist material–ideological problematics that render them vulnerable to premature death[14] — that I wish to take up in the rest of this chapter.

This extended interrogation attempts to delink the grammars of Filipino American discourse from the assumptive mystifications that obscure those grammars' conditions and contexts of articulation. I am suggesting an analytical schematic that (1) foregrounds the historical indelibility of "race" as a nexus of power relations and (commonsense) articulations that compose Filipino subjectivities and collective identities, while (2) referencing the political and material conditions of possibility that enable particular elements of Filipino American discourse to appear intelligible and reasonable when such discursive productions might, under other conditions or framings, be (commonly and popularly) dismissed as incoherent or absurd.

By way of illustration, one pedagogical component of contemporary Filipino American discourse prescribes a peculiar therapeutic regimen that collapses a reifying notion of collective historical trauma ("colonial mentality"), localized forms of social alienation, and intra-"Filipino" community contradictions into pathologies of "identity" and a banal rhetoric of pluralism and diversity. Reductively culturalist renditions of the collective "psychological" legacies of Spanish (and, to a far lesser extent, American) colonialism firmly underscore this production as a fundamentally prescriptive and pedantic venture, offering diagnostic variations on individualized psychocultural wellness as the reconstituting salve for a projected and ostensibly recuperated and psychically "whole" Filipino American identity. Linda

Revilla, for example, initiates her archetypal essay "Filipino American Identity" with the contention:

> Ethnic identity is important because it affects the maintenance and expression of traditional culture, helps individuals enhance their self-concept and self-esteem, and enables individuals to have a sense of belonging to an ethnic group. In addition, it is a necessary ingredient for ethnic consciousness and activism.[15]

Exceeding this functionalist conception of identity as a psychiatric project that mechanistically preserves an ossified "traditional culture" while tautologically facilitating membership in an already extant "ethnic group" (according to Revilla's logic: ethnic identity works to enable membership in a group already consolidated under the rubric of that same ethnic identity), Leny Strobel extrapolates Revilla's schema by outlining a "process of decolonization" for Filipino Americans that evinces no conception of "decolonization" as a complex material — and historically present — lineage of collective (national and indigenous/tribal) insurgency against varieties of institutionalized human domination under European and American imperialisms. In fact, Strobel's "decolonization" is premised on the putative Filipino American self's idealist transcendence of a colonial history's intertwined social materialities, including its contemporary neocolonial and postcolonial formations:

> Decolonization means to reconnect with the past in order to understand the present and to be able to envision the future. . . . Decolonization is a process that makes the mythical and historical past available to the present. Cultural and historical knowledge, language, and personal histories recovered through memory makes the rewriting of the self possible within a decolonized framework. Decolonization strengthens the cultural connection to the Filipino indigenous culture because it is a source of grounding.[16]

Recalling her participation in the early 1990s Sikolohiyang Pilipino (Association for Filipino Psychology) cultural movement, Strobel's warped decolonization pivots on a strident appropriation and alienation of an undifferentiated "Filipino indigenous" (thus the easy appropriation of a "mythical and historical past") that, nonetheless, restores (fabricates?) a foundational premise for "post-1965 Filipino American" identity formation. Most overtly, this therapeutic pedagogy presumes the convenient and tangible usefulness/disposability of "Filipino indigenous culture" to the contemporary Filipino American communion in the United States. For Strobel and others in resonance with her framing, the abstracted "indigenous" is really a compilation of distant cultural artifacts and composes a project of cultural reification that postpones or erases the current life of actual indigenous peoples and movements in (and beyond) the Philippine nation-state, including multivalent political struggles to dissolve or substantially redefine formal Philippine governmental authority and "Filipino" cultural hegemony over the indigenous peoples of Mindanao, Cordillera, and numerous other parts of the archipelago. Further, the generalized naming and appropriation of a Philippine indigeneity fails to account for the specificities of contemporary indigenous peoples' collective political subjectivities, components of which pose a fundamental opposition to Filipino national, ethnic, and diasporic identity formations: for example, the diverse theological–political articulations of Islam among the Moro peoples, rearticulations of Communist and Marxist–Leninist–Maoist thought among a spectrum of movements and organizations/parties throughout the islands, and engagements with electoral politics and governance by some indigenous peoples overtly displace and challenge the sovereignty (and frequently seize the actual political domain) of the Philippine state and suggest a complex set of rhetorical, cultural, and political insurgencies — from reactionary fundamentalist to progressive revolutionary — against the dominance of the Filipino subject.[17]

Strobel's conception of identity formation as a linear progression toward a self-realized Filipino American subject, in addition to alienating, decontextualizing, and abstracting the social meaning of indigenous cultures in the archipelago, is fundamentally an edification of Filipino American cosmopolitan subjectivity —

a tacit premise on which the Filipino American communion is based. Thus, the subjects of her study *Coming Full Circle: The Process of Decolonization among Post-1965 Filipino Americans* are almost entirely college and university students, and the one nonstudent is the salaried director of an arts organization. Embodying the "decolonization" problematic in the biographies of a 1990s Filipino American petite bourgeoisie, Strobel's social scientific Bildungsroman culminates in a prescriptive narrative of the self-actualized Filipino American as a good citizen–subject, that is, as a cooperative partner in the multiculturalist civil formation of the United States: "*To decolonize is to re-imagine the Filipino American community in ways that make it a visible, contributing presence within U.S. society.*"[18]

It is within this rhetorical structure that "decolonization" becomes synonymous — actually symbiotic — with the U.S. (multiculturalist) national project, and as such the authentically self-realized / decolonized Filipino American becomes party to a hegemonic nation building that exceeds the scenes of the American domestic, and revivifies the historical relations of U.S.-proctored "colonialism" and "empire." The dependence on such opportunistic appropriations of an allegedly traditional or indigenous culture for the purpose of installing a stable, U.S.-based cosmopolitanism displaces a radical, if uneasy, possibility: the insurgent production of a Philippine / U.S. Filipino collective historical memory that articulates from within the constitutive violence and traumatic rupturings of American conquest and colonization, coercive modernist "civilization," and the more fundamental surrender of the "independent" Philippine nation-state form itself. (I will examine this possibility more closely in chapter 3.)

While I will introduce a more substantive discussion of Filipino American cosmopolitanism as the project of a historically particular Philippine "national middle class" in chapter 4, it is useful here to appropriate and elaborate the Gramscian schematic in the spirit of Hall's urging. Gramsci's rudimentary conception of the symbiosis between relations of "coercion and consent" in the emergence of hegemonic social formations directly relates to the broadly social — hence historical and material — implications of popular knowledge productions, including and especially projects of communal self-consciousness (articulations of "community"), collective ideology (shared and/or proselytized systems of thought), and folklore (in the above case, recuperations of the Philippine indigenous-"cultural"). Following this formulation, such narratives of Filipino American subjectivity are neither naïve nor benign, but can be seen as entirely conducive with the social logic of the U.S. racist state and its post–civil rights, multiculturalist revisions of U.S. white supremacist cultural formation.

In short, I am privileging the analytical question of whether and how the contingent problematics of Filipino American discourse, across its different moments and sites of production, opportune on (and eventually flourish through) the corresponding hegemonic problematics of contemporary multiculturalist white supremacy, which provide delimited spaces of empowerment and social prestige for the racial subalterns of "classical" American apartheid,[19] while reproducing the institutionality of white life, white bodies, and white subjectivities as the socially ascendant modality of the (allegedly postapartheid) U.S. social formation. Put otherwise, the sanctity and quality of white life, figurative and physical integrity of the white body, and the social and moral ascendancy of the (usually transparent) white subject animate the multiculturalist "turn" in U.S. civil society and form the condition of historical possibility for contemporary Filipino Americanism. The larger social project of representing, communing, and culturally producing a Filipino American historical bloc, then, is essentially defined by a specific conjuncture in the institutional and cultural apparatuses of white supremacy, which are themselves fortified and elaborated by this putative Filipino American communion.

Suggesting a theoretical schematic that is useful to a critical examination of the otherwise obscured connections between the cultural productions of emergent multiculturalist civil "communities" and the legitimated violence of the racist state, Gramsci writes that it is precisely within the terrains of popular knowledge and mass pedagogy that civil society's "common sense" mediates consent to the coercive state. Describing this relation, he writes:

> These two levels correspond on the one hand to the function of "hegemony" which the dominant group exercises throughout society and on the other hand to that of "direct domination" or command exercised through the State and "juridical" government.... The intellectuals are the dominant group's "deputies" exercising the subaltern functions of social hegemony and political government. These comprise:
>
> 1. The "spontaneous" consent given by the great masses of the population to the general direction imposed on social life by the dominant fundamental group; this consent is "historically" caused by the prestige (and consequent confidence) which the dominant group enjoys because of its position and function in the world of production.
>
> 2. The apparatus of state coercive power which "legally" enforces discipline on those groups who do not "consent" either actively or passively. This apparatus is, however, constituted for the whole of society in anticipation of moments of crisis of command and direction when spontaneous consent has failed.[20]

In Gramsci's terms, the labor of generating the masses' "spontaneous consent" to the assumptive political, ideological, and cultural problematics of the existing social formation is a comprehensive popular pedagogical exercise, largely refined and communicated by those "organic intellectuals" of the hegemonic bloc whose vocation it is to teach and (re)articulate the aforementioned "general direction" of social life. Following Gramsci a bit further, the conglomeration of "professional intellectuals" working in generalized allegiance to the "dominant fundamental group" include schoolteachers, novelists, academics, priests, newspaper editors, journalists, lawyers, and others, including various other competing groups of organic intellectuals who embody the interests of social classes and "historical blocs" within a given hegemony.

Gramsci's theoretical purpose in employing this expansive and heterogeneous definition of the intellectual classes, however, is not simply to affirm that in complex societies there are multiple sites of intellectual and cultural production. His conceptual intervention, rather, is to demystify the realm of the popular cultural and popular ideological, that is, to foreground the complex and historically vexed labor of generating "spontaneous consent" as a primary axis of cultural and political labor for hegemonic *and subaltern* social classes and historical blocs. It is the emergence and relative "success" of the pedagogies of common sense, politically galvanized through the production of consent, that in turn composes a particular historical moment in the "life" of Filipino American discourse, which has encompassed an accelerated, unprecedented institutionality and discursive coherence since the 1990s.

Reading the "Voice of Filipino Americans"

The popular vernacular of *Philippine News,* the most widely circulated Filipino American print media form in the world, encompasses a set of political and ideological assumptions that speak more precisely to this key moment in the conceptual life of Filipino Americanism. Since its founding in 1961, the *News* has consistently stipulated its authority as the "Voice of Filipino Americans," in reflection of founder Alex Esclamado's ambitions. Forming a center of gravity through which a class of Filipino American professional intellectuals organizes a collective (pedagogical) voice while projecting a corresponding constituent public, this media organ assumes the ongoing project of defining, controlling, and imagining a discrete Filipino American public. Further, as it has taken on the material form of a corporate media institution (the *News* boasts ownership of the Philippine News Building, its headquarters in South San Francisco), formed a strategic partnership with the *Los Angeles Times*, and developed a significant national distribution (120,000 weekly), the *News* has clearly become one of the foremost ideological apparatuses of Filipino American civil society.[21]

While my symptomatic reading of the newspaper in this chapter is strategically limited to three months' worth of publications in the late 1990s (January–March 1997), this period offers a typical sampling of the discursive structures through which the *News* has fortified its claims to Filipino American "Voice" since the 1986 overthrow of Philippine martial law. Interestingly, a central focus of the newspaper through the 1970s and mid-1980s was to investigate and expose the corruptions and abuses of the Marcos regime, as well as to publish numerous political editorials denouncing Marcos and providing a press outlet for stateside political exiles like Benigno "Ninoy" Aquino Jr., Lorenzo Tanada, Jovito Salonga, Jose Diokno, and Heherson Alvarez. The overall tenor and journalistic makeup of the publication changed gradually and substantially in the post–martial law years, however, particularly after the *News* was purchased by the family of prominent Manila banker Edgardo Espiritu during the same year to which my critical reading of the newspaper is attending.[22]

The procession of my reading of the *News* focuses less on its coverage of discrete, chronologically located events than it does on the repetitive, pedagogical aspects of its inscription of a presumptive — and frequently enunciated — common sense that enunciates and anticipates the assembly of a structure of consent. Thus, this limited examination of the *News* proposes a method and analytical frame through which to examine Filipino American discourse across its apparently dispersed and arbitrary renditions. It is possible, in this sense, to symptomatically read the relative continuity of Filipino Americanism's ideological frames and affective gestures across its different and

displaced pedagogical moments, as well as to situate its particular utterances, political enunciations, and material–discursive
representations within the larger historical project of Filipino
American communion. Here I am following a conception of the
"social production of news" that builds on Gramsci's rudimentary schematic of common sense, while crucially illuminating
the specificity of the "bureaucratic organization of the media"
as a central institutional component in the social intercourse of a
given civil society's readerships and audiences. Hall et al. crystallize this theoretical and methodological approach in their classic
text *Policing the Crisis*:

> If the world is not to be represented as a jumble of random and
> chaotic events, then they must be identified (i.e., named, defined,
> related to other events known to the audience), and assigned to a
> social context (i.e., placed within a frame of meanings familiar to
> the audience).... An event only "makes sense" if it can be located
> within a range of known social and cultural identifications.... This
> bringing of events within the realm of meanings means, in essence,
> referring unusual and unexpected events to the "maps of meaning"
> which already form the basis of our cultural knowledge, into which
> the social world is *already* "mapped...." This process of "making
> an event intelligible" is a social process — constituted by a number of
> specific journalistic practices, which embody (often only implicitly)
> crucial assumptions about what society is and how it works.
>   One such background assumption is the *consensual* nature of soci-
> ety: the process of *signification* — giving social meanings to events —
> both assumes and helps to construct society as a "consensus. [23]

It is within this analytical context that the *Philippine News* is
implicated within the larger pedagogical labors of commonsense
formation and the imaginative labors of consensus building:
What, in this context, does the labor of Filipino American
"sense-making" look like?

The *News* self-narrates as a liberal publication with noble
intentions of "community empowerment." The scope of its
knowledge production and shape of its popular pedagogical
ambitions overtly operate through the discourses and political
common sense of the American post–civil rights national project.

Revising its mission in the aftermath of the Marcos regime's collapse, the publishers of the *News* suggest the rebirth of an activist publication, albeit one newly focused on the promise of the liberal pluralist American dream, rather than on overseas political opposition to a Philippine martial law government.

> [After 1986,] *Philippine News* ... had its work cut out for it, and took it on with much relish. *It was going to be a medium — the vehicle — for the needs and aspirations of Filipinos in America. It was going to serve as a bonding element to fuse the disparate sectors of the community.* It would galvanize its members to take a more active role in political activity. It would become a beacon of enlightenment to help Filipinos fulfil their potential as productive members of society, as well as call recognition to their successes. ...
>
> *Now the challenge for Filipinos is to press harder for America to acknowledge their contributions by giving them a bigger say in the formulation of the national agenda.* Being quiet and staying in the background just will no longer be enough if the Filipino American community is going to get its just share of the fruits of society's labor.[24] [emphasis added]

Departing from this self-inscribed mandate, *Philippine News* maps and depicts a narrative of Filipino American civil ascendancy through persistent textual celebrations and photographic exhibitions of "Outstanding College Students," "Regal Beauties and Leaders" (beauty pageant winners), and "The Filipino Americans' Success in the Social and Cultural Aspects." This political and moral parochialism, situated within the larger schema of a multiculturalist common sense, *produces* while it disciplines a putative Filipino American community, rendering the fundamental assumptions, myths, ideas, and ideologies of U.S. nation building — for example, American exceptionalism, meritocratic upward mobility, political and cultural assimilationism, ideal (racial or protoracial) phenotype, rote patriotism, dutiful electoral participation, valorization of military and police figures — widely accessible, intelligible, and personally appealing to its community of interest.

"Culture," Mobility, and the *Balikbayan*

Philippine News produces the discrete and peculiar national exceptionalism of Filipino American subjectivity through a rather unrelenting fetishizing and sometimes explicit eroticization of the Philippines as a site of easy "cultural" access and pleasurable tourist globetrotting. One such article, "American Tourists Laud Filipino Hospitality," offers the Philippines as an available site of Filipino American *balikbayan*[25] indulgence, and logically extends a notion of the diasporic homeland that rests on pseudo-anthropological constructions of, in turn, the friendly native "Filipino," an awe-inspiring and beautiful (though also immediately accessed and consumed) "Philippine culture," hardworking "maids and chauffeurs," and a mystic Philippine affection for its returning American folk.

> MANILA — Thomas Odol and Lloyd Remo, both U.S. Postal Service Managers of San Francisco, were overwhelmed by the warm hospitality and friendliness of the Filipino. They were filled with awe after seeing the beauty of Philippine culture.
>
> The life style in the city and in the province became interesting to Odol and Remo. They were fascinated by the vast entertainment opportunities, from the disco and ballroom dancing, to the cockfighting and carabao riding. The efficient services of maids and the expert maneuvering of chauffeurs extremely impressed them....
>
> Seemingly spellbound of their wonderful and exciting experiences, they returned back home to the U.S. *Still full of awe and admiration of the Philippines, it took them awhile to get back to reality.*
>
> Leaving their hearts in the Philippines, Odol and Remo promised to go back again this year.[26] [emphasis added]

The short narrative generates a particular and identifiable Filipino American gaze, fortifying the *national* origins of sight and observation through a figurative round trip: the balikbayan's essentialized homeland is a geographically distant yet beautiful reminder of life's simple and indulgent pleasures, in stark contrast to the projected (and inherent) complexities and hardships of Filipino *American* life. As tourists enraptured by the lush scenery and transcendent cultural aesthetic of their cross-

Pacific geography of genealogical origin, Odol and Remo stand in for a Filipino American sentimentality that orbits around the melodrama of the homecoming, here encircled by the petite bourgeoisie pleasures of the balikbayan hero's welcome.

The *News*'s cultural production of the balikbayan as a core discursive figure in the social mosaic of Filipino Americanism, then, enacts a narrative anchoring of the Filipino American subject to the familiar and mundane United States (the *News*'s sturdy "reality") by fabricating that subject's "overwhelmed" unfamiliarity with the quaint deferences afforded to the "American" by the (native, submissive, eagerly servicing) "Filipino." This assertion of Filipino American exceptionality is not only denoted in the narrative nuances of organs like the *News*, but is also explicitly sanctioned through the juridical innovations of the Philippine state. In fact, the figure of the Filipino American balikbayan mirrors the Philippine government's well-recognized enthrallment with "overseas Filipinos," whose remittances compose a major portion of the philippine gross national product, and around whom the Philippine state has literally conceived a field of jurisprudence.[27] The Philippine government's own cultural and juridical productions of the balikbayan subject both "officially" enable and ideologically encourage the emergence of a Filipino American common sense in which the generic nomenclature of the overseas Filipino already implies the privileged — and potentially valorized — status of the "American" Filipino. The text of a 2002 Philippine government press release spills forth the logic of this cultural–juridical work, as if in dialogue with the *News*'s discretely Filipino American discourse of transpacific mobility and consumption:

> President Gloria Macapagal-Arroyo today signed into law a bill amending the Balikbayan law, granting special privileges to overseas Filipino workers and former Filipinos and their families, and four other measures of national interest.
>
> The new Balikbayan law, Republic Act No. 9174, acknowledges the contribution of the overseas Filipino workers and former Filipino citizens to the Philippine economy through the foreign exchange inflows and revenues they generate.

The new law also provides additional benefits and privileges to all overseas Filipino once they come and visit their motherland. Among the perks is the "kabuhayan shopping privilege" allowing tax-exempt purchase of livelihood tools that would enable them to become economically self-reliant members of society upon their return to the country.
Such tools refer to instruments, including computers and accessories, necessary in the practice of one's trade or profession.
The law also entitles the balikbayan and his or her family to tax-exempt purchases in the amount of $1,500 at duty-free shops; discounted rates in domestic carriers; and visa-free entry to the Philippines for a period of one year for foreign passport holders, among others.[28]

Notable in the opening lines of the government press statement is the ambiguous contextualization of the amended law as the province of not only the generically conceived "overseas Filipino worker," but also of those oxymoronically termed "*former* Filipinos and their families." The significance of such utterances — whether or not they are misprints, typographical errors, or meanings "lost in translation" — is their revelation of possibility for a broader, structural conception of Filipino American nationality as both a moment of delineation and distance from the Philippine nation-state or homeland, and as an interpellating subjectivity that significantly exceeds the dry, consumerist-tourist language of the Philippine government's balikbayan jurisprudence.

The figure of the balikbayan, in other words, conveys an assumptive movement and mobility of bodies, identifications, and disposable income across "American" and "Filipino" homelands that, in turn, form a central ideological structure through which the subjects of Filipino American communion foster a material and geographic modality of internal identification with one another. The proper Filipino American subject, abruptly distinguished from the generic category of the globally dispersed Filipino "overseas worker," is *not* reproduced by the social and narrative logic of the "refugee" or prodigal "diasporic" traveler, but rather by the imperatives of a refracted

American exceptionalism or chauvinism (wherein the assumptions and entitlements of mobility compose crucial material and ideological circuits). It is, in part, through the sturdy and multivalent institutionality of the balikbayan figure — and the familiar narratives, stories, laments, and industrialized circuits of travel therein — that Filipino American subjects obtain uniquely privileged currency as the "American" subjects (though not necessarily American citizens) of an otherwise undifferentiated "Filipino diaspora."

The pages of the *News* thus signify the integrity of the Filipino American subject by producing "Philippine Culture" as an alienated geographic and discursive site, objectified and cohered through the imagined communion of American balikbayan, as well as through the incessant circulation and exchange of the Philippine cultural artifact as a major currency of Filipino American discourse. This objectification is compulsively repeated in the production of the Filipino American communal imaginary, in part because the artifacts accumulate as raw material for a conceptual apparatus through which the overtly moralizing imperative to "cultivate" and "promote" an alleged "native" ethnic heritage enacts its essential (and popular) intelligibility. Hence, "(native) Philippine Culture" fragments into programmatic and formulaic rituals of cultural production that, in turn, inscribe the challenge of edifying those Filipino Americans who are marked by the anxiety of their alienation from a mystified and calcified Filipinoness. The *News*'s valorization of one Bay Area dance troupe is typical in its installation of a particular performance artifact as a medium of generational cultural transmission and individualized psychic and physical auto-therapy:

> Karilagan was formed in September, 1995 to promote the Philippine Culture and pass it on to future generations.... Its objective[s] include: cultivating the Filipino culture among its members and to *further enhance their physical and mental attributes* through arts, dance, drama, language and music, providing a medium of self-expression and independence from adverse social pressures.[29] [emphasis added]

The figurative collapsing of Philippine Culture into a marketable, exchangeable, and ritually summoned commodity heirloom, to be "promoted" and "passed on to future generations," suggests a gratuitous — and specifically Filipino American — signification of Philippine Culture as quaint, convenient, and accessible. In fact, this relation of alienation, exchange, and rituality is precisely the logic of the contemporary, liberal multicultural American nationalist project: the viability of American "multiculturalism," as a fundamentally pedagogical (though no less pedantic) post–civil rights discourse that fabricates, assigns, and designates a generalized historical identity to ethnic and racial "minority" groups in a drama of postapartheid nationalist suturing, turns precisely on the facile recognizability of preordained cultural difference as the activity through which the historically marginalized or abject ascend to the status of equal partnership in a nationally imagined, liberal pluralist politicocultural domain.

This structure of multicultural "empowerment" induces eclectic practices of collective self-presentation that not only produce a reified "culture" as a classical public site and spectacle of white nationalist enjoyment/consumption (such as in the well-documented colonialist white supremacist fabrications of Philippine culture and society in the early twentieth-century World's Fairs),[30] but also generate a material culture of communion for the multiculturalist collective self that inspires, arouses, and gratifies as it convenes.

Illustratively, the *News* relies on a well-worn semiotic of tropical feminine fertility to inscribe the autoerotic, exhibitionist logic of Filipino American communion in its narration of the inaugural "Philippine float" for the nationally televised 1997 Tournament of Roses Parade (Pasadena, California):

> New Year's Day 1997 will go down in the annals of Philippine history as the start of an epoch for Filipinos not only because it marked their first-ever participation in the Parade that *symbolized the Filipino spirit* in an event of unparalleled significance, but also because

theirs was a Winner in the initial attempt to take their place in the international limelight....

The Philippine float symbolized the "beauty, strength and heritage of the Philippines." It featured the image of a lovely Filipino woman presenting a lei of orchids and the national flower, sampaguita.... [T]he Filipino is surrounded by a garden of roses, orchids, gerbera daisies, lilies and Gypsophilia, eloquently illustrating the "tropical paradise" that is one feature of the country....

Philippine lawyer Rustie Ricaforte, director of tourism, based in Los Angeles, called the historical Philippine participation in the Rose Parade as "one without equal...." "Our country can no longer be [bypassed] by the world's travelers," he emphasized.[31] [emphasis added]

The colonialist exoticism of the narration (and of the float's own depictions) amplifies the declaration of a triumphal moment in the popular cultural genealogy of a Filipino American enfigurement: the agency, intentionality, and implicit opportunism of such a "Philippine" cultural spectacle are shaken loose from their familiar possession by alien (read: white colonialist) subjects, and repossessed by the rightful "Filipino" owners of the artifact in commemoration of a new Filipino "epoch." This exhibitionism requires the figurative and literal "floating" of a densely unified and homogenous thing: the "Philippine," a notion that vacillates between adjective and noun as it reflects and filters inclusionist desire and the multiculturalist gaze. Here the Philippine float crystallizes the social logic of a Filipino American cultural labor that articulates a viable, national domesticity through spectacular renditions and public imaginations of what cultural theorist Allen Isaac elaborates as the *accessibly foreign and ludic "tropical"* features of a durable (and truly epochal) imperialist multiculturalist project.

Thus enabled by the rubrics, visualities, and social logics of a hegemonic liberal multiculturalism, Filipino American discourse divests the (already oversimplified) cultural categories of Filipino dance, cuisine, song, and bodily ornamentation of their historical embodiment — erasing, obscuring, and/or opportunistically renarrating complex and dense contexts of production and circulation, including the material location of such cultural practices within genealogies of colonization and resistance — and reinvests in them as the public signifiers of a putatively unified communal cultural artifact. I place critical emphasis on this rubric of Filipino American cultural fetish not out of an insistence that it should somehow rehabilitate itself in order to more "accurately" reflect or approximate "real" cultural practices, but rather because this strain of Filipino Americanism mediates the political logic of a contemporary multiculturalist white supremacy. In other words, this trajectory of Filipino Americanism is more than a mere revision of American chauvinist nationalism, it is a *racial* discourse that turns on a Filipino American elaboration and (always incomplete) possession of white (American) subjectivity as that which can possess, fabricate, commodify, and/or reveal the cultural "content" of a subaltern "(Filipino) spirit."

White Supremacy, Liberal Racism, and Multiculturalist Civil Society

Embedded within its gestures of allegiance to the American multiculturalist nationalist project is the *News*'s commitment to defining and policing the boundaries of its imagined community. Selective and strategic coverage of "community events," persistent repetition of the immigrant petite bourgeoisie "success story," and formulation of prescriptive and pedantic narrations of "community" in the newspaper's editorial pages form the armature of its Filipino American civil society. Here I am interested in the deducible and relatively stable set of assumptions underlying this public projection of multiculturalist civil society, to the extent that it is the premises of such a "community" articulation that establish the limits and criteria for inclusion within its projected domiciles.

The most aggressively posited premise of this civil society entails the sanctity of the heteronormative, patriarchal, middle-class nuclear family as the condition of "good" Filipino American public subjectivity. "The family," as idealized within the pages of the *News,* is a steadfastly ahistorical pillar upon which Filipino American civil society flourishes into recognition and public prominence. Morally conservative self-help groups like the Ocean County Philippine Social Club (OCPS), for example, are lionized through such headlines as "OCPS Preserves Family Values."[32] Regular editorial columns by the *News*'s resident public intellectuals emphasize this compulsory familial paradigm, frequently refining their pronouncements with disciplinary and repressive Filipino Catholic varieties of moral conservatism. This compulsory family paradigm invokes a particular Filipino American culturalist *naturalism,* a conceptual move that exceeds narrower notions of "cultural nationalism." *News* editorialist Ludy Astraquillo Ongkeko, Ph.D. (per her byline), reflects this position in many of her writings, including an exemplary editorial that indicts the "rise of female-headed households" as a fundamental cause for the erosion of the Filipino American nuclear family:

> An important underlying reason for greater marital instability is women's increasing economic independence.
> ...I like to think that the Filipino family in this country will not contribute immensely to the breakdown of the family structure. Yes, the family is a fundamental unit of social and economic organization in this culture, but there is always that hope that Filipino cultural and traditional patterns of bringing up a family will prevail despite the odds in these United States.[33]

As if to foreshadow this pronouncement, Ongkeko (in an article written one week prior to the aforementioned editorial) celebrates one couple's "golden wedding anniversary" as an invocation of Filipino American civil society's potentialities for fecundity, wealth, success, and monogamous heterosexual fidelity:

Nowadays, we don't hear too often about decades-old wedding anniversaries.

How about fifty golden years?

Does this sound incredible? Indeed, it does when one sees both celebrants are still youthful and what is even more amazing, their exuberance is a gauge of how they love life and are thankful they are still around to enjoy their great grandchildren. . . .

With 11 children, all married, the Manoloto couple, originally from Pampanga, can lay claim to the beauty in having large families. All their children received their college education. . . .

It was "love at first sight" for Federico. As he glanced at Perla, he told himself, "this is the woman I shall marry." And marry he did, but first, he had to start the courtship with Perla's parents whose consent he eventually won. For her part, Perla reasons out that she acquiesced, her position was borne by her desire to be "obedient" to her parents.

Her love for Federico, she stresses, was one of "developed" love strengthened through the many years solidified by his devotion to her.[34]

Ongkeko's reification of "the Filipino family" as both moral artifact and internally unified sociological category is essential to the multiculturalist civil project at hand: it consolidates a civic unit or building block of Filipino American cultural, social, and biological reproduction through a permanent deferral of the moment of reflexive critique that interrogates, distends, and potentially disarticulates the compulsory heteronormative nuclear family as the harvest of multiple vectors of biopolitical power. ✓

Michel Foucault, in a well-known passage from *The History of Sexuality,* explicates the discursive and institutional structure of the family as a "deployment" of power/sexuality within a social matrix that might be reread through the compulsory civil assimilation of minoritized populations into the American multiculturalist regime. He writes:

> The family, in its contemporary form, must not be understood as a social, economic, and political structure of alliance that excludes or at least restrains sexuality, that diminishes it as much as possible, preserving only its useful functions. On the contrary, its role is to

anchor sexuality and provide it with a permanent support.... The family is the interchange of sexuality and alliance: it conveys the law and the juridical dimension in the deployment of sexuality; and it conveys the economy of pleasure and the intensity of sensations in the regime of alliance.[35]

Foucault reminds us that the allegation of "the family" as a site of moral preservation and heteronormativist vindication — in the Filipino Americanist context, this suggests that *repressive* constructions of sexuality compose a *productive* biopolitical technology — is an exercise of disciplinary and (sexually) normalizing power sui generis. As such, Ongkeko's pleas for the sustenance of the nuclear household amount to more than a conservative bargain with the juridical and cultural apparatuses of American civil society: exceeding the banal prescriptive surfaces of her numerous editorials is a foreclosure of any conceptualization of the Filipino American family as a historically and geographically specific site and moment of crisis, struggle, and violence. There is no room — logically or conceptually — for such potentially explosive and blasphemous critical conversation within a popular pedagogical discourse that exercises community as the production of an internally unified entity that overcomes and overrules constitutive contradiction and conflict. This is to suggest that the Filipino Americanist allegory of the "Filipino family" pivots on a presumption of moral infallibility that precipitates the compulsory family as the vindicated a priori of Filipino American civil society.

Another example culled from the editorial pages of the *News* elaborates the sturdy complicity of this Filipino American familial discourse with the white supremacist logic of liberal multiculturalism. Echoing what sociologist Dana Takagi has argued is one of the fundamental technologies of the Asian American "model minority" signification, the moral integrity of Filipino Americanism consistently turns on its capacity to articulate the compulsory family unit in implicit opposition to the archetypal family pathologies of other ("non-Asian") racially pathologized groups.[36] *News* editorial contributor Corazon Vergara Mandap, Ph.D., thus proposes a series of cultural determinants that facilitate the imminent arrival of a youthful, "U.S. generation" Filipino American petite bourgeoisie:

> Not only do adults achieve, even our students from the elementary, middle, and high schools do. Based on a study I made on the success of Asians of which the Filipinos form a major part, many high school graduates make it to state universities and the University of California system, while many elementary and middle schoolers make it to the top of the classes mainly due to the following factors:
>
> 1. The Filipino family arrangement to support children until they finish a course;
> 2. the extra assistance and guidance given Filipino children in doing their homework, projects, and reviews for exams;
> 3. the high parent expectations set for children to achieve;
> 4. the kind of discipline instilled in them.[37]

Leaving aside the obvious questions regarding the veracity and methodological legitimacy of Mandap's otherwise unspecified "study" of "Asian success," her articulation of "The Filipino Americans' Success in the Social and Cultural Aspects" merits critical engagement as a political and ideological formulation rather than an allegedly social scientific (or "scholarly") one. In addition to rendering a "parenting" archetype that emulates the classical tenets of the white supremacist model minority thesis (in which an undifferentiated Asian immigrant "culture of success" yields well-assimilated, nondelinquent, and high-achieving children),[38] this culturalist articulation must also be read in the historical context of a contemporary American multiculturalism that has emerged in political dialog and symbiosis with post–civil rights neoconservatism.

Mandap's formula for Filipino success, however spurious and dismissible at first glance, is socially significant to the extent that it is an organic late 1990s Filipino American commonsense elaboration of an ideological project first outlined in the 1960s. It was during this period that liberal academics and politicos, enabled in part by their enhanced political–intellectual credibility in the historical moment of the domestic civil rights movement and the acute insurgencies of radical liberationist struggles across the planetary landscape, authored an accumulating body of racist culturalist rationalizations that made (common) sense of the stubborn "postsegregation" social materialities of U.S. white supremacy: persistent residential, institutional, and socioeconomic apartheid, racially configured differences in premature death, and the perpetuity of the U.S. racist state as an arrangement of force that disrupted the optimistic possibilities of a nonracial (or antiracist) sociality. In this moment, a particular strain of liberal racist knowledge production facilitated the organization of a social scientific knowledge industry that was hallmarked by the publication of the now infamous "Moynihan Report" of 1965 (actually titled *The Negro Family: The Case for National Action*). The Moynihan Report was both foreshadowed and accompanied by the wide circulation of an academic (and eventually popular cultural) "culture of poverty" paradigm most closely identified with anthropologist Oscar Lewis's prolific ethnographic work on Puerto Ricans, Mexicans, and others.[39]

Importantly, the explanatory frameworks yielded by the Moynihan–Lewis lineage have insidiously persisted through some of the most prominent contemporary "Filipino Americanist" academic scholarship, most notably in the widely read writing of sociologists Yen Le Espiritu and Diane Wolf. Espiritu's rather reductive explanations of Filipino American familial gender oppression, examined alongside Wolf's alarmingly simplistic rationalization of the high suicidal tendency rates of young Filipina American women, offer similarly extensive articulations of the cultural pathologies and dysfunctions of Filipino "family" and "culture." Wolf, for example, asserts:

> "The family" seems to offer an extremely magnetic and positive basis of Filipino identity for many children of immigrants, yet it is also a deep source of stress and alienation, which for some, has led to internal struggles and extreme despair.[40]

Espiritu, in a similar vein, contends:

> [T]he process of parenting is gendered in that immigrant parents tend to restrict the autonomy, mobility, and personal decision making of their daughters more than that of their sons. I argue that these parental restrictions are attempts to construct a model of Filipina womanhood that is chaste, modest, nurturing, and family-oriented.[41]

While both scholars pay some fleeting descriptive attention to extrafamilial societal factors in their attempts to contextualize their central arguments, both (like Lewis and Moynihan) are fundamentally concerned with the locus of the "Filipino American family" as the primary analytical unit of empirical/ ethnographic study and explanation. Wolf's notion of "emotional transnationalism" installs a reified, culturally unitary notion of "family" and second-generation Filipina American "alienation" that preempts the explanatory possibility that suicidal emotional distress, psychological trauma, and mental illness may not be wholly — or even primarily — "caused" by familial or Filipino cultural pathology. Both authors, moreover, betray a tendency to accept their ethnographic respondents' testimonies about Filipino "intergenerational conflict" and repressive parenting cultures as prima facie explanatory frameworks for conceptualizing Filipino American articulations of gender and patriarchy, as well as for analyzing the apparently astronomical suicidality among adolescent and young adult Filipina Americans. Wolf writes:

> In response to our question as to whether Vallejo (CA) teachers and high school counselors noticed anything particular about their Filipino students . . . particularly the children of immigrants, most responded without hesitation, referring to the intense academic pressure Filipino students of immigrants, especially Filipinas, receive from parents. This pressure was attributed to parents being immigrants, their desire to succeed, and their desire for their children to achieve at least their same middle to upper middle class status.[42]
>
> [S]ome Filipino immigrant parents pursue contradictory tactics with their children's (particularly their daughters') education by pushing them relentlessly to achieve and succeed at first, and then pulling the emergency brake just as they are coming to an important junction, slowing or even stopping them in their tracks and then

sending them in a different direction, often on the local rather than the express train. Instead of continuing to push children to achieve by going to an excellent four-year university...many parents prefer that their children stay at home, even if that means going to a lesser college, if at all.... This process obstructs and derails the drive for excellence parents previously pursued and replaces it with more gendered priorities of control and safety.[43] ⌄

The paradox many young people faced, however, was that while parents wanted/expected their children to come to them with their problems, reflecting Filipino family ideology that one should go to parents with one's troubles, parents were often at the basis of some of these problems. Furthermore, children faced sanctions, punishment, or feelings of guilt in their parents' reactions, leading some of them to withdraw and withhold their problems. This notion of family as the locus of contradictions best summarizes these poignant experiences.[44]

Wolf fails to qualify her attempt at thick description with any rigorous discussion as to whether and how her Filipina subjects' anxieties, antagonisms, and alienations — which she alleges to derive fundamentally from the characteristic repressiveness, Catholic moral punitivity, and embedded generational–cultural distance of Filipino immigrant parents — are qualitatively different from (or for that matter any "worse" than) those of any other category of young adult women and girls. Instead, one is left to take Wolf at her word that these cultural pathologies are not only distinguishing features of Filipina American social experience, but that they also explain an acute proclivity to contemplate or attempt suicide. To Wolf's credit, she admits as much, although she still fails to explain the analytic or methodological validity of her position:

> [W]hile these dynamics *may not differ significantly from intergenerational relations in other immigrant (and nonimmigrant) families,* the emotional outcomes do seem to be significantly different. This may provide insight into the feelings of aloneness and despair which can translate into desperate and suicidal thoughts.[45] [emphasis added]

Wolf's sociological sleight of hand — in which an empirically marked difference of "emotional outcome" suddenly substitutes for sociological "insight" and explanation — rehearses the most durable methodological and logical facets of Lewis's debunked-though-durable culture of poverty thesis, while recomposing the Lewis/Moynihan frameworks to depict a Filipino (or Filipino American) "culture of suicide."

Wolf's laundry list of the pathologies of Filipino "family ideology" exemplifies how the problematic of an emergent Filipino American common sense moves within and between the institutionalized cultural–intellectual spaces of multiculturalist civil society and the U.S. academy:

> Filipino family ideology has taught the students we interviewed that all problems should be kept within the family. A child's problem that is revealed to an "outsider" be (s)he a friend, teacher, or, in the worst case, a counselor, would create gossip and bring shame (*hiya*) and embarrassment to the family because it insinuates that they have a problem. In other words, due to a sense of self that is highly identified with the family, an individual's problems [create] a loss of face for the family as a collectivity, suggesting that parents did not do their job. Since many young people cannot turn to their parents...they feel caught in an extremely lonely bind, with no one to turn to for help.[46]
>
> Attempting to cope with the pressures and problems they feel, the children of Filipino immigrants described a situation of "no exit" — they could not turn to their parents for help nor could they turn to others for fear of further sanctions. This often created intense feelings of loneliness, deep unhappiness, and at times, despair. A few mentioned a religious notion of "suffering in silence" as a way to accept their pain, feeling that if Jesus could withstand carrying or being nailed to the cross, they should be able to handle their own suffering.[47]

Espiritu, building on Wolf's cultural cataloguing, places special emphasis on the *universality* of this structure of "intergenerational" immigrant parental control over the "emotional lives" of second-generation daughters. Deriving some working analytical conclusions from ethnographic data gathered from her San Diego area interviewees, Espiritu writes:

> These narratives call attention to the shifts in the generational power caused by the migration process and to the possible gap between what parents say they want for their children and their ability to

control the young. However, the interview data do suggest that inter-generational conflicts are socially recognized occurrences in Filipino communities.[48]

This narrative suggests that even when parents are unable to control the behaviors of their children, their (dis)approval remains powerful in shaping the emotional lives of their daughters. Although better-off parents can and do exert greater controls over their children's behaviors than do poorer parents, *I would argue that all immigrant parents — regardless of class background — possess this emotional hold on their children.*[49] [emphasis added]

In addition to begging the question of whether Wolf's and Espiritu's depictions of Filipino familial pathologies — even if accepted as "true" — are exclusively or even primarily responsible for the suicidal tendencies and broadly framed, gendered repression of young Filipina women, their analytic framing of the locus of the "Filipino family" remains anchored to a sociological mystification of Filipino "cultural" beliefs/ideologies/practices. Thus, for Wolf, the complexities of suicide as a more rigorously social problem, performance, and/or crisis of subjectivity, and for Espiritu, the analytical questions of how "gender" and "sexuality" articulate as regimes of power within Filipino American social formations, are largely erased in favor of reductive assertions of a Filipino (American) culture of suicide/misogyny.

Addressing a parallel derivative of Espiritu's and Wolf's explanatory frameworks in the "revisionist genre" of historical narrative emblematized by Stanley Karnow's widely read apologia for American colonialism and empire (*In Our Own Image: America's Empire in the Philippines*), cultural and literary theorist E. San Juan Jr. offers a lucid summation of the culturalist thesis-as-common-sense:

> Reduced to a few pivotal notions like *hiya*, internal debt (*utang na loob*), "mutuality of power dynamics," and so on, culture with its complex symbolic economy is divorced from its constellation of determining forces, from the circumstantial network of power. It becomes a generalizing formula utilized to unravel affairs of extreme "thickness" and intricacy, with weighty ethical and moral resonance.

...But the effects of neocolonial exploitation, racism, and gender oppression are absent, marginalized, or concealed.[50]

Remarking on the persistence of the very "culturalist function-alist" tendency enshrined by Filipino Americanists like Wolf and Espiritu, San Juan continues:

> Despite its weakness and for lack of any substitute, this culturalist functionalist paradigm still exercises authority among Filipinologists and their followers. It has now been thoroughly exposed for the following inadequacies, among others: its one-sided attribution of rationality and normative equilibrium to a particular social arrangement, its dismissal of the complex intentionality of individual's (agent's) conduct, and its circular mode of explaining social activity as meaningful insofar as it fulfills a temporally limited normative need such as the reinforcement of a code of values required for social coherence.[51]

Following San Juan, my analytical objective here is to displace the methodological and unspoken ideological premises of such sociological diagnoses of Filipino cultural–familial pathology, rather than to straightforwardly contest their spurious sets of conclusions and explanations: put differently, I am not especially interested in arguing that Wolf's and Espiritu's social scientific productions of "Filipino culture" and "family" are *simply* "untrue" or analytically facile. Rather, I wish to situate their appropriations of Filipina/o youth testimonials of familial antagonisms, cultural difference, and emotional trauma — which cumulatively reflect and reproduce an incipient Filipino American *common sense* rather than an "objective" or empirical social scientific "truth"— within the very genealogy of liberal academic–intellectual production most paradigmatically manifest in the works of people like Lewis and Moynihan, and notoriously refracted in the works of reactionary-to-conservative racist and white supremacist intellectuals like Charles Murray and Richard Herrnstein.[52]

The post-1970s transformation of what had been a relatively obscure "model minority" archetype into a broadly accessible institutional common sense (most widely and notoriously enshrined in the 1966 *U.S. News & World Report* article cited above) was enabled both by the political–ideological hegemony of the Moynihan–Lewis rubric of black–brown cultural pathology (wherein "Asians" stood in as the disciplinary cultural exemplars of "good" minority subjects over and against their black, Mexican, and Puerto Rican counterparts), and by the racial rearticulations of reactionary, conservative, and neoconservative public intellectuals who in part sought to form a white–Asian political bloc in response to momentary crises in the U.S. social formation that often were manifested as "racial" antagonisms in the public sphere.

Thus, Mandap's enunciation of the model Filipino American family can and must be framed as symptomatic of a peculiar *racial* project,[53] which is, in turn, enabled by a genealogy of (liberal) white supremacist racial thought that cuts across nominally "liberal," "conservative," and "neoconservative" social ideologies and political agendas. Her audacious litany of "Filipino Americans' Success in the Social and Cultural Aspects" is, in this context, neither an isolated rumination nor a fanciful moral propaganda, but is an intelligible, resonant, and entirely reasonable stipulation of Filipino American common sense once contextualized by prior (and accompanying) moments of political and ideological struggle. The historical condition of possibility for this discourse's emergence as a viable multiculturalist common sense, in other words, is not reducible to typical essentialist portrayals of ingrained Filipino (Catholic-ordained) moral/sexual/familial conservatism, but is traceable to shifts in hegemonic systems of (racial) alliance that simultaneously fabricate and empower particular social (racial) subjects: consider the 1984 pronouncements of President Ronald Reagan to a privileged audience of "Asian and Pacific-American leaders," which decisively locate the Asian immigrant/settler figure within the American Bildungsroman.

Asian and Pacific Americans have helped preserve [the American] dream by living up to the bedrock values that make us a good and a worthy people. I'm talking about principles that begin with the sacred worth of human life, religious faith, community spirit, and the responsibility of parents and schools to be teachers of tolerance, hard work, fiscal responsibility, cooperation, and love.

It's no wonder that the median income of Asian and Pacific American families is much higher than the total American average. After all, it is values, not programs and policies, that serve as our nation's compass. . . .

America needs our Asian and Pacific American citizens. You've enriched our national culture and our heritage. You've upheld the beliefs that account for so much of our economic and social progress. You've never stopped striving for excellence, despite times not long ago when you experienced terrible discrimination. And let me add that we will continue to fight against discrimination wherever there are any vestiges of it remaining, until we've removed such bigotry from our entire land.

We need your energy, your values, your hard work, and we need them expressed at the polls and within our political system. Those who escaped oppression have a special appreciation for America's freedom, and those who fled poverty cherish America's opportunity. So I urge you to get involved, stay involved, and run for public office. That is another way of helping in this land of ours.[54] ✔

The political architecture of Filipino American common sense both resonates and extrapolates the Reaganist announcement of a fulfilled Asian immigrant assimilationist fantasy and forms a disciplinary apparatus that negotiates the historical tension between Asian Americanist "panethnic" or coalitionist political formations[55] and a Filipino American / Filipino immigrant racial formation that pushes the limits of the assumptive white–Asian bloc. That is, the social logic of Filipino American common sense persistently distinguishes the Filipino American subject from the generic "Asian American" subject — insisting on the specificity of Filipino historical experience and political–cultural affinity with United States nation building through the twentieth century, in distinction from other "Asian" or "Asian American" groups — while ideologically reproducing the cultural, moral, and political apparatuses of a multiculturalist white supremacy.✔ In fact, this is a central feature of the deformed nationalism that animates Filipino Americanism in its creative, revisionist productions of an authentically "American" civil subjectivity.

Outlines of a "Modern Morality Play"

The *Philippine News,* as both a popular cultural and communal pedagogical medium, posits a disciplinary civil pageantry that composes a moral drama of Filipino Americanism. The *News*'s "CommLink" section — a compilation of local news, human interest stories, social events, and gossip — articulates as a nationally scaled community-building imaginary: the purpose of the CommLink pages, the editors assert, is to encourage its readership to "link up with Filipino American groups throughout the country." Tediously detailed with announcements of eclectic and discretely identified "Filipino" and "Filipino American" community events and brief narrations of Mandap's archetypal "Filipino success" in the U.S. setting, CommLink is a textual and pictorial collage of Filipino American professionals, local beauty pageant contestants, and "prominent citizen" profiles, as well as a compilation of sentimental testimonials to various Filipino American philanthropic ventures, marital milestones (especially "silver" and "golden" anniversaries), and "cultural performance" spectacles. The constant repetition of "beauty queen" head shots and professional organization group photos, among other images, forms a space of visual redundancy wherein the accumulated bodies on display become the snapshot apparition — the collective *phenotype* — of an authentic Filipino American civil society.

A typical CommLink piece, "Regal Beauties and Leaders," crystallizes the social logic of this trajectory of collective identification: exhaustively cataloguing the proceedings of the 1996 "Miss Asia International" competition in Rosemont, Illinois, the article lists the names of the beauty pageant winner, several runners-up, the recipients of the pageant's "young professional awards," the winners of the strangely titled "Outstanding Asian awards," and a number of other pageant contestants. One revealing passage locates the event within the animus of multi-culturalist nation building, which I have been arguing is the matrix of Filipino American common sense:

> [T]he award and recognition . . . triggered an overwhelming amount of enthusiasm in the professional community. The experience was a shining example of how the Asian and Latin international community . . . in America can enhance the civic spirit, grow and promote the ideals of democracy.[56]

The *News*'s romantic positioning of the upstanding Filipino American child and adolescent figure is crucial to its narrations of Filipino American civil society. Coverage of such public spectacles as "Beauty and Brains Night," "Miss Teen, Little Miss, and Little Mr. Philippines," and "Calendar Girl" contests, for example, showcase "the beauty and talent of Filipino youth"[57] while establishing identifiable standards for the normative social and political identifications — designated along axes of gender, sexuality, and class — for the presumptive heirs of the Filipino American communal project. Individualized depictions of youth "achievement" are prominent, with lionizing profiles of law and medical school graduates, newly credentialed registered nurses, scholarship winners, and young adults who attain any variety of public recognition by major foundations, state officials, or sporting bodies. Headlines like "Bright Future for Young Golfer," "Attorney General Commends Student," "Firm Hires FilAm Legal Scholar," "Fausto Bags AsianAm Calendar Girl Title," "UC Davis Sweethearts Tie the Knot," and "Francia Graduates from Citadel" prototype the "next generation" vanguard of Fili-pino Americanism as part of a multiculturalist historical bloc: here it is the projection of community and fantasy of civil society inscribed in this fabrication of "youth" that is most conducive to the social coherence of Filipino American common sense.

The composition of Filipino American community through these discursive modalities reflects the political truth of a historical moment: it was during the 1990s that the U.S. nation-building project accumulated a new and critical gravity of political interest and subjective identification vis-à-vis the cultural labors of the still-emerging, maturing, educated professional class Pacific migrations of the post-1965 Immigration Act era. This post-1965 multicultural petite bourgeoisie, in turn, revised the social consensus of a historically white supremacist U.S. civil society (while not essentially displacing its political logic) through (1) its own organic rigors of self-presentation and public comportment (here, the CommLink section of the *News*) and (2) its availability (and voluntarism) as the discursive material for identifiably multiculturalist rearticulations of U.S. national culture. Thus, Filipino American discourse can be seen as both a manifestation of Gramsci's notion of "spontaneous consent" as well as a popular pedagogical work in progress for the extraction of consent from a racially marked immigrant "American" constituency.

Ongkeko's editorial series "When Being Filipino Is a Plus" outlines the ideological structuring of this petite bourgeois multiculturalist bloc, pronouncing the "need to reflect on what has been described as the 'Filipino image'; it stems from Filipino identity, its uniqueness and its own way of defining the pride of being Filipino." The author's rambling endorsement of "class" comportment and assimilationist behavioral propriety follows:

> A close friend who is regarded very highly in the professional circles she belongs to says that one cannot speak of class unless he/she exhibits it. A person need not talk about it. He/she manifests it. I agree.
>
> The earmarks of a classy individual are always there: the inescapable outer signs that signal impeccable taste in the simplest of clothes and fine grooming; unquestionable language, movements — these would need to be proven in charm and grace, not learned overnight but something that would be the outcome of many, many years of being part of it.[58]

Following the discursive blueprint of the *News*'s CommLink space, the description of the properly "impeccable" Filipino American compresses the rituals of communion into exercises of "fine" bodily comportment and fashioning, invoking the early twentieth-century U.S. colonial sponsorship of the male-dominant *ilustrado* bourgeoisie while posturing Filipino American "classiness." Ongkeko is suggesting an embodiment of class at the intersections of the biopolitical (gesture, movement, diction, "grace") and her rendition of an appropriate Filipino American genealogy (an impeccability formed by years of training and self-discipline). The social trajectory of Filipino American communion, for Ongkeko, culminates in a verifiable passport to privileged collective national status: she asserts that in the multicultural post–civil rights moment, it is a social *advantage* to live as a "minority" in the United States:

> Many a time, I'm certain observers like us have . . . seen that the very persons who initially refused to have anything to do with being a Filipino take back their former stand because there are occasions when being Filipino is an advantage.
>
> The advantage of being one can be seen in the outcome of affirmative action when one can sail on being a Filipino because being so means that he/she belongs to the minority; and being so means an advantage because in the past, those slots meant only for the minority had to be filled up. . . . ✔
>
> (Since Proposition 209's passage in California, there might be an erosion of the pluses of affirmative action, but it is hoped that the legal system would take care that this policy be kept alive.)
>
> Although identity might be directed to the façade rather than the niche-constructing self, it is still a decided advantage to be Filipino these days . . . because many doors are open to qualified members of the minority.[59] ✔

While the *News*, during the mid- to late 1990s, consistently advocated in favor of liberal affirmative action policies and periodically criticized various conservative initiatives to dismantle it, a self-generating elitism remained conspicuously embedded within its larger framing of community and identity. Thus, for Ongkeko, the condition of "being a Filipino" sanitizes the racist

society structured in dominance[60] by boldly asserting the gaping
availability of putative institutional advantage — the opportunistic accumulation of social and cultural capital through a
mystified structure of preferential treatment — for "minorities"
who need only take the personal initiative to stroll through
already open doors. Ongkeko's parenthetical optimism regarding California's harbinger Proposition 209 — which remains
the juridical hallmark of the negation of the liberal–progressive
civil rights movement's already compromised concessions from
a historically apartheid national formation — is, in this sense,
far worse than naïve or uninformed: she is suggesting, in resonance with a larger discourse of Filipino American community,
that the essential structure of Filipino American civil personhood turns on both the material (institutional) ascension of
a "minority" petite bourgeoisie (the "classy" representatives
of Filipino Americanism writ large), and a political consent
to the hegemonic logics of the extant American social (and
global) formation. Thus, the fabrication of Filipino American
civil personhood is, *at the very moment of its enunciation,* a
discipline of bodily/affective assimilation and a pedagogy of
faithful political surrender to an American nationalist telos that
has proliferated into multiple multiculturalist narratives of incorporation. Filipino Americans, once "qualified," literally become
institutionalized Americans.

Those who offend and violate the pretensions of this Filipino
American civil communion come to personify and inhabit the
rejected underside of the *News*'s generational civil telos. The
public disavowal and figurative disowning of nonconforming
and wayward individuals fluidly adapts conservative vernaculars of criminality and social deviance, translated as news of
concern to the civil aspirations of the Filipino American imaginary. The *News*'s serial depictions of "gang youth," "criminal
suspects," and other civil irresponsibles become parables of
imminent Filipino American moral failure and civil weakness,
an internal lament that perpetually demands vigilance, discipline,

and accountability to the same ethic of communal discipline that is incessantly represented in the publication's textual and visual tapestry.

The specificity of the Filipino American discourse of criminalization is found in the political form of its rhetorical distancing and conceptual alienation from the state's domestic militarizations and punitive carceralities (e.g., policing, criminal jurisprudence, and imprisonment). This distancing and alienation, on the one hand, does not catalyze a principled Filipino American resistance or opposition to racist criminalization and the white supremacist militarized state. Rather, it articulates a displaced political investment and cultural valorization of the punitive racial formation of the U.S. juridical and policing apparatuses. To clarify: while Filipino American common sense does not and cannot allege the Filipino American's social ownership of the institutionalities of criminal law, policing, and imprisonment — processes that Filipino Americanism's assumptive structure understands as conceived and administered by proper (white) American others — this common sense nonetheless "objectively" narrates partnership and moral approval with their racial technologies and on-the-ground mechanics. The *News*'s conception of Filipino American community echoes and amplifies the policing dictates of the U.S. nation-building project and its racist social formation, a coordination of civil interest that entangles Filipino Americanism in a complex identification with the Gramscian "apparatus of state coercive power."

This affective and political allegiance produces the moral–discursive apparatus of Filipino American common sense as a racist technology of bodily punishment for the sake of "community": Filipino American civil society is to be vigilantly protected from subjects, bodies, and (anti)social practices that contradict, violate, or oppose the juridical ordering of American civil society. Further, this coalescence requires a monotonous and systemic discourse of disidentification from (and default criminalization of) those whose suspect status offends more than the generic legal consensus of the U.S. social ordering, but also undermines the moral integrity and civil comportment of the Filipino Americanist project. A *News* article entitled "Brothers Charged with Vandalism," for example, poses the illicit cultural–performative practice of graffiti tagging as immediately, socially reprehensible, while simultaneously, systemically resolvable:

> Two Filipino suspects from the Northern California city of Fremont were arrested February 5 in connection with an intensive investigation of adult graffiti gangs....
>
> The Hidalgos are allegedly part of a daring, thrill-seeking group of 18–25-year-old men who "tagged" such public property as freeway signs, sound walls, overpasses, BART stations and other property. The graffiti gangs operated mainly in the Fremont and Newark areas....
>
> According to the San Francisco Chronicle, Fremont police Sergeant David Lanier said that the cost of cleaning the graffiti exceeds $150,000....
>
> "It's a thrill," Lanier told the Chronicle. "It's an artistic, individual explosion of ego. It's an addiction."
>
> So addictive, in fact, that police reported that one suspect was caught on police video carving into the wall of his holding cell while awaiting trial.[61]

The coverage of another young Filipino's arrest under suspicion of a pair of bombings in Vallejo, California, visually encloses his likeness with a similar structure of presumptive guilt. The mugshot image of the eye-patched Jason Pascual, enmeshed in a text that paraphrases the criminalizing narrative of the police report, conveys him as the apparition of the anti–Filipino American: he is the abstracted though visually available figure of Filipino American civil society's potential collapse at the hands of irresponsibles, criminals, and other undesirables, particularly when juxtaposed with the *News*'s regular valorization of the socially mobile and civically incorporated. Again, the moral anxiety of Filipino Americanism revolves less around the gravity of the "crime" itself, than it does around the fact that the alleged "criminal" is identified as a Filipino. It is solely this identification that renders the event newsworthy and remarkable for the *News*, and the affiliation of a Filipino suspect with such a heinous accusation in turn marshals the paper's journalistic–moral capacity to represent and (morally) contextualize the person and his suspected social deviancy within the larger discursive labor of a Filipino American common sense:

> Jason Robert Pascual, who police confirmed is Filipino, was arraigned on February 4 along with five others in connection with the January 27 and 29 bombings in the Northern California city of Vallejo.
>
> Vallejo police suspect that Pascual, 22, allegedly placed a backpack filled with 30 sticks of dynamite outside the John F. Kennedy Library which houses a police evidence room. . . .
>
> Although no motive was determined, police believe that (lead suspect Kevin Lee Robinson) intended to disrupt a trial that could have resulted in a "third strike" conviction for him, so he hired the other suspects to bomb the county courthouse along with other targets. . . .
>
> According to a report by the Solano County District Attorney's office, besides Robinson, three suspects . . . are also being prosecuted based on California's "Three Strikes Law."[62]

The moral trajectory exerted by such narratives of social pathology and criminal deviance are the necessary and symbiotic accompaniments to the overtly lionizing and celebratory discourses that more generally characterize the *News*'s reportage and editorializing. Hall et al. provide a useful framing for this symptomatic reading of the *News* and its "crime" production capacities:

> Crime, then, is "news" because its treatment evokes threats to, but also reaffirms, the consensual morality of the society: a modern morality play takes place before us in which the "devil" is both symbolically and physically cast out from society by its guardians — the police and the judiciary. . . . Crime news is not of course uniformly of this dramatic nature. Much of it is routine and brief, because the bulk of crime itself is seen as routine. . . . Nevertheless, the media remain highly sensitized to crime as a potential source of news. Much of this "mundane" reporting of crime still fits our over-all argument — it marks out the transgression of normative boundaries, followed by investigation, arrest, and social retribution in terms of the sentencing of the offender.[63]

Mug shot of "bombing suspect" published in the
Philippine News, February 1997.

Echoing Hall et al.'s appropriation of Gramsci's framing, it is
the *Philippine News*'s socially productive juxtaposition of a
pedagogical mass knowledge and popular cultural production
with the imminent coercive power of the state that interpellates
its constituent subjects and "teaches" or disciplines them into
compliance or "consent" with a logic of communion.

The critical thread running through this symptomatic reading of the *News* thus suggests that the Filipino American
communion, conceptualized as both a material structure of
identification and a narrative structure of collective civil embodiment, is a social project animated by (1) a logic of perpetuity:
the communion must be imagined, symbolically convened, and
physically galvanized in an ongoing confrontation with alleged
obscurity or civil nonrecognition; and (2) a changing circuit of
compulsory moral imperatives: the public coherence and moral
integrity of the communion is actively and continually shaped

by the unending political labors of juxtaposition between appropriate and embarrassing, legitimate and illicit, empowering and regressive Filipino American bodies, subjects, and artifacts. This animus further reveals the relation between the knowledge productions of Filipino American common sense — including its valorizations of the U.S. state's criminalizing and policing capacities — as a deformed American nationalism. A closer reading of this political tendency offers a final point of departure from this symptomatic examination of the *News* and Filipino American common sense.

Voiced through the banal rhetorical structures of liberal multiculturalism and at other times dressed in the formal vernaculars of "ethnic interest group" pluralism, Filipino American common sense coheres through a devout — and often tacit — allegiance to the institutional, moral, and political forms of the U.S. state. By way of illustration, we might briefly consider three seemingly separate and relatively unconnected textual moments: the mundane preamble to the constitution of a national Filipino American umbrella organization, the fleeting utterance of a Southern California Filipino American editorialist, and a professional group's mimetic exercise of imagining Filipina American electoral empowerment. While none of these three articulations is singularly extraordinary in content, overwhelming in its scope of circulation, or politically profound in effecting shifts in the discursive formation of Filipino Americanism, they collectively reflect an ideological ensemble that illustrates the parameters of Filipino American common sense. I foreground these examples in order to distinguish the political trajectory of Filipino American discourse from those identity formations and social movements that engage in the difficult labors of counterhegemony — that is, the work of disrupting, transforming, and/or radically rearticulating the structuring logics (and thus the foundational institutionalities) of a given hegemonic social form. Thus, as accessible surfaces through which a common-sense apprehension of Filipino American social subjectivity is simultaneously assembled (discursively fabricated) and (popularly) produced, these attenuated examples offer a means of entry into a critical method that focuses less on the particularity of individualized "Filipino American" significations than on the underlying structures of ideological connectedness that allow them to be formed as complementary deformations of a durable, if always reifying, nationalist discourse of American exceptionalism.

Prefacing the 2004 revision of its constitution, the National Federation of Filipino American Associations (NaFFAA, founded in 1997) asserts,

> We, members of the Filipino American community in the United States, aware of our civic and social responsibilities as residents and citizens; determined to preserve our Filipino American heritage; concerned with the well-being of our country of origin, the Philippines; inspired to become more active participants in the civic life of our nation; firm in our resolve to muster the vast resources of our community *in order to protect and promote our societal and ethnic interests and contribute to the national well-being of the United States,* do hereby organize ourselves into a national federation and promulgate this Constitution.[64] [emphasis added]

Almost simultaneous with the NaFFAA's postulation of organizational purpose in the fall of 2004, a writer for the Southern California publication *Philippine Mabuhay News* echoes the spirit of this Filipino American nationalist ontology, asserting, "Lalong maraming bumoboto, lalong tataas ang 'prestige' ng Filipino American voters."[65] ("If they cast their ballots in greater numbers, Filipino American voters will achieve greater 'prestige.' ") Here I would contend that the editorialist's rather seamless — and seemingly naïve — affinity with the narrative mystifications of American electoral rituals is less invested in a physical mobilization of Filipino voter turnout at the 2004 polls than it is with signifying an ethic of Filipino American eagerness to engage in the scripted rehearsals of what the NaFFAA names as U.S. "national well-being" (wherein electoral activity, regardless of actual rates of citizen participation, symptomatically validates a functional "democracy"). Meanwhile, also in October 2004, the *Filipino Press* announced the culmination of the San Francisco–based Filipina Women's Network's (FWN) national search for "Filipina Women Who Could Be President," resulting in the "nomination" of two magazine publishers, the CEO of a nonprofit organization, a journalist, a governor of the California State Bar Board, a realtor, and a political consultant/governmental relations specialist as symbolic candidates for the executive office of an imagined Filipina United States. Fronting its seven nominees as the public emblems of a "Filipina Vote" electoral registration drive, FWN describes the campaign's objective as "working towards a system that sincerely values Filipina women and their contributions,"[66] in line with the organization's broader goal of facilitating networking among "Filipina women from corporations, government and nonprofit sectors...focus[ing] on actual career and business experiences, rather than theory, from practitioners, corporate managers and leaders."[67] These archetypal productions exhibit multiple registers of a cross-textual and transhistorical projection of pluralist U.S. civil society. The social dream of the NaFFAA, one of the more prominent and publicly visible Filipino American umbrella organizations in existence, crystallizes the logic of this ideological ensemble in its statement of organizational mission:

> NaFFAA...[was] established in 1997 to promote the welfare and well-being of all Filipinos and Filipino Americans throughout the United States.
> NaFFAA's primary objectives include:
>
> ◆ Promoting active participation of Filipino Americans in civic and national affairs and in all other aspects of mainstream America.
>
> ◆ Promoting awareness of Filipino American contributions to social, economic, cultural and political life in the United States.
>
> ◆ Securing social justice, equal opportunity and fair treatment of Filipino Americans through advocacy and legislative and policy initiatives at all levels of government.

- Strengthening community institutions that promote the cultural heritage of Filipinos.

- Eliminating prejudices, stereotypes and ignorance of Filipino Americans.[68]

Following the political logic of the NaFFAA agenda, the intelligibility and generalized conceptual unity of these moments in Filipino American discourse hinges on a twinning of imaginary labors: first, they orchestrate an archetyping of Filipino American citizenship that romantically narrates the "contributing" and politically cooperative role of a Filipino American "mainstream" to the U.S. nation-building project. In addition to formulating the ideological and existential frameworks through which a putative Filipino American historical bloc obtains its public shape, this knowledge production suggests a transhistorical collective subject that coexists with — and becomes a requisite extension of — the peculiar and specific statecraft of the American social form. In the latter passage, the NaFFAA makes explicit the constituting desire of this civic discourse by rendering an ethic of Filipino American absorption into a hegemonic ensemble of social relations, vis-à-vis declarations of fundamental allegiance to the state and its governing logics and material apparatuses.

Second and relatedly, these discursive surfaces constitute the *cultural* material of a putative Filipino American civil society. That is, these apparently dispersed and disconnected "Filipino Americanisms" convene an internally disciplined Filipino American civic presence that accumulates political currency through overt solicitations of the nominally multiculturalist structural accommodations of the post–civil rights U.S. social formation. This social dream is the irreplaceable and immovable core value of an otherwise dynamic Filipino American common sense, to the extent that the disciplinary (racial) rubric of civic personhood forms the center of political and cultural gravity for a Filipino American civil society that both encompasses and exceeds the formal demands of (American) "citizenship." The

Filipino American figuration is, in this sense, enacted as the *meta-fulfillment* of a multiculturalist nation-building telos. Within the problematic of this deformed nationalism, Filipino American common sense not only refrains from sustained critique of the racist and white supremacist institutionalities of the U.S. state across "Filipino" and "non-Filipino" localities; it is structurally incapable of it. It is to the epistemological premises of this incapacity that I now turn.

Arrested Raciality and the Racial Form of Filipino Americanism

The production of the Filipino American communal subject relies on more than the archetyping of ideal or essential and pathological or criminal Filipino American civic embodiments. It is also, in part, the vexing eclecticism and apparent arbitrariness of Filipino Americanism's engagements with the analytics and socially formative discourses of "race" that compose the problematic through which Filipino American communion articulates. My critical purpose in this section is *not* to systemically outline or render immediately legible a Filipino American "racial project"[69] per se, but rather to indicate that the ideological wandering, internal confusion, lack of conceptual rigor, and generalized theoretical underdevelopment that characterize this putative body of Filipino American "racial" thought produce, in their identifiable totality, a productive and ideologically functional dimension of an emergent common sense that fundamentally coordinates interest with the U.S. racial formation in its contemporary, multiculturalist moment. This aspect of my larger argument is usefully situated within Eduardo Bonilla-Silva's typology of post–civil rights "racial ideology":

> Racial ideology can be conceived for analytical purposes as comprising the following elements: common frames, style, and racial stories. The frames that bond together a particular racial ideology are rooted in the group-based conditions and experiences of the races and are, at

the symbolic level, the representations developed by these groups to explain how the world is or ought to be. And because the group life of the various racially defined groups is based on hierarchy and domination, the ruling ideology expresses as "common sense" the interests of the dominant race, while oppositional ideologies attempt to challenge that common sense by providing alternative frames, ideas, and stories based on the experiences of subordinated races.[70]

While the general outlines of Bonilla-Silva's sociological definition provide sound premises for examining the contemporary "color-blind" rearticulations of racist thought and white supremacist institutionality in the U.S. social formation, his conception of a general dichotomy of ideology and identification between whites and "subordinated races" offers an opportunity to clarify the distinctiveness of Filipino Americanism as a discourse of perpetually displaced raciality: put differently, Filipino Americanism as an articulation of "group life" structurally displaces, exoticizes, and/or postpones the essential political crises and antagonisms of racial identification and subject formation, such that Filipino American discourse not only fails to locate a "group-based condition and experience" within the social frames of a "racially defined group," but in its dilution and postponement of what we might call Filipino Americanist raciality (the rhetorical capacity, political willingness, and discursive capability of Filipino American discourse to engage the social determinations of "race" as an integral aspect of its social modality), Filipino Americanism also undermines the possibility of generating an authentically "oppositional ideology" that positions Filipino group experience as a challenge to a white supremacist common sense.

It may be necessary and useful, in other words, to identify Filipino American racial common sense as constitutively incoherent, in the sense that the nondevelopment of a racial grammar — without which a coherent, much less politically productive, discourse of race literally cannot be assembled — actually enables and enhances the multiculturalist opportunism of Filipino American discourse more generally. I am arguing that the stubborn resistance of Filipino American subject formation to articulate itself coherently within the nuances, political antagonisms, and otherwise socially determining material–ideological apparatuses of racial discourse has little to do with Filipinos' "actual" — that is, phenotypic, genetic, ethnic, or cultural — racial ambiguity or hybridity, and everything to do with a political ambivalence that works to reproduce the fundamental tenets of Filipino Americanism as a deformed nation-building project. It is the arrested raciality of Filipino American discourse that allows it to commune desire and identity through a multiculturalist problematic that significantly relies on what Bonilla-Silva aptly calls the frame of "abstract liberalism" (the use of "ideas associated with political liberalism and economic liberalism in an *abstract* manner to explain racial matters").[71]

Consider, for example, the otherwise meandering stream-of-consciousness response of renowned turntablist DJ Q-Bert to a student research group's eager questions regarding the distinctiveness of an alleged Filipino American "hip-hop generation." Here the obvious (and comic) absurdity of the 1999 interview's content should not be conflated with the epistemological premises of Q-Bert's pronouncements:

> Q-BERT: There's so many Filipinos, it's just like saying "what's a human being?" You know, you have all these different categories: there's fat guys, skinny guys, whatever. You know, it's like, you can't really categorize or generalize what a Filipino is, because they're so diverse.
>
> INTERVIEWER: What do you see as the future of the Filipino American community?
>
> Q-BERT: Like I said earlier, it's gonna go everywhere. You know, you're gonna have dumb fucks, you're gonna have smart guys, you're gonna have cool guys, regular guys, whatever people, rump shakin' on themselves [laughs], you're gonna have whatever you want, you know, it's gonna be positives, negatives, whatever. It's always like that with everything. The bigger something gets, the more it branches.[72]

Within this imagination, the figurative "branching" of Filipino American "diversity" is restrained by neither material borders ("it's gonna go everywhere") nor localized ethical obligations ("it's gonna be positives, negatives, whatever"); rather, to "be" Filipino American is to *flee* the sociopolitical specificities, political crises, and material conditions of possibility of Filipino Americanism's moment of articulation, and to posit a banal, racially unmarked humanism as both the philosophical foundation and future possibility of its cultural–communal production. As cultural theorist Antonio Tiongson Jr. argues, a central aspect of Q-Bert's context of enunciation and broader political credibility is his iconic status as arguably the most recognized "Filipino American" popular cultural figure of the 1990s. Widely acknowledged as a paradigm-shaping innovator in the turntable/deejay form, Q-Bert occupies a central, if not ascendant place in Filipino American youth cultures across two generations.[73]

Most important to this examination, however, is the fact that Q-Bert's prolific work across multiple popular cultural forms — as an internationally recognized turntablist, actor, documentary subject, album producer, and screenwriter — is at least partly premised on his avowed desire to locate his artistic production as a contribution "to every race," and hence to diminish or transcend "all color lines."[74] This banal liberal multiculturalism stands in stark distinction to many of his peer and predecessor DJs, whose work often directly and creatively addresses the nuances of racist state violence as a cultural–political condition of performance.[75] In fact, Q-Bert's blithe rhetoric of diversity and race transcendence references a commonly articulated thread of Filipino American common sense, which attempts to locate the putative Filipino body, genealogy, and historical condition beyond the parochialisms of racial classification, such that "the Filipino" is sometimes positioned outside raciality altogether.

The racial romanticism of "I Am Filipino-American," a manifesto featured on the Web site of epilipinas.com ("dedicated to the promotion of the Filipino culture in North America"), affirms and elaborates the developmental narration of what is, in a sense, the ideal–racial type of post-1965 Filipino American subjectivity:

I am Filipino-American, I came from the 7,000 or so islands of the Philippines. From rice terraces of Banaue and the picturesque Davao City in Mindanao. From Metropolis of Manila, the sprawling city of Cebu, the serene Palawan and the white sand beach of Boracay.

My blood is mixed with the proud Malay race, with Spanish conquistadores, with Americans GIs, British merchants, Chinese traders, Indian Sepoys, the native Aetas and Manobos, and countless other bloods. I can not say I belong to all but all belong in me. I am the melting pot. . . .

I am a Filipino American, I can not [change] my heritage, it is in my blood in my genes and in my past but I will do everything I can to make a difference. I will not let others dictate my place in this society nor prejudice deter me from my goals and destiny.

I am Filipino American, that's who am I.[76]

Echoing former academic and practicing psychologist Maria Root's avowal that "Filipinos belong to no race and belong to all,"[77] such pronouncements narrate Filipino racialization and subjection to the changing regimes of white supremacist modernity through an ahistorical racial common sense. Such utterances work across multiple political purposes, coordinating a fantasy of the Filipino body and its flesh-and-blood genealogy as flexibly and superficially modified by a (usually indeterminate) material history of "race," although never overdetermined or constitutively affected by that history.

Present-tense notions of Filipino American historical agency are thus summoned through the durable epistemic mythologies of individual free will and personal self-determination, and posited outside and against the presumably delimiting outer determinations of racially formed subjectivities and the apparatuses of dominance through which they are (re)produced. Even liberal narrations of Filipino American "empowerment" and "unity," as in New York attorney Reuben S. Seguritan's collection of short editorials and transcribed speeches *We Didn't Pass through the Golden Door: The Filipino American Experience,* stubbornly defer engagement with race as a material social structure through which the U.S. national/racial formation emerges.

This modality of articulating Filipino Americanist historical agency reifies racism, colonialism, and other white supremacist social forms as *past tense* historical episodes that have yielded to a national civil rights telos of increased opportunity and socio-economic mobility. The American multiculturalist mythification is often invoked as a self-evident historical truth, relying on familiar stereotypical litanies of European immigrant assimilation as well as untenable (and sometimes factually incorrect) depictions of African American historical experience and social progress in the post–civil rights age. In a pair of pieces appropriately entitled "Ignoring the Model Minority" and "Learning from the African American Experience," Seguritan writes:

> We must remember that blacks, as the largest minority in the country, have long been subjected to shameful discriminatory laws *in the past.* . . . Though there is much to be desired in policy rectification, blacks today are beginning to find opportunities open to them in workplaces, public services and education.[78]

> Americans have come a long way. [African Americans] were *migrant slaves* until Lincoln's Great Emancipation Decree in the third quarter of the nineteenth century.[79]

> [African American] efforts have paid off. Higher education has placed many of them in positions of power. Many mayors and other government officials have emerged from among them.
> Other migrants — Italians, Polish, Irish, Jews, etc. . . . are well represented in America's political, corporate and academic world. . . .
> While most of America's greats of ethnic background are American-born, they have affirmed their roots and are proud of their heritage, while showing an unshakable faith in *an integrated society that transcends race, color and creed.* . . .
> Let us learn from those who are now entrenched in the seats of power. We must take heed of their strengths: the African Americans' fierce struggle for their rights, the Italians' cultural pride blended with true American spirit, the Jews' drive for excellence and higher education. We surely must have what it takes to achieve what others have already achieved.[80] [all emphases added]

Such narrations reify "race" to the extent that the material complexities and institutional nuances of present-tense racist and white supremacist social apparatuses are reduced to socially ancillary "obstacles" that can and ought to be "overcome" through varieties of ethnic/minority interest group mobilization within civil society's existing institutionalities. In fact, this is the moral and prescriptive thrust of Seguritan's writings, most of which deploy some variety of exhortation that the assumptive Filipino American readership must abandon its ingrained "cultural" inclinations toward laziness and petty interpersonal jealousies, in favor of self-actualized, calculated political "unity." He contends, in "Re-Asserting Affirmative Action," "Our Image Problem," and "Why Not a United Political Force,"

> Among Asians, the Filipinos are the least unified or the least concerned with bonding together as one people.[81]

> No doubt, there have been efforts to unify us, yet somehow something almost always rises from out of the mud to drag them down. Jealousies, petty squabbles, backbiting, intrigue, misplaced values. ... Sadly, this is the kind of drama our communities seem to put up time and again so that we are unable to assert our political strength at times when we need to.[82]

> In his diary, [José] Rizal bewailed the indifference, the extravagant penchant for dissipating drinking socials, and lack of earnestness and sense of unity [among fellow *ilustrados* in late nineteenth-century Madrid. This observation seems as applicable, particularly to Filipino Americans, today as when it was made in Rizal's time, more than a century ago.[83]

> We have to learn this early, that political participation is key to political empowerment and the earlier we learn our lessons from involvement in [the] American democratic process, the greater benefits will be derived by our community.
>
> That is why a call to form a single political force for Filipino Americans is relevant at this point.... For Filipino Americans, the 1990s should mark the beginning of our *political maturity and influence.*[84] [emphasis added]

The logic of Seguritan's and other such narratives[85] dictates that the remnants of "discrimination" against Filipinos in the United States are to be decisively confronted and disrupted by a rational, self-determining, militant liberal Filipino American collective subject capable of coordinating its political self-interest and "obtaining" or possessing power as a social bloc. Such prescriptions hinge on a deferral and ultimate dismissal of racism and white supremacy (including the U.S. racist state and white supremacist national culture) as epiphenomenal to the "Filipino American" present tense. That is, liberal Filipino Americanism renders "empowerment" as a condition to be achieved under a flagship unity, within the power pathways always already available under the institutional auspices of a mystified U.S. liberal democracy. The possibility of a robust (rather than periodized and opportunistic) antiracist politics and cultural production, on the other hand, is postponed for the sake of a "political maturity" that attains the formally nonracial (though substantively white normative and white supremacist) subjectivity of American modernity's liberal humanism.

Filipino American common sense leverages its political and moral currency through facile simplifications of race as (1) a historically ossified descriptive category of difference and (2) the self-explanatory grounds for liberal multiculturalist prescription (hence "empowerment"). This structural postponement of a Filipino / Filipino American racial analytic enables a vacillating, though no less fantastic racial narcissism: this affective and discursive structure enables Filipino Americanism's imagination, self-narration, and normativization of the collective (racial) body it inhabits and reproduces in virtual perpetuity. [In addition to obscuring the racial and protoracial social and cultural antagonisms and relations of dominance among and between regional, tribal, and ethno–racial groups in the Philippines (as well as in the alleged diaspora), this Filipino American racial narcissism installs a "mestizo" normativity that both reinscribes (while reembodying) the reified status of the white political subject as rational (read: racially unaffected if not unmarked) "human" and figuratively biologizes multiple histories of conquest into a romantic hybridity of "bloods."| This move extrapolates the contemporary American nationalist construction of multiculturalist liberalism (epilipinas.com's "I am the melting pot"), a political gesture that amplifies the compulsory disciplinarity of "good" Filipino American civic comportment. The grandiose historical and ontological racial vision of *Philippine News* founder Alex Esclamado provides an appropriate coda to this critical discussion in a speech delivered at the March 1997 Filipino Intercollegiate Networking Dialogue (FIND) in Stonybrook, New York. Deploying a vernacular of transhistorical Filipino globality, Esclamado's rhetorical flourish reconstructs the arrested raciality of Filipino Americanism as a supremacist claim:

> My friends, we have a big task to transfer to you, and that is the future. The future is yours. The community has grown. Now is the time to empower you.
>
> The world is yours.
> You are a superior race. You are.
> Why not?[86]

Conclusion:
From Renaissance to (Racial) Terror

The field of Filipino American discourse, inscribed through multiple texts and cultural productions, has proliferated with the post-1990s emergence of a Filipino American cultural and civil renaissance. This renaissance — landmarked by such momentous events as the 1994 election of a Filipino American state governor (Benjamin Cayetano, Hawaii), increased institutional sanction of "Filipino American Studies" as a coherent academic subfield, and such popular cultural landmarks as the 2000 premiere of the feature-length film *The Debut* — has mediated a political labor of communion whose grammars of intelligibility intend to represent, produce, and organize the organic sociality of a Filipino American civil society. According to Gramsci:

> Every social stratum has its own "common sense" and its own "good
> sense," which are basically the most widespread conception of life
> and of man. Every philosophical current leaves behind a sedimen-
> tation of "common sense": this is the document of its historical
> effectiveness. Common sense is not something rigid and immobile,
> but is continually transforming itself, enriching itself with scientific
> ideas and with philosophical opinions which have entered ordinary
> life. "Common sense" is the folklore of philosophy, and is always
> half-way between folklore properly speaking and the philosophy, sci-
> ence, and economics of the specialists. Common sense creates the
> folklore of the future, that is as a relatively rigid phase of popular
> knowledge at a given place and time.[87]

I have been concerned in this chapter with how the Filipino
Americanist production of a Gramscian common sense encompasses an internally complex and dynamic body of accessible
symbols, political–historical narratives, and discursive structures that effectively extends the reach and relevance of a
hegemonic nationalist (rather than oppositional or counterhegemonic) multiculturalist sensibility. In its interpretation and
(popular) envisioning of the "Filipino American's" absorption
into the constitutive racial and white supremacist logics of the
post–civil rights U.S. nation-building project, this emergent Filipino American common sense offers a conception of community
that is disciplinary and pedagogical: the movements of Filipino American communion posit a social ambition of nationalist
multiculturalist raciality, while also inducing a Filipino American
sociality that cannot (and must not) engage the always violent
and terrorizing analytics of raciality.

This situated emergence of Filipino American common sense
is a historical echo of the Fanonian genealogy of "cultural
alienation" invoked in the previous chapter. The manifest ontological violence of this resonance — which Fanon contends is a
focal point of the colonial project and its larger (neocolonial,
postcolonial, and protocolonial) historical implications — forms
multiple, mobile matrices for the multiculturalist civil and political projects of the post–civil rights and multiculturalist iterations

of U.S. global white supremacy. It is within this structure of rearticulation that the labors and imaginations of Filipino American communion become the contemporary reanimation of the incipient colonial civil society enacted in the early twentieth-century U.S. program of "benevolent assimilation." ✓

While I will offer a more sustained reflection on this resonance and echoing in chapter 4, I conclude this chapter with a point of departure and clarification, guided by my own abiding interest in the projects of radical community building and interdisciplinary, multitextual activist praxis: I am interested neither in an absolutist notion of postmodernist flux, fluidity, and unfixability (of either "community" or collective "subjectivity") nor in the identity/community building project of a "strategically" waged essentialism. Rather, I am interrogating the Filipino American communion's points of fixity in order to contextualize potential lines of betrayal — treason to a deformed nationalism — that might substantively disrupt and displace the production of the "Filipino American" as a labor of allegiance to the United States and its perpetual global projects of dominance. In this sense, we might position the Filipino American civil figure as an embodiment of historical implication in the multiple white supremacist domesticities of the U.S. national project, which was itself elaborated and protracted through the initial transpacific genocidal ventures waged at the turn of the twentieth century. It is to this period of racial apocalypse that we now turn.

— 3 —

"Its Very Familiarity Disguises Its Horror"

White Supremacy, Genocide, and the
Statecraft of Pacifica Americana

> We should not overlook the fact that genocide is a
> problem not only of war but also of peace.
> —Raphaël Lemkin, 1944

The Illegible Encounter

How might we understand the material genesis of the post-nineteenth-century Filipino condition as a marshaling of capacities for dominance that cannot be sufficiently described through the conventional rubrics of empire, colonialism, or warfare? In this chapter, I contend that the massively fatal political antagonisms that precedent and enable the developmentalist narratives of "Filipino American" liberal multicultural subjectivity also form a central and immovable pillar in the historical architecture of Filipino arrested raciality. As elaborated earlier, I am conceptualizing arrested raciality as a structurally disrupted articulation of racial and protoracial historicity: this disrupted racial articulation is constituted by the grammatical *presence* of racial signification in Filipino discourses and the simultaneous *sanitization* of that signification by a labor of critical illiteracy (that is, this illiteracy is a social production, not an innocent symptom of ignorance). Filipino arrested raciality, then, is a

98

political–intellectual praxis in the sense that it enables Filipino (American) socialities by strategically undertheorizing and misconceiving the overdetermination of the Filipino condition by the long symbiosis of the overlapping historical technologies of race, violence, and global white supremacy. Here I ask: in what ways does the historical and discursive structure of arrested raciality reproduce through a genealogy of white supremacy that, once adequately addressed and historically reframed, might productively disorganize and rearticulate the grounding rubrics of Filipino subjectivities, communities, and politicalities in their various institutional and casual forms?

Moving from the framework of this interrogation, this chapter addresses an analytical structure, cultural vernacular, and historical architecture that is essential to Filipino American sociality and that also broadly implicates the condition of Filipino political and cultural productions across its different historical geographies. I am concerned with the fundamental illegibility of the particular and utterly foundational Filipino encounter with the material formation of U.S. white supremacy as both (1) a perpetual militarized conquest of (cultural, political) territories in ostensibly domestic ("conquered") and materially alien or global ("frontier") sites; and (2) a genocidal national and (global) racial project that is multilayered and versatile in its institutional mobilizations and singular in its production of particular conditions of historical inescapability for peoples who are and have been subjected to the material logics of genocide.

This elaboration of genocide as a central modality of U.S. nation building and white supremacist globality follows Mahmood Mamdani's insistence on a historical inventory that accounts for the specificities of place, time, cultural articulation, and political logic:

> If the genocidal impulse is as old as the organization of power, one may be tempted to think that all that has changed through history is the technology of genocide. Yet, it is not simply the technology of genocide that has changed through history, but surely also how that

impulse is organized and its target defined. Before you can try and eliminate an enemy, you must first define that enemy. The definition of the political self and the political other has varied through history. The history of that variation is the history of political identities, be these religious, national, racial, or otherwise.[1]

Framed in response to Mamdani's useful complication of genocide studies, this chapter contends that the post-1898 Filipino condition is constituted by a genealogy of Manifest Destiny as a *perpetually* genocidal nation-building project. I suggest that this condition of Filipino engagement with the United States constitutes a relation of irreparability, illiteracy, and absolute antagonism that is unresolved by the allegations of Filipino Americanism as a grammar of multicultural nationalist identification and communion. Historian Reginald Horsman's characterization of U.S. racial nation building during the mid-nineteenth century offers an initial point of departure for this analytic:

> By the 1850s the American sense of idealistic mission had been corrupted, and most of the world's peoples were condemned to permanent inferiority or even to extinction. General world progress was to be accomplished only by the dominating power of a superior race, and a variety of lesser races were accused of retarding rather than furthering world progress. A traditional colonial empire had been rejected, but it was believed that the expansion of a federal system might ultimately prove possible as American Anglo-Saxons outbred, overwhelmed, and replaced "inferior" races.[2]

Indicating the white supremacist logic of militarized conquest, especially in the form of undeclared wars against indigenous peoples, Horsman contends that the constitution of American racial–national identity carries the endemic properties of a genocidal — and, by its own definition, epochal — global project:

> [A]s Anglo-Saxons sought out the most distant corners of the globe, they could ultimately replace a variety of inferior races. The Anglo-Saxonism of the last half of the century was no benign expansionism, though it used the rhetoric of redemption, for it assumed that one

race was destined to lead, others to serve — one race to flourish, many to die. The world was to be transformed not by the strength of better ideas but by the power of a superior race.[3]

Following the extended implications of Horsman's historiography, I am invoking Manifest Destiny as a rubric of American white supremacy and U.S. nation building in the long historical sense, and especially as a project that encompasses and surpasses the disputed body counts of a white supremacist colonial conquest in the Philippines that mobilized capacities for human extermination comparable in speed, technology, and scope only to the precedent and contemporaneous continental wars against the indigenous peoples of North America.

The Stakes of the Historical Present: "Colonial Tutelage," the "Special Relationship," and Their Antecedents

To clarify this conceptual framing by means of juxtaposition, it is useful to revisit the remarks of historian Stanley Karnow, who infamously deploys the terms of paternity and redemption in his apologia for U.S. colonialism and neocolonialism in the Philippines. Waxing nostalgic in the wake of the People Power movement and Corazon Aquino's subsequent rise to the Philippine presidency in 1986, Karnow writes:

> Most Americans may have forgotten, perhaps never even knew, that the Philippines had been a U.S. possession; for those who remembered, Cory [Aquino] symbolized anew that *special relationship.* During its half-century of colonial tutelage, America had endowed the Filipinos with universal education, a common language, public hygiene, roads, bridges and, above all, republican institutions. Americans and Filipinos had fought and died side by side at Bataan and Corregidor and perished together on the ghastly Death March. The United States was still in the Philippines, the site of its two largest overseas bases, and more than a million Filipinos lived in America. By backing Marcos, even as an expedient, the United States had betrayed its protégés and its own principles, but, as if by miracle,

> Cory Aquino had redeemed her nation — and redeemed America as
> well.[4] [emphasis added]

Karnow's text offers a convenient, shorthand rendition of the
neocolonial common sense of the Philippines–U.S. entanglement,
reflecting a durable and accessible historical narrative that enables
the articulation of Filipino American discourses — as well as
Filipino discourses about "America" — as mystifications of the
convergence of the United States and the Philippines in a shared
and reconcilable (if conflicted and periodically violent) history of
unevenly symbiotic national formations.[5]

As if to authorize Karnow's historical fabrication of twentieth-
century Filipino–U.S. solidarity, Filipino American historian
Fred Cordova romances the watershed of World War II as
another genesis moment of political union and nationalist coalescence between Filipino Americans, the United States, and the
feminized Philippine homeland in need of vindication and rescue.
For Cordova, it is the remarkable spectacle of Filipino Americans
mobilizing domestically for war as putative "American" nationalists under sanction of the U.S. military and for the honor of
ancestral homeland — " 'Remember Bataan!' That slogan was
echoed throughout every Filipino American community in the
U.S.... as Pinoy men, women, and children geared up for the
long war effort"[6] — that constitutes the time of redemption for
Filipino American history. Resonating Karnow, Cordova writes:

> Even at its earliest stages, World War Two was very real for Filipino
> Americans, especially Philippine-born immigrants. They had lost
> their "homeland," symbolic of their American-indoctrinated belief
> in freedom and democracy. Filipino Americans had just witnessed
> the fall of the Philippines....
>
> As the war progressed, the racial climate towards persons of Fili-
> pino ancestry changed dramatically in the U.S. The Philippines —
> despite its devastation and the atrocities inflicted on wounded sol-
> diers and innocent civilians — became America's staunchest ally in
> the Pacific war. Brown men from the Philippines were no longer
> called "Little Brown Monkeys" in America. *Overnight, they gained
> some respect as "Little Brown Brothers."*[7] [emphasis added]

I am interested in interrogating the dense postscript of Cordova's blithe valorization of Filipino racial modernity vis-à-vis an exaggerated Pacific partnership in U.S. imperial warmaking and the figurative "Filipino American's" alleged evolution from being the minor simians to the minor siblings of an emergent American global hegemony.

I am also concerned with the stakes (as distinguished from the content) of Filipino Americanism as a living and commonly accessible archive of political–cultural labors that plays a central role in historically locating and philosophically fixing the Filipino condition in a relation of political continuity and relative historical congruency with the animus of U.S. nation building in the alleged aftermath of its defining white supremacist institutionalities: racial chattel slavery, frontier conquest, and racial colonial domination. While previous chapters have outlined the contours of this contemporary archive, some examples from Root's 1997 anthology *Filipino Americans: Transformation and Identity* usefully crystallize the slippery and unconvincing discursive acrobatics that have conventionally produced the Filipino American rubric and that, most importantly, forfeit the analytical, cultural, and political possibilities of situating the post-twentieth-century Filipino condition as a potential disarticulation of the American (hence "Filipino American") nationalist telos:

> I have taken the liberty of defining *Filipino American* in the most inclusive sense. We are immigrants-now-citizens, American born, immigrant spouses awaiting eligibility for green cards, mixed-heritage Filipinos, students or workers on visa, *tago ng tago* (undocumented), and transnationals moving between the Philippines and the United States. Thus, *Filipino American* is a *state of mind* [emphasis added] rather than of legality or geography. Under the same roof, family members hold different meanings for and attachments to being Filipino American.[8]

> Whether planful or accidental, centuries of invasion and visitation by traders, seafarers, missionaries, warfarers, and colonists guaranteed that Filipinos across the archipelago would fuse multiple ethnic

> influences and physical features. Across families, the family portrait defies neatly delineated boundaries; *Filipinos belong to no race and belong to all.*[9] [emphasis added]

> For the purposes of this chapter, Filipino American ethnic identity is assumed to be the product of our historical and cultural backgrounds and the process of negotiating and constructing a life in the United States.[10]

The rhetoric of Filipino American identity and self-definition reflects the contingent, though flexible and persistent, multiculturalist common sense that organizes articulations of collective subjectivity through vulgar notions of cultural artifact and commodity ("ethnic identity" as "product" of history and culture), compulsory allegiance with liberal variations of American nationalism, and deeply depoliticized conceptions of racial hybridity (in this case, suggesting that "centuries of invasion" have produced a Filipino subject somehow undetermined and unpossessed by the relations of dominance constituted by "race").[11] ✓

As such, Filipino American discourse is neither unique in the political implications of its archival compositions — it is in most ways a rather typical articulation of banal multiculturalism — nor is it separable from the liberal nationalist racial analytic that has succeeded and effectively displaced the overlapping insurgencies of the progressive antiracist tendencies of the civil rights movement and the radical-to-revolutionary anticolonial, anti-imperialist, and anti–white supremacist praxis of U.S.-based liberation movements: within this nationalist racial analytic, "Filipino American" forms an allegation of historical coalescence that recuperates "racial" (ethnic, national, religious) difference from its institutionalized fatalities and reconciles it with the compulsory absorptive tendencies of liberal nation building. In an attempt to erode the premises of this Filipino American analytic, I initiate my critique from theoretical grounds similar to those staked by Nerissa Balce in her illuminating essay "Filipino Bodies, Lynching, and the Language of Empire," where Balce convincingly argues that "popular discourses on Filipino savagery, the rise of lynchings in the South, and the emergence of a U.S. imperial policy in the Pacific *are the historical milieu of the term 'Filipino.'* "[12] [emphasis added]

I contend, on the one hand, that the very grammar of Filipino Americanism perpetually invokes that which its self-referential political foreclosing disavows: at the nexus of this strategic coalescence and conflation of the "Filipino" and the "American" sits an essential relation of death, an unfathomable violence that renders the discursive field of Filipino Americanism untenable in both its formal grammars of articulation and its larger premises of political coherence. A radical critique of this peculiarly Filipino American common sense, I would suggest, similarly entails (in fact, necessitates) a political disarticulation of the United States as a nation-building project that is always and only anchored to the social logic, historical present, and institutional capacities of white supremacist genocide. For the purposes of this argument, I am considering the material genealogy of the Filipino condition and its formative structure of contact with the American national project through a theorization of genocide as a modality of dominance that is not containable to discrete swatches of linear historical time, or isolatable to peculiar spectacles of homicidal atrocity.✔

In other words, while the most profound militarized and institutional mobilizations of genocidal nation building occur in specific historical moments and under the organic contingencies of those moments, and thus deploy on particular (indigenous) territories and political–cultural geographies in ways that are concretely identifiable, it is the indelible political condition inaugurated and perpetually constituted by white supremacist genocide as a fundamental relation of dominance that perpetually constitutes the historical present. Because it is necessarily constituted by the political afterlife, material "haunting,"[13] and institutional legacies of its initiating intimacy with genocide in the decade following the Spanish-American War, the contemporary articulation of the Filipino condition continuously calls upon notions of historical passage, epochal distance, national development, and (racial) unaffectability to fortify a rubric of rational self-determination and disciplinary self-government.

To elaborate Silva's situating of affectability as a central term in the historical conceptual structure of race, the conventional discourse of the Filipino (American) condition persistently refutes the idea of the Filipino as "the kind of mind subjected to both the exterior determination of the 'laws of nature' and the superior force of European minds,"[14] and in turn, perhaps most fundamentally, permanently defers intimacy with genocide as its essential condition of possibility. This deferred intimacy not only inscribes the Filipino condition as decisively *alienated* from the defining terms of production for indigenous political philosophies, subject formations, and sovereignty/liberation struggles that have focused on the presence of genocide as a constitutive social logic of the alleged "postconquest" moment, but it figuratively reforms the Filipino as something that emerges after the unnamed time of unfathomable death. In resistance to this impulse, I move from historian Omer Bartov's conclusion that "the world we live in is the same world that produced (and keeps producing) genocide," and that "because we know now the barbaric essence in modernity, its potential of scientifically and legally sanctioned and state controlled evil,"[15] it is useful and necessary to (*a*) strategically disrupt conceptions/narratives of the Filipino condition that cannot sufficiently account for the historical present of its genocidal American encounter, and (*b*) generate political and theoretical trajectories that position the putative Filipino in a state of irreconcilability with the U.S. nation-state and its ongoing conditions of possibility.

It is in this context that the U.S. conquest of the Philippines at the turn of the twentieth century is not reducible to a minor extension, derivative, or distension of the continental North American genocidal campaigns that have produced — and perpetually reproduce — the American national order, but is its own complex articulation of white supremacist (and eventually colonialist) genocide that has overdetermined the changing domains of political and cultural intercourse through which the Filipino condition strives for (what it postulates as) viable self-identification and discursive coherence. It is the generalized undertheorization and nondiscussion of this structure of overdetermination that both characterizes and decisively enables the state of Filipino arrested raciality.

I am also interested in considering the multilayered military, political, and cultural labors of U.S. genocidal nation building — a process that precedes, accompanies, and temporally exceeds the institutional formalities of American colonialism in the Philippines — as a constituting site of production for Filipino (and particularly Filipino American) sociality in its current forms. That is, the historical present of the American genocide in the archipelago marks the grounds on which the Filipino condition attempts to *make sense of itself,* despite and because of its consistent deferrals of intimacy and disavowals of entanglement with this genealogy of white supremacy. Thus, rather than merely invoking and commemorating a contained, remarkable, and discrete historical period of U.S. genocide in the Philippines, the remainder of this chapter is suggesting a delicate and perhaps dangerous relocation of Filipino political and cultural genealogies that understands the logic of human/social extermination as both a central historical premise and perpetual condition of possibility for the Filipino global condition generally, and the work of "Filipino American" cultural and communal productions more specifically. ⌣

The currency of a Filipino American identity, history, community, and politic is at once the reification of a deeply troubled contact point between Frantz Fanon's paradigmatic "native" and "settler," while also a rhetorical valorization of a postconquest rapprochement between the U.S. nation and its undifferentiated Philippine subjects. Fanon's critique of the "native intellectual" elaborates the qualitative conditions of domination and disruption that ruin possibility for authentic dialog within the historical dialectic of conquest. In this analysis, the very idea of the "Filipino American" — incessantly produced as a coherent and presumed historical subject — collapses on the possibility of its own internal disarticulation, the potentially rupturing antagonism between the "Filipino" and the "American." My overarching concerns here resonate Fanon's desire for a radical departure from the durable cultural rubric that outlives the discrete time of formal colonial domination, framed by his critical lamentation that "the colonized's endeavors to rehabilitate himself and escape the sting of colonialism obey the same rules of logic."[16]

Rather than accepting the premises of coherence on which Filipino American discourse is based, I wish to view the grammatical structure *and* archival content of the Filipino American rubric as the signifier of an originary relation of death and killing, the ongoing inscription of a genocidal condition of possibility for the Filipino's sustained presence in (and in proximity to) the United States. While most scholars and researchers acknowledge the mass-scale killing and sophisticated campaigns of extermination and displacement waged by the United States during (and after) the so-called Philippine-American War (1899–1905, depending on the author), few have explored the implications of this death and destruction as constitutive and productive elements of the contemporary Filipino condition.

A Brief Genealogy of "Genocide": The Politics of Definition and Reframing

An extended reflection is appropriate and necessary here, an opportunity to consider the generalized political–intellectual refusal of, and sometimes moral objection to, the descriptive and theoretical use of the term "genocide" to address historical circumstances other than those already commemorated as such. Beyond references to the liquidation campaigns against indigenous peoples in the Americas and, more universally, the industrialized elimination of Jews under Hitler's German National Socialism, few incidents of (ethnically/racially) targeted, mass-scale physical and cultural extermination have obtained the canonical status of authentic human holocaust. Yet it is one of the twentieth century's constitutive contradictions that the proliferation and evolution of technologies of killing — at varying scales of mass-based mortality — is irrevocably tied to the varieties of social formation produced and reproduced by "modernity" itself.[17] In this sense, the question of how genocide manifests as a military and social logic of and for modernity is critical for an adequate reflection on the historical and institutional location of Filipinos in relation to U.S. social formation. Some concise historical contextualization and critical definitions facilitate this task.

It has been widely acknowledged by legal and historical scholars, as well as indigenous liberation and human rights activists, that the United Nations adoption of a resolution on the "prevention and punishment" of genocide in 1948 is juridically characterized by the very acts it fails to implicate. By way of contrast, the U.N. Secretariat's earlier, preapproval draft of the document was far more comprehensive in scope and contained the outlines for strong and effective enforcement of its content. According to Churchill, this draft of the resolution stated:

> [A]cts or policies aimed at "preventing the preservation or development" of "racial, national, linguistic, religious or political groups" should be considered genocidal, along with a range of "preparatory" acts, including "all forms of propaganda tending by their systematic and hateful character to provoke genocide, or tending to make it appear as a necessary, legitimate, or excusable act."[18]

In fact Rafaël Lemkin, a Polish legal scholar retained by the U.N. Secretariat's office who is widely acknowledged as the originator of the term, defines genocide extensively in chapter IX of his 1944 text *Axis Rule in Occupied Europe*. Far from narrowing his legal, historical, and conceptual definition of genocide to apply exclusively (or even primarily) to the acts of the Nazi regime, Lemkin employs the German example as a case study, ultimately developing a multilayered and nuanced conception of genocide that provides a relatively strong legal basis for analysis, criminal prosecution, and redress across historical moments and political specificities.[19] While only a complete reading of Lemkin's chapter can adequately contextualize the scholarly and jurisprudential importance of his work, a brief passage will suffice for the purposes of the argument I am making here:

> Genocide is, as we have noted, a composite of different acts of persecution or destruction. . . . The entire problem of genocide needs to be dealt with as a whole; it is too important to be left for piecemeal discussion and solution in the future. Many hope that there will be no more wars, but we dare not rely on mere hope for protection against genocidal practices by ruthless conquerors. Therefore, without ceasing in our endeavors to make this the last war, we must see to it that the Hague Regulations are so amended as expressly to prohibit genocide in any war which may occur in the future.
>
> Moreover, we should not overlook the fact that genocide is a problem not only of war but also of peace. . . . If [national minority] groups should not be adequately protected, such lack of protection would result in international disturbances, especially in the form of disorganized emigration of the persecuted, who would look for refuge elsewhere. . . .
>
> An international multilateral treaty should provide for the introduction, not only in the constitution but also in the criminal code of each country, of provisions protecting minority groups from oppression because of their nationhood, religion, or race. Each criminal code should have provisions inflicting penalties for genocide practices. In order to prevent the invocation of the plea of superior orders, the liability of persons who order genocide practices, as well as of persons who execute such orders, should be provided expressly by the criminal codes of the respective countries. Because of the special implications of genocide in international relations, the principle of universal repression should be adopted for the crime of genocide.[20]

Lemkin's insistence on a relatively strong juridical structure of international accountability for genocide as a "composite" of practices, usually though not exclusively carried out by members

of the state, was arguably the characterizing feature of the proposal he submitted for the U.N. Secretariat's perusal. Further,
as activist and scholar Darryl Li has indicated, many of the
conceptual and definitional shortcomings of Lemkin's juridical
formulation of genocide — such as his refusal to include "political groups" in the draft of the Convention and his generalized
fetishization of the "nation" and "national groups" as the primary (if not the exclusive) sources of human community, culture,
and creativity — were effectively addressed by other experts who
participated in writing the Secretariat's draft.[21]

Upon receiving the U.N. Secretariat's text, however, some of
the former European colonial states and the emerging super-
powers coalesced and conspired to strip the document of its
definitional scope and legal context. In a rare moment of Cold
War political collaboration, United Nations representatives from
the United States and the U.S.S.R. specifically bullied Lemkin out
of the approval process and, in dialogue with representatives
serving on the U.N.'s Legal Committee and Ad Hoc Committee on Genocide, successfully advocated for the elimination of
the provision regarding the wholesale destruction of "political
groups."[22] Behind-the-scenes maneuvering also resulted in the
deletion of provisions for a permanent international tribunal
(instead allowing each state to autonomously develop its own
juridical measures to internally litigate accusations of genocidal
conduct) and also erased the entire second article of Lemkin's
original draft. Critically, it was this article that spoke to the
question of cultural genocide, defining it as

> the destruction of the specific character of a persecuted "group" by
> forced transfer of children, forced exile, prohibition of the use of
> the national language, destruction of books, documents, monuments,
> and objects of historical, artistic, or religious value.[23]

The elimination of this provision was central to the eventual
ratification of the watered-down proposal, particularly as it
alleviated the United States of its burden of accountability

for multiple historical acts of mass-based killing and cultural destruction within its continental and transpacific frontiers.[24] The final text of the U.N. Convention on the Prevention and Punishment of the Crime of Genocide amounts to a largely unenforceable (or at best, arbitrarily enforceable) juridical measure that refracts a consensus of abstract moral outrage, while undermining the possibility for institutionalizing concrete avenues of legal and political accountability for acts of genocide. The Convention's inherent delimitations of jurisprudential power and legal phrasing make it radically ill-suited for addressing and officially acknowledging, much less prosecuting, genocides committed by hegemonic or otherwise globally dominant states and their extra-state partners in violence (e.g., agricultural firms, oil corporations, and precious metal conglomerates). By way of prominent example, Article 2 states:

> In the present Convention, genocide means any of the following acts committed with intent to destroy, in whole or in part, a national, ethnical, racial or religious group, as such:
>
> (*a*) Killing members of the group;
>
> (*b*) Causing serious bodily or mental harm to members of the group;
>
> (*c*) Deliberately inflicting on the group conditions of life calculated to bring about its physical destruction in whole or in part;
>
> (*d*) Imposing measures intended to prevent births within the group;
>
> (*e*) Forcibly transferring children of the group to another group.[25]

As historian Frank Chalk and sociologist Kurt Jonassohn contend, "although it marked a milestone in international law, the U.N. definition is of little use to scholars."[26] In addition to excluding political groups and social–economic classes from the realm of target populations, Chalk and Jonassohn continue, the Convention "makes no distinction between violence intended to annihilate a group and nonlethal attacks on members of a group."[27] This lack of specificity is only compounded by the fact that the resolution has had almost no practical effect in enabling or enforcing legal accountabilities for either localized or mass-scaled campaigns of human liquidation and/or enslavement that would otherwise fit squarely within the conceptual framework of genocide. Thus, despite such efforts as William Patterson and the Civil Rights Congress's unprecedented 1951 *We Charge Genocide* petition to the U.N. accusing the U.S. government of committing genocide against the domestic black population, and Jean-Paul Sartre and Arlette El Kaïm-Sartre's 1968 summation of evidence of U.S. genocide in Vietnam through the International War Crimes Tribunal,[28] the U.N. Genocide Convention does not succeed as legislation on its own terms.

While the juridical and historical context of the Convention's practical impotency is far too complex to adequately summarize here, legal sociologist Leo Kuper's concise critique of the document's singularly disabling terminology provides an appropriate distillation for the purposes of what follows in this chapter:

> The crime of genocide under the Convention is not committed simply by the destruction, in whole or in part, of a racial, national, ethnic or religious group. *There must be the intention to destroy.* The Convention defines genocide constituted by specific acts "committed with intent to destroy, in whole or in part, a national, ethnical, racial or religious group, as such." The "inadvertent" wiping out of a group is not genocide....
>
> The inclusion of intent in the definition of genocide introduces a subjective element, which would often prove difficult to establish. ...This limited the grounds which would be necessary to constitute genocide, so that the destruction of a group for profit or because of personal rivalry between tribes could not be charged as genocide.[29] [emphasis added]

While most scholars, activists, and state officials have effectively forfeited a radical critique of the U.N. Genocide Convention in exchange for acknowledging its significance as a landmark in human rights discourse, Chalk and Jonassohn's analytical 1990 study outlines the resolution's entanglement in (1) the internal politicking of the U.N.'s member countries and (2) broader contestations over global hegemony, including implicit and explicit assertions by individual nation-states of the militarized right to kill at contained and mass-based scales. In this sense, the ratified document has actually institutionalized a profound juridical contradiction — that between a broadly implicating conception of mass-based human extermination, on the one hand, and a pragmatic provision of de facto amnesty to those states that have carried out some of the most heinous forms of wholesale categorical killing, on the other. Chalk and Jonassohn write:

> [A]lthough the UN condemnation of genocide has undoubted symbolic value, it has never had any practical effect. There are several reasons for this. In negotiating the convention the member countries wanted to make sure that it applied only to the losers of World War II. . . .
>
> Another reason for its ineffectiveness is the nature of the United Nations itself. It is composed of sovereign member countries who are interested in using it as a political platform, but who are strongly opposed to the establishment of international judiciary and policing powers that would override their own sovereign powers. Since the perpetrators of genocidal killings are almost always sovereign states, it seems unlikely that the UN member countries would act against one of their own — and [as of 1990] they have not yet done so, in spite of the fact that there has been no lack of opportunities.[30]

The contentious history of the U.N. Genocide Convention indicates the difficulty of arriving at a widely accepted theoretical, much less juridical, definition of genocide. While this chapter is not invested in presenting a definitive and closed definition of the term (a refusal based on the conviction that any redefinition of genocide that aspires to guide and shape social activity must stem from collective community and activist conversation as well as rigorous and critical scholarly praxis), it does offer an intervention on existing genocide discourse in generating a conceptual departure from conventional accounts of the "Philippine–American War." In this sense, it is worth considering three different sources for a working conceptualization of genocide through which the remainder of this historical meditation may proceed.

Native American scholar activist Ward Churchill's (Keetoo-wah Cherokee) "functional definition" of genocide provides a useful point of departure, particularly in its elimination of the legal rubric of "intent" and insistence on a categorization of genocide that centers a complex notion of a people's "right of existence" and thus brings focal historical attention to the actuality of "destruction," regardless of intentionality:

> *Proposed Convention on Prevention and Punishment of the Crime of Genocide (1997)*
>
> Although it may or may not involve killing, per se, genocide is a denial of the right of existence of entire human groups, as homicide is the denial of the right to live of individual human beings....
>
> *Article II.*
>
> In the present Convention, genocide means the destruction, entirely or in part, of any racial, ethnic, national, religious, cultural, linguistic, political, economic, gender, or other human group, however such groups may be defined by the perpetrator.[31]

Churchill's full formulation in the closing chapter of *A Little Matter of Genocide* defines three primary forms of genocide: the physical, biological, and cultural.[32] Much of his elaboration builds on Lemkin's 1944 conceptualization, as well as the U.N. Secretariat's early draft of the Convention. Several dimensions of Lemkin's definition are worth foregrounding in relation to the technologies of genocide that shaped the U.S. conquest of the Philippines. Lemkin writes:

> *I. Genocide: A New Term and New Conception for the Destruction of Nations*
>
> Generally speaking, genocide does not necessarily mean the immediate destruction of a nation, except when accomplished by mass killings of all members of a nation. It is intended rather to signify a coordinated plan of different actions aiming at the destruction of essential foundations of the life of national groups, with the aim of annihilating the groups themselves. The objectives of such a plan would be disintegration of the political and social institutions, of

culture, language, national feelings, religion, and the economic existence of national groups, and the destruction of the personal security, liberty, health, dignity, and even the lives of the individuals belonging to such groups....

II. Techniques of Genocide in Various Fields

Social

The social structure of a nation being vital to its national development, the occupant also endeavors to bring about such changes as may weaken the national spiritual resources....

Cultural

In order to prevent expression of the national spirit through artistic media, a rigid control of all cultural activities [is] introduced....
[T]he population [is] also deprived of inspiration from the existing cultural and artistic values.

Economic

The destruction of the foundations of the economic existence of a national group necessarily brings about a crippling of its development, even a retrogression. The lowering of the standard of living creates difficulties in fulfilling cultural-spiritual requirements. Furthermore, a daily fight literally for bread and for physical survival may handicap thinking in both general and national terms.[33]

While Lemkin's discussion is largely structured by an international analytic, in which the ostensible objects of genocide are national groups or recognized national minorities, the Civil Rights Congress's groundbreaking 1951 petition to the U.N. shifts the juridical and analytical lens to address the peculiarities of the United States as a site of internal or "domestic" genocide.

The opening lines of *We Charge Genocide,* edited by William L. Patterson (National Executive Secretary of the Civil Rights Congress), address the U.N. General Assembly with an enunciation of the petition's unprecedented stakes:

The responsibility of being the first in history to charge the government of the United States of America with the crime of genocide is not one your petitioners take lightly. The responsibility is particularly grave when citizens must charge their own government with mass murder of its own nationals, with institutionalized oppression and persistent slaughter of the Negro people in the United States on a basis of "race," a crime abhorred by mankind and prohibited by the conscience of the world in the Convention on the Prevention and Punishment of the Crime of Genocide....

If our duty is unpleasant it is historically necessary both for the welfare of the American people and for the peace of the world.[34]

In addition to constituting the first rigorous, internationally circulated historical contextualization of the U.S. racist state as a *genocidal* racist state, *We Charge Genocide* constructs a useful anatomy of white supremacist nation building that explicates the intimate, symbiotic link between "democracy" and antiblack genocide. Read alongside Churchill's and Lemkin's renditions, portions of the petition provide eloquent and theoretically useful elaborations of the U.S. genocidal formation that challenge the inherent limitations of the ratified U.N. Convention:

Seldom in human annals has so iniquitous a conspiracy been so gilded with the trappings of respectability. Seldom has mass murder on the score of "race" been so sanctified by law, so justified by those who demand free elections abroad even as they kill their fellow citizens who demand free elections at home. Never have so many individuals been so ruthlessly destroyed amid so many tributes to the sacredness of the individual. The distinctive trait of this genocide is a cant that mouths aphorisms of Anglo-Saxon jurisprudence even as it kills.

The genocide of which we complain is as much a fact as gravity. ...In one form or another it has been practiced for more than three hundred years although never with such sinister implications for the welfare and peace of the world as at present. Its very familiarity disguises its horror. It is a crime so embedded in law, so explained away by specious rationale, so hidden by talk of liberty, that even the conscience of the tender minded is sometimes dulled.[35]

While *We Charge Genocide* formally bases its legal argument on the 1948 U.N. Genocide Convention, it critically contextualizes and reinterprets the Convention's key terms in order to bring an appropriate analytical gravity to the consideration of U.S. apartheid, state-conducted and state-sanctioned racist violence, and the conditions of antiblack oppression and repression generally. Passages from the petition's opening outline of charges against the U.S. government reflect the Civil Rights Congress's recognition of the need for historical and methodological specificity in confronting the particular technologies of genocide innovated by the U.S. social and state formation:

Killing Members of the Group

We shall submit evidence proving "killing members of the group," in violation of Article II of the Convention. We cite killings by police, killings by incited gangs, killings at night by masked men, killings always on the basis of "race," killings by the Ku Klux Klan, that organization which is chartered by the several states as a semi-official arm of government and even granted the tax exemptions of a benevolent society.

Our evidence concerns the thousands of Negroes who over the years have been beaten to death on chain gangs and in the back rooms of sheriff's offices, in the cells of county jails, in precinct police stations and on city streets, who have been framed and murdered by sham legal forms and by a legal bureaucracy....

Economic Genocide

We shall prove that such conditions so swell the infant and maternal death rate and the death rate from disease, that the American Negro is deprived, when compared with the remainder of the population of the United States, of eight years of life on the average.

Further we shall show a deliberate national oppression of these 15,000,000 Negro Americans on the basis of "race" to perpetuate these "conditions of life...."

We shall offer evidence that this genocide is not plotted in the dark but incited over the radio into the ears of millions, urged in the glare of public forums by Senators and Governors. It is offered as an article of faith by powerful political organizations, such as the Dixiecrats, and defended by influential newspapers, all in violation of the United Nations charter and the Convention forbidding genocide.

The Negro Petitioners

Many of your petitioners are Negro citizens to whom the charges herein described are not mere words. They are facts felt on our bodies, crimes inflicted on our dignity. We struggle for deliverance, not without pride in our valor, but we warn mankind that our fate is theirs. We solemnly declare that continuance of this American crime against the Negro people of the United States will strengthen those reactionary American forces driving towards World War III as certainly as the unrebuked Nazi genocide against the Jewish people strengthened Hitler in his successful drive to World War II.

… We solemnly warn that a nation which practices genocide against its own nationals may not be long deterred, if it has the power, from genocide elsewhere. White supremacy at home makes for colored massacres abroad. Both reveal contempt for human life in a colored skin.[36]

The full petition includes documentation of numerous cases of racist killing and "imposition of genocidal living conditions,"[37] including lynching, police murder, "psychological terror and mass intimidation on the basis of 'race,'"[38] institutionalized exposure to fatal and preventable disease, denial of education, and racist criminal justice. Reaching a crescendo with its elaboration of the role of "monopoly capital" as the "prime mover of the mammoth and deliberate conspiracy to commit genocide against the Negro people in the United states," and the culpability of the U.S. government in "[committing] genocide for profit, a conspiracy engineered and directed by monopoly and executed by its state power on a federal, state, county and municipal level,"[39] *We Charge Genocide* constructs an anatomy of U.S. white supremacist genocide that both directly responds to, and critically reconceptualizes, the existing parameters of the U.N. Genocide Convention.

It is worth emphasizing that the work of Patterson and the Civil Rights Congress is being revisited at the current moment by a growing community of radical intellectuals, including anthropologist and Africana studies scholar João Costa Vargas (*Never Meant to Survive: Genocide and Utopias in Black Diasporic Communities*)[40] and Native American (Cherokee) feminist scholar Andrea Smith (*Conquest: Sexual Violence and American Indian Genocide*).[41] Vargas, Smith, and others bring appropriate attention to the work of Patterson and the Civil Rights Congress, while enabling a critical revisiting of *We Charge Genocide* as a document for the historical present. The remainder of this chapter will move from an analytical and conceptual framing of genocide that draws broadly from the texts of Lemkin, Patterson, and Churchill, meditating on the Philippine genocide as the unspoken genealogical nexus of the Filipino condition.

Genocide as Archive:
The Dawn of Pacifica Americana

The long and present moment of the putative Filipino subject's absolute inseparability from the movements and compulsions of U.S. nation building, statecraft, and governmentality emerges at the nexus of an American military mobilization that carried out strategic campaigns of indiscriminate killing, cultural desecration, and ecological destruction. It is empirically indisputable that the emergence of the contemporary Filipino condition is rooted in the symbiosis of modernity's engulfing developmentalist telos with the particular, historic encounter in the archipelago wherein the toll in human lives (overwhelmingly common "civilians" rather than *ladrones* [bandits], guerillas, or *insurrecto* [insurgent] soldiers) was astronomical, yet is forever beyond the historical record: estimates of native people killed during the first four years of the U.S. occupation and conquest range anywhere from a few hundred thousand to two million.

Luzviminda Francisco's 1973 essay in the *Bulletin of Concerned Asian Scholars*, "The First Vietnam: The U.S.–Philippine War of 1899," remains perhaps the most lucid analysis of this initiating moment. While her purpose in this piece is more commemorative and polemical than rigorously historiographic or theoretical, Francisco's rendition of this time of conquest enables multiple lines of elaboration and questioning. Most significantly, her narration of the U.S. encounter as a fundamentally racist militarization places the conquest within a continuum of white supremacist — and particularly anti-indigenous —

American statecraft that illuminates the nation-building project as genocidal in its articulated intent and material outcomes:

> An American congressman who visited the Philippines, and who pre-
> ferred to remain anonymous, spoke frankly.... "You never hear of
> any disturbances in Northern Luzon...because there isn't anybody
> there to rebel.... The good Lord in heaven only knows the number of
> Filipinos that were put under ground. Our soldiers took no prisoners,
> they kept no records; they simply swept the country and wherever
> and whenever they could get hold of a Filipino they killed him."[42]

It cannot be overemphasized that the post facto nomination of this Philippine–American nexus as a "war" in the conventional sense distorts the terms — rhetorical and military — on which the genocide was waged. Variously termed by U.S. state and military officials as a necessary response to indigenous "insurrection," "rebellion," and "criminal" guerilla struggle, and at other times euphemized as a series of "skirmishes," the conquest was gener-ally conceptualized in the familiar terms of white supremacist Americana as (1) the logical extension of the dominance of an ultimately redemptive Anglo-Saxon racial civilization, and (2) an ascendant global–historical encounter with inevitability for uncivilized, premodern, and undomesticated "natives." Soci-ologist Julian Go concisely outlines the continuities of warfare, white supremacist colonial governance, and racial genocide in this particular instance:

> The first U.S. military governors in the Philippines (Wesley Mer-
> ritt, Elwell S. Otis, Arthur MacArthur, and Adna Chafee) had
> had considerable experience in administering Indian policy, and the
> Philippine–American War was often scripted as but another "Indian
> war...." Furthermore, congressmen, pro-imperialists, and organiza-
> tions such as the Friends of the Indian society typically collapsed
> Native Americans and Filipinos into the same category, arguing that
> the rule of the latter was not unlike the rule of the former.[43]

Historian Stuart Creighton Miller's durable 1982 text *Benevo-lent Assimilation: The American Conquest of the Philippines, 1899–1902* painstakingly details the on-the-ground conditions in which this rubric of racial and civilizational "rule" concretely

animated the nationalist discourses of U.S. civil society, electoral politics, and military decision making. While Miller never
fully elaborates the genocidal logic of the conquest, his archival
and historiographic work seems to clearly indicate that genocide was in fact the structuring cultural, political, and military
contingency of the moment.

Surveying various periodicals in which U.S. military veterans
commented on the still-unfolding war on the archipelago frontier, Miller details some of the crucial labors of white supremacist
consensus-building that enabled racial genocide as a practice of
embryonic American hegemony:

> In short . . . [U.S. military] veterans believed that "Injun warfare" was
> necessary against such "savages." One Kansas veteran stated this sen-
> timent quite directly to a reporter polling his regiment as it awaited
> discharge. "The country won't be pacified until the niggers are killed
> off like the Indians." Howard McFarlane agreed it was necessary
> "to blow every nigger into a nigger heaven." Adapting an old fron-
> tier adage, another veteran explained that "the only good Filipino is
> a dead one. Take no prisoners; lead is cheaper than rice."[44]

That such genocidal white supremacist candor was rather soberly
inscribed on the pages of the *New York Evening Post, Omaha
Bee, Public Opinion, Literary Digest, Arena,* and the *Kansas City
Times* in the spring months of 1899 suggests that the contours
of a white nationalist racial common sense were significantly —
if not centrally — organized by a moral–political obligation of
conquest, "pacification," and military domination, whether articulated as bloodthirsty Indian/"nigger" killing, or "benevolent
assimilation" colonialism.

This white supremacist common sense was central to the U.S.
nation-building project during the nineteenth century and was
both well institutionalized and fully operational by the time of
the Philippine conquest. Native scholars Lenore Stiffarm (Gros
Ventre) and Phil Lane Jr. (Yankton Sioux/Chickasaw) add:

> By the mid-19th century, U.S. policymakers and military comman-
> ders were stating — openly, frequently and in plain English — that

their objective was no less than the "complete extermination" of any native people who resisted being dispossessed of their lands, subordinated to federal authority, and assimilated into the colonizing culture. The country was as good as its word on the matter, perpetrating literally hundreds of massacres of Indians by military and paramilitary formations at points all over the West.[45]

Declarations and admissions of (and periodic liberal laments over) this national–racial commitment to campaigns of effective human liquidation anchored in spectacular racial violence are supplemented by the U.S. state's own archival records, including a wealth of congressional testimonies by veterans of the Indian and Philippine wars. This archive constructs a history of the germinal Philippine–U.S. encounter that illuminates the genealogical basis for the kind of critical and radical racial analytic that might productively disarticulate Filipino arrested raciality. A brief foray into this body of knowledge production suggests the ineluctable, fatal symbiosis between the epochal ambitions of genocidal U.S. nation building and the emergence of the Filipino condition as a subject of incipient, post–Spanish colonial "modernity."

The political architecture of U.S. colonialism is distinguished by its ideological and institutional commitment to militarized white supremacy. In fact, the statecraft of U.S. dominance in the Philippines was defined, in its opening sequences, through rhetorics of racial paternalism that authorized the mass-based destruction that quickly followed the initial stages of occupation. The April 4, 1899, statement of the Schurman Commission, convened by President McKinley three months earlier, precisely establishes the mandate of genocidal frontier warfare as the incumbent obligation of an avowedly benevolent U.S. state. Composed of Jacob G. Schurman, Rear Adm. George Dewey, Gen. Elwell S. Otis, Charles Denby, and Dean C. Worcester, the Schurman Commission was formed under the auspices of facilitating "the most humane, pacific, and effective extension of authority throughout these islands, and to secure, with the least possible delay, the benefits of a wise and generous protection of life and property to the inhabitants."[46] As is often the logic of emergent racist colonial formations, this rubric of imposed white civil society and white supremacist governmentality *necessitated* the oblivion of military pacification and absolute indigenous submission. The Commission's 1902 proclamation to the Philippine people asserts:

> [T]he attention of the Philippine people is invited to certain regulative principles by which the United States will be guided in its relations with them. The following are deemed of cardinal importance:
>
> 1. The supremacy of the United States must and will be enforced throughout every part of the archipelago, and those who resist it can accomplish no end other than their own ruin.[47]

Such open anticipation of absolute suppressive violence was already utterly common to the institutional nuances and self-articulations of late nineteenth- and early twentieth-century U.S. statecraft, within and beyond its ambitions of territorial expansion. Even official critics of the embryonic U.S. colonial state such as Sen. George F. Hoar describe the maneuvers of the U.S. military as more comparable to a quelling of domestic insurgency than a "war." In fact, this distinction is central to Hoar's political rationale for ceasing colonization and bartering Philippine independence:

> We are not at war. We made peace with Spain on the 14th day of February, 1899. Congress has never declared war with the people of the Philippine Islands. The President has never asserted nor usurped the power to do it. We are only doing on a large scale exactly what we have done at home within a few years past, where the military forces of the United States have been called out to suppress a riot or a tumult or a lawless assembly, too strong for the local authorities.[48]

While Hoar was among the most fervent "anti-imperialist" U.S. statesmen of his era, known also for decrying state-conducted and state-sanctioned violence against African Americans and Native Americans,[49] his opposition to the U.S. conquest is notable for its effectively unchallenged description of a genocidal national–colonial project. That is, Hoar's acute (and ultimately failed) challenge to the American statecraft of Philippine conquest hinges as much on his eloquent outrage over (what he understood to be) the excessive brutality, unbecoming incivility, and spectacles of carnage induced by the colonial pacification as it does on his loftier philosophical advocacy for a people's right to independence. His candor on the floor of Congress inadvertently provides an archival testimonial of U.S. genocide in the Philippines, and his utterances thus merit significant historical attention and theoretical recontextualization:

> What you have done so far has been to get some few thousand children actually at school in the whole Philippine dominion. To get this result, you *have certainly slain many times that number of parents.*[50] [emphasis added]

> You have devastated provinces. You have slain *uncounted thousands* of the people you desire to benefit. You have established reconcentration camps.... You make the American flag in the eyes of a numerous people the emblem of sacrilege in Christian churches, and of the burning of human dwellings, and of the horror of the water torture....
>
> The conflict in the Philippines has cost you $600,000,000, thousands of American soldiers — the flower of our youth — the health and sanity of thousands more, and *hundreds of thousands of Filipinos slain.*[51] [emphasis added]

Hoar's rhetorical flourish should not be confused with empirical exaggeration or distortion, as all official indications suggest that the deployment of U.S. military troops was no mere parade of force, but was shaped at its inception to strategically extract maximum Filipino mortalities as well as territorially focused cultural–ecological disaster.

Brig. Gen. J. F. Bell's organization of the campaign in the Batangas province both echoes and extrapolates the implications of the Schurman Commission's ominous disclosure of the political expediency and military necessity of a logic of indiscriminacy. His orders to the brigade in "Telegraphic Circular No. 3" clearly couple a notion of "native" political incorrigibility to the fabricated inevitability of a genocidal "peace," and circumstantially indicate the military–juridical premises of indiscriminate killing:

> A general conviction, which the brigade commander shares, appears to exist that the insurrection in this brigade continues because the greater part of the people, especially the wealthy ones, pretend to desire but, in reality do not want peace. That when all really want peace we can have it promptly. *Under such circumstances it is clearly indicated that a policy should be adopted that will as soon as possible make the people want peace, and want it badly.*
>
> *It is an inevitable consequence of war that the innocent must generally suffer with the guilty, for when inflicting merited punishment upon a guilty class it is unfortunately at times impossible to avoid the doing of damage to some who do not individually deserve it. Military necessity frequently precludes the possibility of making discriminations.*[52] [emphasis added]

Bell's orders authorized precisely the form of racial frontier warfare that was already common and tactically accessible to many of his soldiers (i.e., veterans of the continental campaigns against indigenous peoples), while also institutionally fortifying the anticipated scale and intensity of the extermination still to come. Detailing a crucial shift in the protocols of the Batangas brigade's overall conduct, Bell empowers a broad autonomy of tactical force that effectively eliminates the military chain of command, facilitates the maximum killing capacity of the individual soldier, and (ostensibly) boosts the warmongering morale of the rank and file. Bell's orders dated December 9, 1901, read:

> Commanding officers are urged and enjoined to use their discretion freely in adopting any or all measures of warfare authorized by this order which will contribute, in their judgment, toward enforcing the policy or accomplishing the purpose above announced.
>
> It is not necessary to seek or wait for authority from these headquarters to do anything or take any action which will contribute to the end in view. It is desired that subdistrict commanders accord to their subordinate officers and commanders a degree of confidence and latitude in operations similar to that herein conferred upon

them.... Subordinate commanders and young officers of experience should not be restrained or discouraged without excellent reason, but should be encouraged to hunt for, pursue, and vigorously operate against armed bodies of insurgents wherever they may be found. Considering the comparative morale of our troops and insurgents, and the lack of reliable ammunition and training on the part of the latter, it is not believed there exists any just cause for exceptional caution or apprehension in attacking them boldly.[53]

While Bell's prominent role in the so-called Philippine–American War is widely acknowledged, it is difficult to overstate the fact that his tactical approach to the conquest was structured by a conception of coerced vulnerability to mass-based mortality that, far from being an abnormal or extreme form of U.S. military mobilization, was absolutely constitutive of the white supremacist social logic of American state violence at the cutting edge of its overlapping nation-building and colonial projects.

Testimonies from the 1902 "Hearings on Affairs in the Philippine Islands," held before the Senate Committee on the Philippines, repeatedly and rigorously affirm the U.S. state's commitment to this genocidal social logic. Documented in the three volumes of *Senate Document 331* (1903), covering the expanse of several thousand pages, the 1902 hearings encompass the words of enlisted soldiers, veteran (colonial) statesmen, and military officers of the highest ranks.[54] A significant portion of the testimonies directly address and elaborate the focal antagonism of Manifest Destiny statecraft — white Anglo-American civilization's confrontation with nonwhite, un- or under-civilized social and cultural formations — in the novel extracontinental site of the Philippine archipelago. William Howard Taft, appointed civil governor of the islands in 1901, succinctly frames the racial–historical telos of white supremacist genocide in the early part of his testimony to the Senate:

SEN. THOMAS M. PATTERSON: When a war is conducted by a superior race against those whom they consider inferior in the scale of civilization, is it not the experience of the world that the superior race will almost involuntarily practice inhuman conduct?

> Gov. TAFT: There is much greater danger in such a case than in dealing with whites.[55]

Taft, who later acceded to the office of the presidency and was subsequently appointed chief justice of the U.S. Supreme Court, echoes and affirms the discourse of historical inevitability, military necessity, and political rationality that constitutes genocidal frontier warfare in the opening movements of the Philippine colonial project. While he and his accomplices in the military rarely unleash the rhetoric of bloodthirstiness and overt racist brutality that is prototypically expected of those engaged in the initial stages of conducting an epochal genocide, their testimonies cumulatively provide the rhetorical, philosophical, and ethnographic blueprint for a transpacific rearticulation of white supremacist (colonial) nation building.

Brig. Gen. Robert P. Hughes, in the initial portion of his testimony, broadens the reach of the conquest's genocidal rationality by establishing the inapplicability of conventional rules of engagement to the military's encounter in the archipelago:

> My theory of war is that it should be made entirely civilized and just as light as possible to succeed in getting the result your government expects. I went there supposing these people to be sufficiently civilized to follow the ordinary rules of civilized warfare. I became convinced, greatly to my sorrow, that they would not follow the rules of war.[56]

Hughes, as is common in the testimonies of many of his cohorts, explicates this alleged dismay by offering an impressionistic ethnography of Filipino gender pathology and warmaking impotency. Asked by Sen. Thomas M. Patterson at a later point in the hearings to explain the radical disparity in the ratio of American to Filipino fatalities during the first years of the war, Hughes's illustration of the absolute typicality of slaughter delineates the continuities between Brigadier General Bell's infamous Batangas orders and the normal military protocols in other parts of the archipelago:

SEN. THOMAS M. PATTERSON: There were ten Filipinos killed or wounded where there was one American, and you say that disparity increased [as the war progressed].

BRIG. GEN. ROBERT P. HUGHES: . . . I always felt as if we were hitting a woman in fighting those people. They did not know the first earthly thing about how to fight.

SEN. PATTERSON: Then the percentage, the difference between their killed and wounded and ours —

BRIG. GEN. HUGHES: I was going on to say that you can occupy those people in front and send a command — really your attacking force — around by flank and fire on them, and I have known them to be caught that way time and time again. They never seemed to learn. . . .

SEN. PATTERSON: And the disparity between the killed and wounded of the Americans and the Filipinos continued to increase as time went on?

BRIG. GEN. HUGHES: Yes. . . .

SEN. PATTERSON: That would indicate either one of two things — either that the war has been pretty much of a slaughter or else the Filipinos were brave to a fault. . . .

BRIG. GEN. HUGHES: I do not think you are correct in that.

SEN. PATTERSON: How do you account, then, for the immense disparity in killed and wounded between the two forces?

BRIG. GEN. HUGHES: The difference is that our men can shoot. As I said before, the ordinary Filipino could not hit a stack of barns.[57]

Despite the Senators' periodic attention to widespread practices of torture (particularly the "water cure" or water boarding) by U.S. military officers on native prisoners of war,[58] it appears throughout the hearings that there is, at most, only subdued concern over the scale of military slaughter that is exhibited in the gaping ratio of fatalities between U.S. soldiers and their indigenous antagonists.

Sgt. Leroy A. Hallock's response to questioning from Sen. Joseph L. Rawlins is fairly typical in echoing Hughes's depiction of Philippine natives as veritable rifle fodder:

SEN. JOSEPH L. RAWLINS: How many men of your company had been killed during the entire time you were stationed at Leon in Panay...?

SGT. LEROY A. HALLOCK: Two men.

SEN. RAWLINS: How many natives were killed during the same time by American soldiers?

SGT. HALLOCK: I could not state the number.

SEN. RAWLINS: About how many?

SGT. HALLOCK: It would be very hard for me to tell.

SEN. RAWLINS: Give us a general idea, if you can.

SGT. HALLOCK: Well, if we got into a skirmish we could not tell how many men were killed or wounded.

SEN. RAWLINS: Were there a good many killed?

SGT. HALLOCK: There were more killed than there were Americans.

SEN. RAWLINS: How many do you know of yourself having been killed?

SGT. HALLOCK: Do you mean altogether in the fights we had there?...

SEN. RAWLINS: That your company participated in — yes; the regiment.

SGT. HALLOCK: In the neighborhood of 200 or 300, I should say, for a guess....

SEN. RAWLINS: How many Americans were killed in those three fights?

SGT. HALLOCK: I should say 20.[59]

Another exchange, in this case between Senators Patterson and Rawlins during the testimony of Maj. Gen. Arthur MacArthur (appointed military governor of the Philippines in 1900 and veteran of the frontier wars in western North America), similarly reveals the matter-of-fact nature in which the highest levels of the U.S. state described and sanctioned the genocidal trajectory of the incipient "Philippine–American War":

SEN. THOMAS M. PATTERSON: What is the proportion of the killed to the wounded?...

SEN. JOSEPH L. RAWLINS: The summary of the enemy's loss [is] 800 killed and 30 wounded; while the summary of our loss is, killed, 40; wounded, 72.[60]

Far from marginalizing the utterances and missives of Brigadier General Bell (and, even more notoriously, Gen. Jacob "Hell-Roaring Jake"/"Howling Jake" Smith) as wild deviations from the otherwise sober and civilized statecraft of benevolent colonization, the content of the hearings suggests that there was really no fundamental difference between the conquest of Batangas and the procedures of genocidal warfare in the Philippines more generally. The additional example of the first thirteen months of intensified warfare in Mindanao, in 1900–1901, further depicts the scale, speed, and proportion of killing that took place across the Philippines more generally. Historian Leon Wolff summarizes:

> In thirteen months roughly covering the period under discussion, the following figures were officially tabulated: there were 1,026 engagements, 245 Americans killed, 490 wounded, 118 captured; while 3,854 rebels had been killed, 1,193 wounded, and 6,572 captured.[61]

While there are, of course, territorial (a.k.a. provincial) specificities concerning the range and acceleration of military conquest, as well as significant differences in the estimated (and in many cases largely speculative) body counts accumulated by provincial campaigns, there is little reason to believe that either the overarching mandate of extermination or the more particularized tactics of indiscriminate killing were exceptions to the rule.

Here it is worth emphasizing that the destructive violence marshaled by the genocidal conquest was centrally directed at the substantive and traumatic, if not altogether irreparable, disarticulation of indigenous cultures and ecologies, including residential and familial systems, economies of intimacy and economic exchange, and the obliteration of local land bases themselves. This production of cultural genocide is widely noted by indigenous activists, critics, and scholars to be a dimension of conquest that is crucial to the broader assertion of colonial and imperial dominion. It is precisely the modality through which this violence is discursively organized and materially deployed that initiates the reification and coerced exoticism of indigenous cultural forms. Native scholar and antiviolence activist Andrea Smith (Cherokee) has cogently argued:

> Native communities argue that Native people cannot be alienated from their land without committing cultural genocide.... When the dominant society disconnects Native spiritual practices from their landbases, it undermines Native peoples' claim that the protection of the landbase is integral to the survival of Native peoples and hence undermines their claims to sovereignty.[62]

Manifest Destiny, in its transpacific articulation, fully advanced the well-worn program of land alienation and cultural genocide. The testimony of Corp. Daniel J. Evans offers a concisely stated example of a military reasoning that surfaces throughout the 1902 Senate hearings — at times betraying the sanitizing or euphemizing rhetoric of the military witness — and helps broaden the scope of this historical meditation beyond a fixation on fatality calculations and estimates:

> SEN. ALBERT J. BEVERIDGE: [W]hat is your observation as to the treatment of the people engaged in peaceable pursuits, as to kindness and consideration, or the reverse, from the American officers and the men?
>
> CORP. EVANS: They were never molested if they seemed to be peaceable natives. They would not be molested unless they showed some signs of hostility of some kind, and if they did, if we struck a part of the island where the natives were hostile and they would fire on our soldiers or even cut the telegraph lines, the result would be that their barrios would probably be burned.[63]

Resonating with Evans's recounting of the normalcy of the U.S. military's tactic of mass-based barrio arson, Brig. Gen. Bell's military order to specifically target native religious leaders extends the sweep of appropriate targets for neutralization and liquidation and illustrates the centrality of cultural genocide to the genesis of U.S. colonial rule. Bell's "Telegraphic Circular No. 3" asserts:

> Chief and most important among this class of disloyal persons are native priests. It may be considered as practically certain that every native priest in the provinces of Batangas and La Laguna is a secret enemy of the Government, and in active sympathy with insurgents.

These are absolutely our most dangerous enemies — more dangerous even than armed insurgents — because of their unqualified influence. They should be given no exemptions whatever on account of their calling.[64]

This logic of absolute subjection to the insatiable standards of the conquest's demands for native "loyalty" permeates the institutional discourses and archival records of the occupation. Available juridical evidence also demonstrates that the military precedents of the colonial legal order essentially reproduced the U.S. state's (continental) frontier jurisprudence by forming a durable structure of native criminalization.[65]

Given the extreme mismatch in the terms of military engagement (emergent industrial and automatic weaponry vs. underarmed guerilla outfits) as well as the heinous disproportion in casualties, the juxtaposition between two 1901 military memoranda is instructive. The first document, tediously titled "Memorandum in regard to trials by courts-martial and military commissions of persons in or connected with the Army in the Philippine Islands for offenses against natives, showing offenses, sentences, and remarks (if any) in reviews of proceedings touching subject of cruelty to natives,"[66] denotes the conviction of five American soldiers for unlawful murder and two for the manslaughter of Filipino natives between 1898 and 1901. The second document, "Memorandum in regard to trials of Filipinos by military commissions for cruelty against soldiers,"[67] records the conviction of twenty-seven Filipinos for murder and two for the manslaughter of U.S. soldiers between January 1, 1900, and March 13, 1902. The juxtaposition of these figures — which imply that it was, in fact, "Filipino natives" who were the most egregiously criminal homicidal actors during the years of conquest — indicates the expansive nature of U.S. white supremacist statecraft at the cutting edge of its genocidal movements.

Symbiotic with the carnage of frontier warfare, in this sense, is the equally ambitious and violent project of establishing the dominion of white supremacist institutionality in the colonial setting. It is within this articulation of institutionality that the integrity of indigenous subjectivity — particularly as an oppressed human subject possessing the nominal political right of self-determination and freedom from external (colonial) domination — is structurally undermined by the racial rationality of a genocidal war making and civil society-building logic.

In this context, perhaps the most remarkable passage from Sen. George F. Hoar's aforementioned speech on the floor of the 57th Congress involves his frank summation of figures so astronomical as to escape any analytical language other than that of genocide. Examined alongside *Senate Document 331*, Hoar's comments provide valuable insight regarding (1) the fairly broad accessibility and circulation of the information relating the archipelago genocide, as well as (2) the broader civil and governmental context in which such information could be received and (politically and morally) assimilated into a national white supremacist common sense. Again, it is worth emphasizing that Hoar's estimation of Filipino fatalities here encompasses only the first few years of the conquest and speaks only to the provincial sites of Batangas and Luzon. Perhaps more importantly, while most of his peers rejected Hoar's moral and political position, none disputed the essential truthfulness of his description of what was occurring in the Philippines:

> It has been shown, I think, in the investigation now going on that the secretary of the province of Batangas declared that one-third of the 300,000 of the population of that province have died within two years — 100,000 men and women.
>
> The *Boston Journal*, an eminent Republican paper and a most able supporter of the imperialistic policy, printed on the 3d of May, 1901, an interview with Gen. James M. Bell. . . . He said in May, 1901, and he advocated the policy in the interview, too, that one-sixth of the natives of Luzon have either been killed or have died of the dengue fever in the last two years. Now, what is the population of Luzon? It is about 3,000,000, is it not? . . . Then one-sixth is 500,000.
>
> I suppose that this dengue fever and the sickness which depopulated Batangas is the direct result of the war, and comes from the condition of starvation and bad food which the war has caused. The

other provinces have not been heard from. If this be true we have caused the death of more human beings in the Philippines than we have caused to our enemies, including insurgents in the terrible civil war, in all our other wars put together. The general adds that —

"The loss of life by killing alone has been very great, but I think not one man has been slain except where his death served the legitimate purposes of war. It has been necessary to adopt what in other countries would probably be thought harsh measures, for the Filipino is tricky and crafty and has to be fought in his own way."[68]

Again, there is no historical consensus as to the number of native mortalities ultimately accumulated by the U.S. conquest. While Hoar's deductive estimate of 600,000 deaths in Luzon and Batangas reflects the broadly anecdotal nature of many attempts at calculating Filipino casualties at their broadest scale, it is generally accepted that such numbers are entirely within the realm of possibility and are almost certainly underestimations of the human damage wrought by the Philippine-American War.

Given the shoddy-to-nonexistent records of Filipino casualties maintained by U.S. officials in the Philippines during the first decade of the twentieth century, the conventions of empirical social science do not offer an adequate methodological lens through which to comprehend and analyze this historical moment. Rather, the most convincing affirmations of this white supremacist statecraft as a demonstrably genocidal racial–colonial formation arrive cumulatively and discursively, conveyed by the historical archive as (1) the reflection (and periodic construction) of a racist and genocidal white nationalist–imperialist common sense, and (2) the multivalent, internally contradictory, though still cohesive self-enunciation of a formative period in U.S. state building, as its frontier-taming rigors of white civilization-making and native social liquidation cross the Pacific.

Thus, the infamous orders issued by Gen. Jacob H. Smith in late 1901 that culminated in the massacre of native Filipinos at Samar inscribe the genocidal truth of the emergent Pacifica

Americana and should not be analytically or historically isolated as uniquely or even exceptionally egregious in either the
clarity of their intent or their authorization of particular tactics
through which ostensible military objectives are to be fulfilled.[69]
Testimony during the trial of Major L. W. T. Waller, who was
court-martialed for his role as an accomplice to Smith in the
mass murder of alleged *insurrectos* at Samar, revisits the famous
directive:

> [U]pon the trial of Major Waller, of the Marine Corps, testimony was
> given by Waller, corroborated by other witnesses, that Gen. Jacob H.
> Smith instructed him to kill and burn; that the more he killed and
> burned the better pleased General Smith would be; that it was no time
> to take prisoners, and that when Major Waller asked General Smith
> to define the age limit for killing, he replied, "Everything over 10."[70]

Waller's acquittal was punctuated by comments to the *New York
Times* that exhibited his incorrigible commitment to the spirit of
Smith's orders, and which clearly articulated the esprit de corps
of the occupying forces:

> I have fought in every country in the world except Australia, but
> Samar — well, Hades is a Winter resort compared to Samar. I left
> Samar a howling wilderness. They tried to make it that for us, but
> we made it a howling wilderness for them.[71]

Smith's own admissions during his court-martial confirm Waller's
(and others') testimony:

> [Smith] admits by his counsel that he issued orders to make Samar a
> howling wilderness; to kill all natives capable of bearing arms, and
> that boys of ten years and upward were included because they were
> as dangerous as their elders.[72]

While the evident vulgarity of Smith's rhetoric offended the sensibilities of peers and government officials alike, there is no
evidence that the spectacle of the general's eventual conviction by court-martial dissuaded the progress of the military's
protocolonial genocide. To the contrary, the fact that Smith was
actually not tried for murder, but rather for "conduct to the
prejudice of good order and discipline" (which amounted to a

"KILL EVERY ONE OVER TEN."
Criminals because they were born ten years before we took the Philippines.
The New York Evening Journal.

"Kill Every One over Ten," *New York Evening Journal,* May 5, 1902, page 1.

court-martialing for a *verbal* blunder), implicitly sanctioned the content of his orders while punishing the rhetoric in which they were dressed.[73] Further, the terms of his conviction resulted only in a written reprimand, and his forced retirement under order of President Roosevelt in July 1902 was actually met with a sense of subdued objection from fellow army officers, many of whom implied that had the court anticipated the president's imposition of Smith's retirement, it would not have convicted him at all.[74]

Jacob H. Smith's emblematic orders, and the larger genealogy of genocide to which they belong, inaugurate a retheorization and renarration of the Filipino condition that considers the productive capacities of a globally produced white supremacist social logic. I am suggesting that the trajectory of U.S. nation building is, on the one hand, indelibly genocidal in both its periodic mobilizations of military and extra-state paramilitary racial violence *and* the conditions of historical possibility that it perpetually fortifies as its premises of existence. On the other hand, I am arguing that the genocidal logic of U.S. white supremacy, inscribed across its range of institutionalities, necessarily facilitates and overdetermines the knowledge production, subject formation, and political projects of those who inherit and embody this social logic.

Either formal or casual delineations of any distinction between "legitimate" war making and racist or protocolonial genocide, are generally nonexistent in both the governmental and military discourses of the United States. That is, U.S. national discourse — from the jurisprudential to the popular/mass cultural — is generally illiterate when it comes to addressing the multiple dimensions and complexly entangled histories of the American continental and global project as a mosaic of mobilizations for, and institutionalizations of, genocidal and protogenocidal force. In this context, it is especially noteworthy that the production of U.S. genocide across North America and in the Philippine archipelago preceded the era of fully industrialized warfare and the manufacture of weapons of mass destruction: the process of genocidal conquest was utterly *labor intensive,* requiring extraordinary physical expenditures and strategic improvisation in the struggle to neutralize and exterminate guerillas and civilians and to exert tentative military control over the frontier. The strident euphemisms of military historian Brian Linn offer a prototypically valorizing nationalist gaze at the innovation of military practices in the archipelago theater:

> Indeed, the key to the Army's success was its lack of adherence to rigid doctrines or theories and the willingness of its officers to experiment with novel pacification schemes. ... In the Philippines there were no helicopters or radio communications to insure that each subordinate followed his instructions to the letter. ... This lack of official control aided pacification. It not only forced individual officers to be responsible for the pacification of their areas, but also prevented interference from their superiors:[75]

"Pacification" here is a versatile signifier for the very condition that remains outside the historical record: as such, Linn's professed methodological and epistemological adherence to "official" U.S. Army documents constructs a history of warfare that reifies indigenous actors, unilaterally valorizes the American conquest, and generates a narrative of "fascination" with military conquest at the limits of Manifest Destiny and American modernity.[76]

> A final lesson for students of guerilla warfare is the necessity of achieving a decisive military victory over guerilla forces. Although benevolent policies such as education, self-government, and social reforms may win over the populace and demonstrate an alternative to the revolutionaries, they cannot succeed until military superiority is achieved.... As long as the guerillas could rely on civilian support, whether inspired by patriotic motives or fear, pacification was impossible.[77]

I would argue that the philosophical and ideological architecture of Filipino arrested raciality, particularly in enabling such profound silence and disavowal regarding the historical genocide under examination here, is fundamentally a reinscription and refraction of this broader American illiteracy. What, then, are the political–intellectual implications of the historic and geographic progression of American white supremacy and its genocidal logic, initiated in the territories of indigenous peoples throughout North America, sustained in the coterminous transatlantic holocaust and chattel enslavement of Africans, and momentarily culminating in the razing conquest of the newfound Philippine archipelago?

Conclusion: To Live the "Zone of Death"

The essential and inescapable violence of the encounter with American modernity continues to shape the time, subjectivity, and sociality of the Filipino condition. Anthropologist Arthur

Kleinman provides a useful schema for conceptualizing violence as an active historical force, a constitutive aspect of the social, through which institutions and infrastructures are partially though still fundamentally shaped:

> Rather than view violence, then, simply as a set of discrete events... the perspective I am advancing seeks to unearth those entrenched processes of ordering the social world and making (or realizing) culture that themselves are forms of violence: violence that is multiple, mundane, and perhaps all the more fundamental because it is the hidden or secret violence out of which images of people are shaped, experiences of groups are coerced, and agency itself is engendered. Because the cultural prefiguring and normative social workings of violence shape its consequences as forms of suffering and means of coping, such violence must also be at work in the institutions that authorize response and in the ordinary practices of engagement. Policies and programs participate in the very violence they seek to respond to and control.[78]

Herein lies the entanglement of the Filipino condition with the generative legacy of genocidal contact with the United States. In seeking to constitute a historical subject that reconciles the killer with the killed, the discourse of Filipino Americanism persistently reassembles, rationalizes, and coheres the Filipino condition as a social existence outside the realm of racial affectability — specifically, as a subjectivity that is *not* perpetually tied to a genealogy of white supremacist genocide. This knowledge production, in turn, generates a peculiar and powerful Filipino American sentimentality: a structure of affect and historical sense that dislocates the constitutive, genocidal racist violence of the Filipino–American relation into silence and invisibility. The very coherence and accessibility of this Filipino American sentimentality is precisely what forms the existential condition of necessity for an identity construction — "Filipino American" narrowly, "Filipino" broadly — that is otherwise perpetually undermined by a historical structure of irreconcilability with (white supremacist) modernity, American nation building, and white institutionality.

Filipino American sociality thus inscribes and periodically exaggerates a certain historical fantasy: through the magical disappearance of mass-scale death, it posits a decisive movement that dislocates an originating genocidal violence and laboriously articulates the grounds of a metaphysical reconciliation between the Fanonian "native" and "settler." This is a contrived peace, overshadowed by its historical condition of possibility in genocide, and generative of an altogether different (though no less profound) structure of violence. To appropriate Fanon's anticolonial critique, the very grammar of things "Filipino American" collaborates in the social logic of a genocidal colonialism (and its descendants in underdevelopment, imperialism, and neoliberalism). Fanon's meditation here returns the image of the paradigmatic colonial subject, the linguistically assimilated native intellectual:

> To speak means to be in a position to use a certain syntax, to grasp the morphology of this or that language, but it means above all to assume a culture, to support the weight of a civilization. . . .
> A man who has a language consequently possesses the world expressed and implied by that language. What we are getting at becomes plain: Mastery of language affords remarkable power.[79]

The legacy of physical extermination and cultural–ecological devastation entails far more than the formal inception of an oppressive and exploitive colonial regime: in the emergence of genocidal Pacifica Americana, one also finds the birth of a modernist racial pedagogy, wherein the native becomes the preeminent embodiment of modern/national progress and its unstoppable historical telos. For Fanon, this condition constitutes the field of cultural death in which the colonial native intellectual works, advancing the mission of white modernity through a dialectical process of "adoption" and "renouncement."

> Every colonized people — in other words, every people in whose soul an inferiority complex has been created by the death and burial of its local cultural originality — finds itself face to face with the language of the civilizing nation; that is, with the culture of the mother country.

> The colonized is elevated above his jungle status in proportion to his adoption of the mother country's cultural standards. He becomes whiter as he renounces his blackness, his jungle.[80]

Proximity to blackness and the jungle become primary signifiers of backwardness, premodernity, the dead past. The epochal killing of the initial contact, having allegedly and decisively ceased, is now replaced with the relative benevolence of liberal state institutions and a state-sanctioned cosmopolitan civil society, the grammar of modernity having obscured while extending the logic of cultural displacement. Humanistic progressivism — the lifeblood of cultural conquest — restores the supremacy of modernity's presumptive white subject in magnanimous fashion, inviting the native's selective and always partial membership. Goldberg writes:

> [T]he spirit of modernity is to be found most centrally in its commitment to continuous progress: to material, moral, physical, and political improvement and to the promotion and development of civilization....
>
> Basic to modernity's self-conception, then, is a notion...of a Subject that is abstract and atomistic, general and universal, divorced from the contingencies of historicity as it is from the particularities of social and political relations and identities....
>
> Enter race. It pretends to universality in undertaking to draw otherwise disparate social subjects together into a cohesive unit in terms of which common interests are either found or fabricated.... [R]ace offers itself as a category capable of providing a semblance of social cohesion, of historical particularity, of given meanings and motivations to agents otherwise mechanically conceived as conduits for market forces and moral laws.... It is an identity that proves capable of being stretched across time and space, that itself assumes transforming specificity and legitimacy by taking on as its own the connotations of prevailing scientific and social discourses.[81]

Perhaps the nexus of what I have been calling the "Filipino–American relation" is the convergence between the physical extermination of an object native people and colonialism's contingent production and incorporation of native intellectuals as subjects of modernity and agents of modernization. In turn, cultural displacement — long understood by indigenous peoples worldwide as a primary form of genocidal conquest — is manifest in the formal structure, grammar, and institutional locations of Filipino American discourse. This field of knowledge production and cultural meaning, in its ritualized subsumption of epochal death in exchange for a troubled historical rapprochement with U.S. national formation, thus becomes a complex bearer of the legacy of mass extermination. Here it is the very gesture of American belonging, simultaneously a sentimental and theoretical move, that constructs the transpacific "return" of the native intellectual, interpellated by the colonizer's syntax and personifying modernity's fatal dialectic of civilization and genocide.

The pedagogical mission of white modernity, advancing in and through the white supremacist institutionality of colonialism and the violent displacements of its transplanted social forms, is persistent and clear: within the genealogy of genocide, the production of social truth simultaneously authorizes mass-scale killing while inscribing the historical death of indigenous cultures and communities as the precondition for a backward people's authentic (modern) freedom and their access to the rational faculties of (political and subjective) self-government. The analytical gap that erases genocide as the condition of the Filipino–American relation — and hence as the material historical premise of Filipino American discourse in its various forms — also rests on a false categorical distinction between physical killing and cultural death. Narrow conceptions of colonial conquest, even when conceding the historical possibility of mass-scaled population liquidation, proceed as if the logic of white supremacist colonization's genocidal capacities is centrally (or even exclusively) fixed on the realm of the physical body, culminating in contained fashion with the violent end of the native's functioning biological husk.

To conceptualize white supremacist conquest through a more dynamic and dense genealogical notion of genocide as archive, however, refocuses the attention of the historical present on modalities of disruption and/or forced liquidation of indigenous cultural institutions and their modes of social organization, during and beyond the designated moments of intensified genocidal mobilization. This framing suggests a historical conception of "death" that, in resonance with a complex and historically nuanced notion of genocide, disassembles the reifications of the cultural formations, bodies, and historical subjects that are the focal targets of white supremacist civilization-building. The cultural formation, body, and historical subject of racist genocide (the very same that survive and may even at times flourish within genocide's epochal enabling of white supremacist institutionalities, from neocolonial government to postcolonial social formation) may "live" perpetually in a condition of historical death that is the essential global racial condition of succeeding social forms.

Beyond the alleged military requirements of large-scale killing in this misnamed American "war" against a scandalous, treacherous, and generally criminal (hence apolitical) guerilla resistance, it was the irrepressible compulsion of modernity — its "racist culture" of mass-homicidal, manifest whiteness[82] — to fantasize (and wage) genocide for white life's sake. The 1902 congressional testimony of Brig. Gen. Robert P. Hughes is especially illuminating here, with its abrupt opposition between "towns" (the property of white sociality) and "barrios/sitios/villages" (the residency of the uncivilized) structuring the military–racial rationale for punitive scorched earth campaigns:

> SEN. RAWLINS: . . . [I]n burning towns, what would you do? Would the entire town be destroyed by fire or would only offending portions of the town be burned?
>
> GEN. HUGHES: I do not know that we ever had a case of burning what you would call a town in this country, but probably a *barrio* or a *sitio*. . . .

SEN. RAWLINS: What did I understand you to say would be the consequences of that?

GEN. HUGHES: They usually burned the village.

SEN. RAWLINS: All of the houses in the village?

GEN. HUGHES: Yes; every one of them.

SEN. RAWLINS: What would become of the inhabitants?

GEN. HUGHES: That was their lookout.

SEN. RAWLINS: If these shacks were of no consequence what was the utility of their destruction?

GEN. HUGHES: The destruction was as a punishment. They permitted these people [guerillas] to come in there and conceal themselves and they gave no sign. . . .

SEN. RAWLINS: The punishment in that case would fall, not upon the men, who could go elsewhere, but mainly upon the women and little children.

GEN. HUGHES: The women and children are part of the family, and where you wish to inflict a punishment you can punish the man probably worse in that way than in any other.

SEN. RAWLINS: But is that within the ordinary rules of civilized warfare? Of course you could exterminate the family, which would be still worse punishment.

GEN. HUGHES: These people are not civilized.[83]

Following the white supremacist logic of the conquest's rhetorical apparatus and on-the-ground military conduct, the native population of the Philippines was not being loosely and simplistically compared with or grammatically reduced to "Indians" and "niggers" through a transplanted racial analogy that was readily accessible in the white supremacist lexicon of statesmen, generals, commanding officers, and rank-and-file soldiers.

In this state of contrived war, where the distinctively American rendition of modernity's aggressive movement through place and time entailed the *production of* (racialized) enemy/others, "Indians" and "niggers" constituted social rubrics of absolute exposure to technologies of social, cultural, and biological disintegration, and thus orbited around a logic of *categorical* death. The constitutive bottom line of American modernity, and U.S. nation-building processes more generally, is that the material pathways and historical trajectories toward good sociality — at the local and global scales — require multiple productions of categorical death.

The difference here between categorical death (which moves through the genealogy of genocide as its premises of elaboration) and Orlando Patterson's well-known conception of social death (which is concerned with the social constitution of slave societies[84]) is that the logic of the categorical pushes at the limits of the social–biological subject (including the socially dead subject or putative social nonsubject): categorical death frames a modality of nonexistence that exceeds the spectacles of accumulated corpses and mass graves, initiates a historical technology of killing that perpetually demands the extraordinary climaxes of white sociality and white supremacist institutionality, and, in the case of the Philippine conquest, alienates the social possibility of the self-enunciated "Filipino" from the materiality of genocide and accompanying struggles to resist, abolish, and survive it.

It was within the genesis moment of the Filipino–American relation that the very nomenclature of the "Filipino" embodied the continuity of conquest en masse, offering a Pacific native population that both occupied and deformed the genocidal nationalist discourse of "Indians" and "niggers."[85] The Filipino occupied the central distinction of living — categorically and ontologically — for the productive (socially exterminating) measures of racial nation building and for selective, coercive assimilation into a white (American) modernity — the very crystallization of categorical "life."

> [A]s early as April 1899, General Shafter gave grisly portent to the future conduct of the war: "It may be necessary to kill half the Filipinos in order that the remaining half of the population may be

advanced to a higher plane of life than their present semi-barbarous state affords."[86]

Focusing this broad conception of categorical death, the material notion of a "zone of death" provides theoretical and structural coherence for understanding the stakes of Filipino American discourse amid its anxious rationalizations of the Filipino condition through characteristic discourses of national membership, entitlement, and belonging.

Taking the terroristic campaign in Batangas province as a defining theoretical rubric, the institutionality of the "dead line" offers a moment of clarity in delineating the historical contingencies of genocidal conquest for subject populations. Francisco's crystallization offers an analytical catalyst for precisely this kind of framing:

> In the "zone of death" outside the camp "dead line," "all rendered themselves liable," according to [Brig. Gen. J. F.] Bell. All property was destroyed, all houses put to the torch and the country was made a "desert waste...of death and desolation." According to statistics compiled by U.S. government officials, by the time Bell was finished at least 100,000 people had been killed or had died in Batangas alone as a direct result of the scorched-earth policies, and the enormous dent in the population of the province (which was reduced by a third) is reflected in the census figures.[87]

Resonating Francisco's narration, Miller broadens the social–ecological impact of the "dead line" to include the constituting elements of indigenous cultural existence:

> The entire population outside of the major cities in Batangas was herded into concentration camps, which were bordered by what Bell called "dead lines." Everything outside of the camps was systematically destroyed — humans, crops, food stores, domestic animals, houses, and boats. Actually, a similar policy had been quietly initiated on the island of Marinduque some months before.[88]

Francisco and Miller enable an analytic of archive that radically resituates the historical protocols of the Filipino–American relation in its formative moments. Rather than proceeding from the assumptive politic of conquest as a historically contained episode in a Philippine telos of national independence and emergent racial unaffectability (hence access to what Silva calls the rational racial subjectivity of the "transcendental I"[89]), we can apprehend such archival moments as Brig. Gen. Bell's December 1901 order to establish the Batangas "zone of death" as the blueprinting of an epochal social logic within which the Filipino condition is rigorously overdetermined by the perpetual, immanent violence of a white supremacist social formation and its genocidal statecraft. It is the genesis of the compulsory social carceral — literally, an incarceration premised on the absolute (in this case territorial) adjacency of extermination and "pacified" native sociality — that animates the Filipino relation to Pacifica Americana. Bell's orders state:

> In order to put an end to enforced contributions now levied by insurgents upon the inhabitants of sparsely settled and outlying barrios and districts by means of intimidation and assassination, commanding officers of all towns now existing in the provinces of Batangas and Laguna, including those at which no garrison is stationed at present, will immediately specify and establish plainly marked limits surrounding each town bounding a zone within which it may be practicable with an average sized garrison to exercise efficient supervision over and furnish protection to inhabitants (who desire to be peaceful) against the depredations of armed insurgents. . . .
>
> Commanding officers will also see that orders are at once given and distributed to all the inhabitants within the jurisdiction of towns over which they exercise supervision, informing them of the danger of remaining outside of these limits, and that unless they move by December 25 from outlying barrios and districts . . . to within the limits of the zone established at their own or nearest town, their property (found outside of said zone at said date) will become liable to confiscation or destruction.[90]

It is possible — and I would argue politically necessary — to read within the incredible banality of Bell's orders a clear pronouncement of the definitive end of native life as such, and the onset of an ontological condition that indelibly — that is, categorically — marks the Filipino's putative raciality as a significution of genocidal "benevolent assimilation." At the nexus of this set of protocols, then, is the possibility for an articulation of subjectivity that does *not* require fabrications of historical coherence, self-determining rationality, or congruence with white sociality. Instead, the Filipino condition may potentially enable an extended meditation on the symbiosis between genocide and the genealogies of social formation, state making, and civic institutionality that genocide both historically facilitates and perpetually accompanies.

At the temporal and historical limit of the Filipino–American relation remains the desolation of the dead line. This is the manifest and allegorical border of "pacification," the condition of possibility for the production of the very discursive field with which this book is concerned. The impossibility of simply grasping, negotiating, or reconciling with the dead line — as it delineates categorical death for those who wander, approach, and/or cross — forms the underside of Filipino American sociality's institutional (and ritualized) logic of progress, especially as underwritten by notions of participation and historical presence within the nuances and global distensions of U.S. social formation. Where goes the historical subject that dies, disappears, emerges, and reproduces in and through this genocidal encounter with the United States? Here we find a potentially radical point of departure for the theorization and political articulation of the Filipino condition generally, and the Filipino–American relation more specifically: a critical labor that must be permanently and productively enabled and provoked by the racial apocalypse to which it is anchored.

— 4 —

Suspended Apocalypse

Toward a Racial Analytic
of the Filipino Condition

> The national bourgeoisie, with no misgivings and with
> great pride, revels in the role of agent in its dealings
> with the Western bourgeoisie.
> — Frantz Fanon, 1963

The Political – Cultural Logic
of a "National Bourgeoisie"

The notion of suspended apocalypse identifies a political–cultural logic that rearranges, deforms, and dislocates a Filipino genealogy of subjection and death. Far from functioning simply as a distortion of historical truth or indication of collective false consciousness, this logic forms the discursive structure of a "post-genocidal" subjectivity, the grounds on which to make sense of the Filipino condition through its conceptual congruence with the overlapping and complementary political–cultural structures of global liberal multiculturalism and white supremacist governmentality. In this chapter, I deploy the rubric of suspended apocalypse to historically site and genealogically resituate Michel Foucault's conceptualization of governmentality as the changing technologies and institutionalities through which "relations of subjugation can manufacture subjects."[1] Departing from the previous chapter's extended reflection on the touchstone genocide shaping the onset of Pacifica Americana, this discussion addresses some of the contemporary and living artifacts of Filipino arrested raciality as persistent claims to civic legitimacy, composing an anxious (and still largely androcentric) response to what Warwick Anderson references as the U.S. colonial project's foundational diagnosis of "Filipinos as infantile, immature subjects, unready yet for self-government of body or polity — as *formes frustes* [incomplete manifestations of disease] stalled on the trajectory from native to citizen."[2]

The self-assembly of the overlapping Philippine and Filipino American "national bourgeoisie" hinges on a perpetual dispute with the "little brown monkey's/brother's" incapacities for self-possession, a conflict that takes the shape of a redemptive obligation to fulfill the (rational, self-determining, racially unaffected) projected Filipino's historical promise. Located most profoundly in the formation and social reproduction of a Philippine transpacific national bourgeoisie, or more descriptively, the cultural nuances articulating the organic interchange and overlap between a Philippine petite bourgeoisie and "Filipino American" professional class, the discursive structure of Filipino Americanism enunciates a Filipino condition politically outside of and historically unaffected by the apocalypse of the American encounter. The conditions of possibility through which Filipino Americanism coheres as a viable multiculturalist pronouncement centrally entails an allegation of essential *compatibility* with the institutional logics of U.S. nation building in its local/domestic and global articulations. In the space of this chapter, I am critically and theoretically engaging two dimensions of this ongoing, troublesome historical project.

First, and most broadly, I am concerned with tracing a genealogy of the avant garde of Filipino arrested raciality, relying significantly on a reading of the Fanonian analytic of the "national bourgeoisie" that assembles and emerges within the antagonisms of decolonization and formal Philippine independence. Meditating on several exemplary historical moments, I rehearse a rudimentary contextualization of the compulsory assimilationist/

comprador political subjectivities generated through the apparatuses of neocolonialism, neoliberalism, and U.S. global hegemony. More importantly, in order to concretely illustrate the political architecture of this avant garde I attempt to initiate a critical theoretical framing of the white supremacist racial comportment of American colonialism in the Philippines: specifically, the social and governmental order that it induced through the protocols, political–cultural forms, and protracted administration of Philippine national independence. Here my argument is both indebted to and departing from the work of such scholars as Warwick Anderson, Neferti Tadiar, Allen Isaac, Michael Salman, Victor Bascara, Vicente Rafael, Reynaldo Ileto, and others who have examined the racial technologies of the U.S. colonial project in the archipelago.

The acute focus of my critical approach here is on the avant garde of Filipino arrested raciality as an embodied revelation of the historical animus of liberal Americanist multiculturalism. This national bourgeoisie distends the genealogy of U.S. white supremacist nation building by revealing its political capacities along two generally under-recognized trajectories: (1) the capacity of U.S. white supremacist institutionality to mobilize and produce a global nationalist ascendancy and *reembodied* American politicality — by the latter I mean the practical and proprietary whiteness of American and Americanist "politics" as a technology of rule that can be vested and comported in different "nonwhite" racial bodies across the global political landscape; and (2) the capacity of a multiculturalist content revision — hence constitutive fortification — of white institutionality, by which I mean the forceful universalization of the white social body's self-protective biological and conceptual integrity as the generalized premises of institutional coherence and reproduction. Here I see white institutionality as the overdetermining modality of U.S. global dominance in its different historical periods.

While the theoretical method of this first concern is invoking the Fanonian analytic to name and historically–geographically locate the Filipino national bourgeoisie, my account does not (in fact cannot) adhere to an orthodox conceptualization of "class." The social formation of the Philippines as an American colony, and later as a putatively independent nation-state, is defined by a categorical ambiguity between the elite, ruling, and nominal middle classes. Effectively, the very rubric of a historical Philippine "national bourgeoisie" or petite bourgeoisie, in the Fanonian sense, references the continuum of power, influence, and social prominence that is constantly traversed by those who would be considered traditional elites (large landowners, government officials, wealthy families, doctors, lawyers) and others who would more squarely fall under the categorization of the middle classes (shop owners, small landowners, carpenters, artisans, and professional intellectuals, or *ilustrados*). Resil Mojares, by way of example, writes that on the eve of the U.S. conquest of the Philippines, "Cebu province was a socially irregular, unstable, and inchoate landscape. Nineteenth-century economic changes created new social groups, revised old social relations, and primed the appearance of the new social formations."[3] With such a historical caveat in mind, the method of my engagement is less concerned with offering a rigorous descriptive inventory of who definitively *composes* the Philippine "national bourgeoisie" than it is with understanding its *performances* of collective subjectivity and nationalist integrity.

In revisiting Fanon's critique of the national bourgeoisie in his essay "The Trials and Tribulations of National Consciousness," this chapter is attempting to offer some needed theoretical nuance to Philippine historian Teodoro Agoncillo's classical historical schematization of the Filipino "colonial mentality" in his durable text *History of the Filipino People*. Agoncillo writes in chapter 20, "Results of the American Occupation":

The economic invasion of the Philippines brought the American mode of living close to the Filipinos. American goods and services were at first considered luxuries. After forty-five years of occupation, they became necessities. . . . Is your pair of shoes Stateside? Is your car imported from the States or assembled here in the Philippines? Such questions, though silly and pretentious, are common. If it is Stateside it is the best. . . .

The mental attitude that despises one's own and loves anything foreign is the natural result of American "altruism" bolstered by propaganda. . . . [T]he Americans softened the Filipinos by pampering their stomach. . . .

The softening of the Filipino spine, which resulted from too much American canned goods, in turn resulted in the persistence of the colonial mentality. Having developed an extreme liking for things American without critical evaluation of their intrinsic worth, the average Filipino considers it blasphemous to criticize the United States or any American.[4]

While Agoncillo's language is blunt and his characterizations simplistic, his essential political–intellectual contribution is worth illuminating: Agoncillo is naming (and simplifying) the slippery common denominator that ideologically and psychically coheres the Filipino national bourgeoisie. Recognizing that labored ignorance and intellectualized disavowal are the inherent dangers of critically or radically interrogating those sets of political and cultural assumptions that are so taken for granted that they generally escape extended analysis, Agoncillo's text is (in places) trained on an absolute discomforting of the Filipino petite bourgeoisie. *History of the Filipino People* has been required reading for Philippine college and university students for decades (since its initial publication in 1960), and this is primary evidence of the resonance — if not the demonstrable "accuracy" or ultimate political effectiveness — of its polemical historical narration. While I will refrain from offering an extensive inventory of textual examples that illustrate the core social truth articulated in Agoncillo's text, this chapter does attempt to outline how the Philippine national bourgeoisie is both the "class" refraction and pedagogical production of U.S. genocidal conquest and its colonialist genealogy.

Pushing beyond the limitations of Agoncillo's schema, the structuring and socially productive sentimentality through which "America" convenes a gravity of "adoration" and political identification not only defines the historical animus of the Filipino national bourgeoisie; it also establishes the political–discursive conditions of possibility for ostensibly *critical* rearticulations of the Filipino condition, including progressive, counterhegemonic, and radical political iterations of disaffected elements of the Filipino American petite bourgeoisie. Here I am not merely focused on a schematic identification of the political tendencies of a neocolonial or "postcolonial" petite bourgeoisie, but I am also interested in revisiting the generally unspoken sentimental premises on which certain critical Filipino discourses — including those of progressive U.S.-based Filipino solidarity organizations — are formulating their means of rhetorical and political address.

The second major theoretical and pedagogical concern of this chapter concerns the problem of whether and how Filipinos, Filipino immigrants, and Filipino Americans "fit" into the historical and sociological narratives of contemporary Asian immigration and Asian American racial formation. The nominal liberalization of immigration restrictions under the 1965 Immigration Act is almost universally conceptualized as the watershed moment of the Asian American emergence in the United States, and Filipinos are presumptively tethered to this generalized immigrant narrative. In this context, I am raising theoretical questions that disassemble the conceptual limitations of the Asian Americanist narration of the post-1965 migrations: How might we reconceptualize and renarrate the contemporary Filipino transpacific migration and post-1965 Filipino American civil and community formation by thinking historically and theoretically beyond (and significantly against) narrative reifications of the 1965 Act's juridical inscriptions of the "Asian immigrant" figure? Might the historical conditions of Filipino immigration and migration substantively displace the "Asian

Americanization" of the post-conquest Filipino condition, such that Filipinos cannot be appropriately located within the engulfing rubrics of Asian American "panethnicity"?[5] To put a finer point on these questions, I am concerned with the ways in which this juridical schematization of "post-'65" Filipino immigration — which at times shifts into an empiricist and economic determinist rationalization of the social formation of Filipino American communities — works to obscure and erase the constitutive uniqueness of the Philippine experience with formal U.S. colonialism between 1899 and 1946. In departure from the conventions of Asian Americanist articulations, I follow the critical gesture of Michael Salman, who writes:

> [H]istorians of the United States have been slow to take colonialism seriously as a relationship of interaction between Americans and other peoples. . . .
> Concurrent with U.S. historians' tendency to isolate themselves and their subjects from the rest of the world, most of the vibrant comparative scholarship on colonialism and colonial discourse during the past two decades has bypassed subjects related to U.S. history.[6]

To clarify my conceptual framing in relation to Salman's critique, I am distinguishing the moment of formal colonialism from the larger rubrics of American empire, imperialism, militarism, neoliberalism, and neocolonialism in order to further resituate the historical genealogy of the Filipino condition. Tracing the emergence and political animus of the Philippine national bourgeoisie enables a theoretical framing that illuminates the symbiosis between (*a*) the relations of dominance inscribed by a half-century of subjection to the U.S. white supremacist colonial state, and (*b*) the genesis and elaboration of Filipino Americanism as an intentionally deforming signification of the Filipino condition, a labor largely inhabited by the transpacific national bourgeoisie through its sentimental solidarity with the U.S. nation-building project.

Thus, in resonance with the analytical and theoretical focus of chapter 2, I am concerned less with the empirical content of

Filipino Americanism than with the political disclosures and narrative logics this archive offers in particular historical moments of genealogical formation. It is these political disclosures and narrative logics that cohere Filipino Americanism as an archive of experience, in turn producing and disciplining social formations across different political and cultural geographies. To consider this archive as something commonly accessed and ordinarily lived, I would argue, attends to the importance of framing the discursive terrain of the Filipino condition as a range of political contestations and institutional entanglements rather than a reifying "objective" or reductive empiricist description of a people's social and economic circumstance. Here it is the specificity of the colonial legacy, and the continuity between U.S. colonialism and the historical present of the Philippines, that extends the implications of the previous chapter and elaborates Filipino arrested raciality as a symptom of contemporary multiculturalism's constitutive (if always troubled) partnership with the political, cultural, and social logics of white supremacy.

Suspended Apocalypse: A Fanonian Approach

Fanon, writing at the crest of global struggles for decolonization and national independence across Africa, Asia, and the Americas, famously lambasts the national bourgeoisie of the underdeveloped world for its generalized refusal to fully engage in anticolonialist insurrection and revolutionary struggle. "The unpreparedness of the elite," Fanon asserts, "the lack of practical ties between them and the masses, their apathy and, yes, their cowardice at the crucial moment in the struggle, are the cause of tragic trials and tribulations."[7] Attributing a definitive *anti-anticolonialist* historical subjectivity to the national bourgeoisie (and hence refusing a reductive reading of its ideological confusion or "false consciousness"), Fanon sketches a characteristic neocolonial logic that reinvents colonialist subjection through the "intermediary" opportunisms and conservative nationalist pretensions of this "native" class formation.

Reflecting the conceptual and epistemological apparatuses that reform colonialist institutionalities into their neocolonial variations, Fanon's nationalist bourgeoisie is hounded by its history of disengagement from the risks, dangers, and possibilities of anticolonial "popular praxis" and perhaps most profoundly by its "incapacity to attribute [anticolonialist struggle] any reason."[8] Fanon further contends that the colonialist — and cosmopolitan white supremacist — imprinting of this native elite as an intellectual bloc constitutes one of the central political antagonisms of "independence."

> The characteristic, virtually endemic weakness of the underdeveloped countries' national consciousness is not only the consequence of the colonized subject's mutilation by the colonial regime. It can also be attributed to the apathy of the national bourgeoisie, its mediocrity, and its deeply cosmopolitan mentality.
>
> The national bourgeoisie, which takes over power at the end of the colonial regime, is an underdeveloped bourgeoisie. Its economic clout is practically zero, and in any case, no way commensurate with that of its metropolitan counterpart which it intends replacing. In its willful narcissism, the national bourgeoisie has lulled itself into thinking that it can supplant the metropolitan [colonialist] bourgeoisie to its own advantage. But independence, which literally forces it back against the wall, triggers catastrophic reactions and obliges it to send out distress signals in the direction of the former metropolis. . . . The national bourgeoisie in the underdeveloped countries is not geared to production, invention, creation, or work. All its energy is channeled into intermediary activities.[9]

Thus, it is not merely the epochal violence of colonialism's "cultural alienation" (see chapter 2) that shapes the political ontology of the national bourgeoisie, but the productive and interpellating technologies of white supremacist institutionality that (1) significantly fabricate the national bourgeoisie as an offspring of colonialism's episteme and material social forms while (2) altering the genetic code of "nationalist" consciousness in the time of formal independence, decoupling it from the rigors of revolutionary decolonization. Fanon contends that the self-assembling of the national bourgeoisie is both a criminal nationalist venture in its reembodiment of the "rapacity of the colonists,"[10] and a somewhat pathetic (though utterly unsympathetic) historical figuration of both neocolonial dependence and nationalist pretension.

Fanon's durable critical theorizations have been widely and differently received in political intellectual conversations across a spectrum of socially transformative and progressive engagements, from radical feminist thought to indigenous liberationist praxis. His incisive polemical gestures against the historical trajectory of the postcolony's national bourgeoisie, however, have not yet been sufficiently revisited as a point of departure for a genealogy of the production of a global multiculturalist "class" formation that specifically feeds on the post–civil rights discursive shifts in the national racial discourse of the United States. Herein, the structuring assimilation of the transpacific Filipino petite bourgeoisie to the global logics of U.S. nation building, alongside the still emerging vernaculars and political architectures of Filipino Americanism, catalyze a symptomatic reading of the contemporary "multicultural" embodiments of white supremacist dominance and violence. Following the national bourgeoisie of Fanon's political schema, which inhabits the oppressive and exploitive institutionalities of the colonial order in a rendition of illegitimate or perverse inheritance, the post–civil rights multiculturalist ordering of white supremacist nation building consistently and (class) selectively incorporates and elevates the onetime subjects of racist domination to positions of full participation, if not actual leadership, in the hegemonic apparatuses of cultural, state, and socioeconomic formation.

Fanon's is a useful critique for this historical moment in the life of global white supremacy, owing to his choice of protagonists in the venerable text *The Wretched of the Earth*. His meditation on the political animus of the national bourgeoisie and its resident configuration of "colonized intellectuals"

also forms a useful analytical matrix through which to critically interrogate the self-conceptualizations of the post–U.S.
conquest Filipino condition: Under what political conditions,
and through what discursive structures, has it been possible for
Filipino subjectivities to articulate *through* white supremacist
institutionalities and epistemologies — for example, the university, the nation-state, the English language — even as they
periodically represent political positions that purport to resist
or oppose the vestiges of racial colonialism?[11] How does a particular Filipino comportment of rational (racial and protoracial)
subjectivity and ("national" and existential) self-government historically perform the Filipino condition as an ahistorical artifact,
that is, as a subject capable of *not* recognizing itself as indelibly, inescapably, and perpetually produced by the logics of white
supremacist colonialism, U.S. nation building, and transpacific
racial genocide?

   This theoretical interrogation, which I am framing through
the analytical and historical rubric of a Filipino suspended
apocalypse, foregrounds Filipino arrested raciality as the premise of a self-governed, rational subjectivity and the persistent
institutional renarration of the Filipino condition through an
existential and analytical *postponement* of the genocidal historical encounter with the United States. Here I intend a multilayered
notion of suspension: in verb form, it implies the denial, deferral,
and contingent (hence momentary and incomplete) expulsion
of the apocalyptic American encounter in relation to the labors
of constructing historical memory, cultural common sense, and
collective Filipino politicalities. On the other hand, the adjective form of suspension suggests that the apocalypse of Filipino
engulfment within the historical logics of U.S. white supremacy,
genocide, and colonialist nation building is never quite fully,
definitively, and finally denied, deferred, and expelled; thus, the
American apocalypse remains "suspended over" the Filipino
condition and its self-articulations, out of direct view, though
nonetheless structurally situated above and behind, continuously

shadowing and altering the very historical subject that refuses to accommodate it.

Rereading Fanon's acute critique of the national bourgeoisie as a delineation of the colonial and neocolonial "class" inscription of Filipino suspended apocalypse is to revisit the accoutrements of "Philippine Independence" as a territorially distended pageantry of American (white) institutionality, somewhat morbidly allegorized by the date on which the flag of the independent Philippine Republic was first raised: July 4, 1946. The granting of Philippine independence as a simulation of American liberal democracy formed the basis for a post–World War II and Cold War era coalition between the U.S. government and an incipient Philippine national bourgeoisie, over and against contemporaneous — and still ongoing — struggles against American imperialism and the independent Philippine state.[12] Historian Reynaldo Ileto, in the incisive essay "The Philippine–American War: Friendship and Forgetting," contends that contrary to conventional modernist narrations of a colonial-anticolonial dialectic:

> [A] war with the United States simply does not fit into the historical trajectory from colonialism to independence, tradition to modernity. The goals of the *ilustrado* leaders of the 1898 revolution [against Spain] *were* apparently fulfilled through U.S. intervention. The repressive, anti-liberal regime of the Spanish friars *was* apparently replaced by U.S. tutelage towards eventual self-rule. Good government was established in Taft's New Era. By the time of Gov. Francis Burton Harrison's policy of Filipinizing the bureaucracy, and the passage of the Jones Bill promising eventual independence, it looked like the goals of the 1898 revolution were within reach through peaceful means rather than war.[13]

Following Ileto's crystallization of *ilustrado* nationalist desire, and conceptualizing the U.S. "promise" of independence as the logical outcome of a genocidal white supremacist statecraft, the bureaucratic Filipinization of colonialist institutionalities establishes a material foundation for the logic of suspended apocalypse.

To clarify by way of example: in the decade following the onset of Philippine independence, Philippine lawmakers established the Committee on Anti-Filipino Activities (CAFA), an organization that overtly drew its inspiration from Sen. Joseph McCarthy's infamous House Un-American Activities Committee (HUAC). Reflecting and extending the McCarthyite agenda, CAFA pursued intellectuals suspected of affiliation or sympathy with the Communist Hukbalahap rebellion and Partido Komunista ng Pilipinas (Communist Party of the Philippines), and was accompanied by the Philippine state's anti-communist alliance with the Roman Catholic Church throughout the archipelago.[14] The example of CAFA, as an index of the statecraft of Philippine independence, illuminates the labors of Filipino political mimesis as self-conscious practices of induction into a global white supremacist body politic — that is, the naturalized conjunction of nation-statehood with internal "domestic" warfare against political, racial, and cultural pathologies signifies a particular fulfillment of the *ilustrado* national telos and forms the premises of the putative Filipino subject's definitive departure from the absolute vulnerabilities and unspeakable terror of genocidal conquest. In this sense, it is U.S. colonial domination, and its resident technologies of "benevolence," that reform Filipino vulnerability and terror through the rigorous mechanics of a multiculturalist/neocolonialist white institutionality.

While it is beyond the scope of this chapter's conceptual and theoretical focus to sufficiently outline the neocolonial nuances of Philippine independence since 1946, it is worth emphasizing that the incessant postindependence juridical codifications of U.S. hegemony in the archipelago — most conspicuously marked by the changing territorial occupations of the U.S. military and overbearing presence of American corporate and financial capital — loom as the durable points of political and governmental solidarity between the Philippine national bourgeoisie and the U.S. neocolonial and neoliberal global order. This state-mediated order both instantiates and consistently encompasses the U.S. economic and governmental proctorship of the Philippine government and its formal ruling class.

The political animus of the Philippine national bourgeoisie, however, should not be altogether conflated with the policies, decisions, and rhetoric of the formal Philippine ruling class, despite the significant overlap between them. To the extent that it is not, as an undifferentiated whole, charged with the responsibilities of Philippine statecraft, the national bourgeoisie's historical coalescence with the United States encompasses a political and cultural labor that exceeds the work of formal government and state building. Remarking on the hallmark of Filipino pro-Americanism during the vexed moment of Philippine resistance to Japanese occupation during World War II, nationalist Philippine historian Renato Constantino suggests that it is the cultural and ideological turn in the Philippine social formation, not the unilateral political dictates of a ruling elite, that possesses and shapes the common sense of the national bourgeoisie:

> The erosion of the ideals of the revolution had indeed been great. The basic error of the collaborators who were not real traitors and the guerillas who were genuinely fighting against fascism was to pin their hopes on the return of America. MacArthur's "I shall return" was the slogan of the period.... The guerillas who fought the Americans in the 1900's were for freedom. The guerillas of the 1940's were fighting Japan for America. Americanization had taken away from us and especially from our leaders the capacity to think and act for ourselves; our efforts were therefore tragically misdirected.
>
> Collaboration in our leadership, American-oriented resistance among the guerillas, and the people's loyal waiting for the Americans to return were all indications of a successful miseducation. They were evidences of the almost complete Americanization of our society. We regarded America's war as indivisible from our war.[15]

It is the multiple and compounded crises of genocide, U.S. colonialism, nascent Philippine nation-statehood, and wartime (Japanese) occupation that organically shape the cultural-ideological labors of the Philippine national bourgeoisie. These labors, in turn, make sense of the moment of compounded historical crisis by translating and resignifying the political collaboration of Philippine elites with the U.S. empire through a broadly popular, though also "class" elaborated, allegation of allegiance to the unspecified promise of the American "return" — a return that was always already imminent in the colonialist institutionality of emergent Philippine nationhood.

Cultural "Americanization" and the rigorous pedagogical institutionality of the colonialist social program that Constantino famously decries as the systemization of the "miseducation of the Filipino"[16] is the technology through which the Philippine national bourgeoisie is not only schooled, but is also the apparatus through which it comes to realize itself as a "class" formation. (Notably, Constantino's notion echoes the critical race rhetoric of African American educator Carter G. Woodson in his groundbreaking *The Miseducation of the Negro,* published in 1933 and significantly shaped by Woodson's political disillusionment in the Philippines while serving as a high-level administrator of the new public schools during the early years of U.S. colonialism.[17]) Constantino delineates the genesis of the national bourgeoisie as such:

> The first and perhaps the master stroke in the plan to use education as an instrument of colonial policy was the decision to use English as the medium of instruction. English became the wedge that separated the Filipinos from their past and later was to separate educated Filipinos from the masses of their countrymen.... With American textbooks, Filipinos started learning not only a new language but also a new way of life, alien to their traditions and yet a caricature of their model. This was the beginning of their education. At the same time, it was the beginning of their mis-education, for they learned no longer as Filipinos but as colonials. They had to be disoriented from their nationalist goals because they had to become good colonials.[18]

A schematic, critical explication of the Fanonian analytic facilitates a genealogical tracing that might further clarify the fruits of the Philippine national bourgeoisie's labor in the nominal aftermath of U.S. colonialism. Fanon's focal point in "The Trials and Tribulations of National Consciousness" is the dilemma induced by a national bourgeoisie that is both conceived and trained by the precedent colonial power to assume the administration of the onetime colony at the moment of national independence. The rigorous underdevelopment of the former colony during the period of conquest and occupation requires, in Fanon's vision, a second (though no less historically determining) revolution that transforms "national" social relations in the wake of formal decolonization. It is in the context of this revolutionary necessity, internal to the embryonic neocolony, that Fanon contends:

> [T]he historical vocation of an authentic national bourgeoisie in an underdeveloped country is to repudiate its status as bourgeois and an instrument of capital and to become entirely subservient to the revolutionary capital which the people represent.[19]

Fanon's dramaturgy renders the "vocation" of the national bourgeoisie in this second, social revolution of the postcolony as encompassing a particular, revolutionary nationalist enactment of class suicide: the possibility of legitimate social transformation, Fanon argues, requires the effective abolition of this bourgeoisie as a colonialist artifact, hence the erosion of the socially determining "class" formation that enables neocolonialism.

> In an underdeveloped country, the imperative duty of an authentic national bourgeoisie is to betray the vocation to which it is destined, to learn from the people, and make available to them the intellectual and technical capital it culled from its time in colonial universities.[20]

Fanon's socialist revolutionary dream, of course, rudely awakens to the ugly truth of a neocolonial national bourgeoisie that "turns away from this heroic and positive path...and unabashedly opts for the antinational, and therefore abhorrent, path of a conventional bourgeoisie, a bourgeois bourgeoisie that is dismally, inanely, and cynically bourgeois."[21] Fanon laments the emergence of an authentic *neocolonial* bourgeoisie that, in its newfound vanities of national "independence," finds its deepest, mimetic identifications in the "Western bourgeoisie from which it has slurped every lesson."[22] Finally, this neocolonial class coalesces with its proctor bourgeoisie in the imperial metropole by shaping the geography and economy of the former colony according to the needs and fancies of its onetime colonizers.

A late twentieth-century example echoes and revises the telos of Fanon's composite national bourgeoisie through the political theater of the Philippine governing and academic bourgeoisie. In 1991 the Philippine Senate, amid heightened debate and a budding national crisis, refused to renew the U.S.-Philippines Military Bases Agreement of 1947. The Military Bases Agreement had been the keystone of the neocolonial military relation throughout the half century of formal Philippine independence and was generally understood as codifying the most strategically indispensable U.S. military occupation in the Pacific theater during the Cold War era. The ballyhooed 1991 rejection of the agreement, along with the devastating eruption of Mt. Pinatubo months before the vote (which effectively destroyed Clark Air Force Base),[23] prefaced the nominal closure of the Subic Bay Naval Base in 1992.[24]

The Subic Bay Base closure was, in fact, generally celebrated by Filipino/Filipino American leftist and nonleftist intellectuals and politicos alike and was seen as a vindication of the common-sense principles of national sovereignty. Conspicuously absent from this celebratory discourse, however, was a historical contextualization of the determinant role of the Philippine national bourgeoisie and political ruling class in initially endorsing, drafting, and negotiating the 1947 Military Bases Agreement, and then enforcing and renewing it for half a century until circumstances of convenience (and a putative "surge of nationalism" in the Philippine Senate) led to the 1991 nonrenewal over and against the desires of the most hawkish U.S. officials. (Then-Secretary of Defense Dick Cheney called the Philippine Senate's rejection vote "a real tragedy for the Philippines.")[25] In fact, the Philippine Senate vote carried by the slimmest of margins (12–11), and the Senate rejection contradicted the sentiments of President Corazon Aquino, who stridently supported the extension of the Subic Bay lease.

Rather than signifying a groundswell of Philippine nationalist revivification, then, the tentative repulsion of the U.S. military presence actually carried forward the profound ambivalences of national independence under neocolonial subjection and its protocolonialist trappings of militarization. In fact, while it is often obscured in the nationalist narrative and popular common sense of the base closure as a vindication of Philippine sovereignty, both the initiation and nominal cessation of the U.S. military occupations at Clark and Subic Bay demonstrate the durable historical solidarity of interest between the Philippine national bourgeoisie, the Philippine ruling elite, and their U.S. benefactors and political proctors. The solidarity of the Philippine military and political elite with the global ambitions of U.S. nation building is clearly articulated in the March 5, 1992, congressional testimony of Adm. Charles R. Larson, commander in chief of the U.S. Pacific Command.

Speaking before the House Subcommittee on Asian and Pacific Affairs (a unit of the Committee on Foreign Affairs), Larson was the key figure in a hearing entitled "Implications of the U.S. Withdrawal from Clark and Subic Bases." His summation of the relation between the U.S. and Philippine armed forces in the aftermath of the formal base closure, rather than mourning the end of U.S. military occupation in the archipelago, appears to offer a guarantee of a more authentically "neocolonial" military relation:

> The Philippine Government's decision to terminate our stationing agreement has changed the situation there and in the Western Pacific. We are fully engaged in complying with the requirements of departure and relocation. We will continue an appropriate military-to-military relationship with the Armed Forces of the Philippines in accordance with our treaty obligations. As such, I still Co-chair the U.S.–Philippine Mutual Defense Board with the Chief of Staff of the Armed Forces of the Philippines. That body manages military aspects of the

Mutual Defense Treaty, which is the bedrock of our allied relationships. How that relationship is maintained depends in large part on the future actions of the Philippine Government.[26]

Later in the question-and-answer portion of his testimony, Larson outlines the U.S. Navy's plans for a "post–Subic Bay" hegemony over the Pacific region. Responding to Rep. Robert Lagomarsino's question, "What is the Navy going to do after we leave Subic Bay?" Larson responds:

What we are going to do, Mr. Lagomarsino, is to redistribute the critical functions that Subic Bay performed to other areas in the Pacific where we already have an infrastructure so we won't have to build new bases.

We will send our Logistics Command...into Singapore. They have said they will accept them. That gives us a very strategic location to carry out repair, maintenance and logistics coordination functions for all the naval forces in the Western Pacific.[27]

Larson continues by detailing the Navy's plans to extend its active operations into Japan (Yakusuka and Sasebo), Guam, South Korea, and the British dependency of Diego Garcia. At the end of his session with Congress, Larson allegorizes this macroscale entanglement through an indulgent reference to his more personalized Philippine intimacies:

We will remain committed to them under our Mutual Defense Treaty, and we will be committed to them to help train and modernize their armed forces....*I have a lot of very close friends in their government and in their military, and I expect that to continue.*[28] [emphasis added]

It is precisely the intimacy of Larson's "friendships" with the Philippine governing and military elite that bears remark here, to the extent that his congressional testimony carries the mark of a remarkable (neo)colonial entitlement — an "expectation" of continued amicability and cooperation among the (neo)colonized, carried over and against their formal repulsion of the U.S. military bases. To meditate on the genealogical tracing of Larson's testimony, the juridical life — and death — of the 1947 Military Bases

Agreement represents a master stroke in the American fabrication of a Philippine ruling elite that identifies its "independence"
with the epiphany of a benevolent American emancipation and
proceeds to articulate this Americanist identification *through a
discourse of sovereignty:* that is, the institutional positionality
and ontology of the Philippine ruling class is inseparable from
a "national independence" that was — and in multiple ways
continues to be — overwhelmingly (if not unilaterally) enabled
and reproduced by a dominant colonial/neocolonial sovereign.
Thus, the putative evacuation of the U.S. military from Subic
Bay in 1991, not unlike the achievement of nominal Philippine
national sovereignty in 1946, is best understood as a painstakingly orchestrated pageantry of consensus, overseen by the U.S.
government/military, brokered by a "friendly" Philippine elite,
and endorsed by the consensus-building knowledge productions
of the Philippine national bourgeoisie.

Far from composing a facile, determinist correspondence
between the Philippine "ruling elite" and the "national bourgeoisie" to which it is politically and genealogically connected,
the work of building a Philippine consensus around the dominion of Pacifica Americana is precisely the "organic" intellectual
task of the national bourgeoisie. That is, the primary pedagogical
and cultural mission of the national bourgeoisie is to render the
complexities and contradictions of brokered compromise and
rearticulated pro-Americanist allegiance (*a*) popularly intelligible, and (*b*) politically righteous and historically rational. The
work of generating "consensus," in this instance, is virtually synonymous with the labor of building, engaging, and ultimately
defining the "common sense" of Philippine national formation.
For example: interviewed at the height of the Subic Bay debate,
the breathless words of Philippine editorialist and political sci-
entist Alexander Magno (later appointed director of the Development Bank of the Philippines by President Gloria Macapagal-
Arroyo) echo the core values of this consensus/common sense,
while unwittingly echoing the anxieties of infantilization that

permeate the labors of Filipino arrested raciality in its "nation-alist" form:

> To reject this base treaty is not by any means a practical move. But the emotional release, the assertion of power and independence will be great. It will be therapeutic, a national primal scream that may mature us.[29]

In fact, this "national primal scream" was the audible enunci-ation of a national bourgeoisie that assumed the obligation of valorizing a shift in the *form* of a militarized neocolonial and white supremacist U.S. Pacific hegemony: within two years of the Base closure, in the historical wake of the Philippine Senate's grandstanding claim that their rejection vote had eliminated the "last vestige of American colonialism,"[30] the Subic Bay U.S. military infrastructure had been effectively transformed into a U.S. corporate infrastructure, replete with the prototypic forms of neoliberalism. It was converted into a "freeport" administered by a new governing apparatus inhabited by the national bour-geoisie (the Subic Bay Metropolitan Authority), and successfully solicited a $452 million investment from thirty-six private cor-porations, including Enron ($115.4 million), which operated a "30.5 megawatt diesel-fed power plant," and Coastal Petroleum ($105.8 million), which operated "the petroleum, oil and lubri-cant depot facility" left behind by the U.S. Navy.[31] Compounding this reformation into the institutionalities of global capital, the Subic Bay Base was reopened for periodic "joint military exer-cises" with the U.S. Navy in 1999 (under a new Visiting Forces Agreement)[32] and has since been mandated by the Philippine gov-ernment for strategic and "emergency" use by the U.S. armed forces.[33] The U.S.–Philippine women's solidarity organization Gabriela Network summarized the conditions of Subic Bay in 1998, seven years after the nominal closure of the bases:

> In 1992, the number of prostituted children was only estimated at 60,000. Now the number has risen to 100,000. Presently, there is an estimated 400,000 prostituted women all over the country. This number does not yet include the non-registered "commercial sex

workers," seasonal prostitutes (prosti-tuition) and those outside the country working as "entertainers" and those victimized by sex trafficking (mail order brides and serial sponsorships). The government cannot deny that the social hygiene clinics and licensing of "entertainment establishments" is part of the infrastructure in support of sex tourism. It was the US Navy which institutionalized this practice to protect its servicemen from sexually-transmitted diseases. The government, today, is implementing this to protect and encourage foreign tourists. . . .

And now, the US military is staging a comeback via the Visiting Forces Agreement subserviently signed by the Ramos government in anticipation of the growing unrest of the Filipino masses in this time of intense crisis. With VFA and 22 more ports opened for military exercises, the number of prostituted Filipino women and children will continue to escalate and spread all over the Philippines.[34]

As different trajectories of activist and scholarly work continue to form around the shifting terms of U.S. militarization across the world,[35] it is increasingly clear that a crucial political and theoretical task for those invested in radical, feminist, antiracist, and liberationist conceptions of peace and demilitarization is to critically address and, ultimately, politically disassemble the neo/postcolonial national bourgeoisie across its variable iterations.

The ensemble of social relations constituting and reproducing this national bourgeoisie, a "historical bloc" in the Gramscian sense, remains severely undertheorized within even the most critical examinations of neoliberalism and globalization. Following and extrapolating the historical trajectory of Fanon's schema, the national bourgeoisie is not merely a pathetic and despicable derivative "class" generated by the colonialist order and its neocolonial aftermath, but is also, eventually, the collective rearticulation of colonial white supremacy in localized, "native" form. This is precisely the historical possibility coded into Constantino's observation of U.S. colonial schooling:

With American education, the Filipinos were not only learning a new language; they were not only forgetting their own language; *they were starting to become a new type of American.*[36]

To take seriously Constantino's notion that U.S. colonial schooling was an institutional modality through which the Filipino
reinhabited the racial comportment of the modern "American" subject/body is to also catalyze a subtle expansion in
the scope of Fanon's "cultural alienation": within the historical present of this colonial analytic, the Philippine national
bourgeoisie cannot be understood or politically addressed as
a secondary or marginal figure in the global apparatuses of
genocidal globalization and white supremacist neoliberalism,
but must instead be conceptualized as a nexus of institutional
and cultural coherence for a fatal global ordering: on the one
hand, in resonance with Fanon's composite figure, the Philippine national bourgeoisie is at minimum an accommodationist
enterprise, voluntarily wedged in a contingent and relatively
privileged relation to neocolonial politicocultural dominance:
"Networking and scheming seem to be its underlying vocation."[37] On the other hand, unlike the Fanonian figuration
of the national bourgeoisie, which is in conflicted proximity
to the immediate violence and material legacies of a popular anticolonialist struggle, the Philippine national bourgeoisie
has no organic, overarching familiarity with any such violent struggle to overthrow and abolish U.S. colonialism: that
is, the celebrated (masculine) lineage of Philippine *ilustrado*
nationalists and petite bourgeoisie anticolonialists memorial-
izes the repulsion of the Spanish colonial order, while the
"post-1898" national bourgeoisie is an *emancipated* class, persistently exhibiting its capacity to adequately inhabit the white
institutionalities of U.S. "democracy."

The terms of this emancipation continue the relations of
"parental"/racial proctorship and domination. In addition to
blueprinting, through the Bell Trade Act and other measures,
a neocolonial political economy, it is the governmentality of the
Philippine national bourgeoisie that serves notice of its devout
valorization of the United States-as-colonizer. Vicente Rafael
elaborates:

> White love [or what President McKinley notoriously called the policy
> of "benevolent assimilation"] holds out the promise of fathering, as
> it were, a "civilized people" capable in time of asserting its own
> character. But it also demands the indefinite submission to a program
> of discipline and reformation requiring the constant supervision of a
> sovereign master.[38]

In an eloquent elaboration of this point, Agoncillo recalls the
public oratory of Manuel Roxas, the first president of the new
Republic of the Philippines. Here Roxas's pronouncements can
be seen as a pedagogical composition that configures the premises of self-identification and political coherence for a national
bourgeoisie that is always already posed to fracture on its constitutive racial anxieties and modernist incongruities; this is, in
other words, a statecraft of and for an incipient national bourgeoisie that is the constituency of legitimization for the larger
Philippine nation-state–building project:

> In his inaugural address on July 4, 1946, as the first President of
> the Republic, Roxas waxed enthusiastically, recalling with pride and
> with thanks the coming of the Americans in 1898 and urging the
> people to have absolute faith in the goodness of America. "To do
> otherwise," he said, "would be to foreswear all faith in democracy,
> in our future, and in ourselves." Thus, the Filipinos should, happen
> what may, follow the American lead.... "*Our* safest course, and I
> believe it is true for the rest of the world as well, is in the glistening
> wake of America whose sure advance with mighty prow breaks for
> smaller craft the waves of fear."[39]

The Philippine national bourgeoisie hinges its existence on a particular nation-state form, an allegation of sovereignty that is profoundly alienated from the genealogies of anticolonial or Third
World revolutionary struggle marked in Fanon's *The Wretched
of the Earth*. Philippine independence, manifest *through* rather
than *against* American governmentality, relies with relative uni-
laterality on the political sanction and economic proctorship of
the Cold War, post–Cold War, and War on Terror articulations
of the United States of America.

I am suggesting that, in fundamental accompaniment to conventional notions of Philippine ruling/elite class corruption (vis-à-vis martial law and institutionalized governmental misconduct), the sustenance of the Philippine national bourgeoisie (and its organic intellectual components) is irreconcilably measured and edified by a strong (conspicuous, self-conscious, and incessantly pronounced) historical consent to U.S. dominance over the archipelago and, necessarily, the rest of the world. Thus, the Philippine national bourgeoisie exceeds the Fanonian "intermediary" role in the administration and politicocultural consolidation of the neocolony. This class represents, in its "nationally" emancipated articulation, the Pacific cutting edge of white supremacist empire, or differently phrased, the collective and massively embodied promise of accommodation to the United States as a global nation-building project. Thriving on the suspended moment of the Philippine–American encounter, and willfully dispelling or disavowing the multiple registers of human apocalypse that the encounter represents (psychic, ecological, biological, and political), this national bourgeoisie is the template for white supremacist empire's metamorphosis into an interpellating pedagogical form, completing the historical circuit that links military conquest to proctored national emancipation.

To reiterate a key point: the Philippine national bourgeoisie is the pedagogical and political production of genocidal American colonialism and a central figure in its aftermath of paternally designated nation-statehood. In this context, it is perfectly logical that the valorized notion of "Philippine independence" lacks even the mythology of a (nationally) self-actualizing anticolonial struggle, as evidenced by the strained and somewhat bizarre annual celebrations of the nation's 1898 "independence" from Spain, which overwhelmingly obscure or erase the colonial half century that followed.[40] (The 2003 Sangandaan International Conference in Manila, with its centering of the history and legacies of U.S. colonization, offered a momentary though significant departure from this discourse.)[41] Absent any intimacy with an authentic anticolonial (political or paramilitary) struggle to obtain formal independence from the United States, this national bourgeoisie lacks the constituting political pretensions of Fanon's composite neocolonial bourgeoisie: the Philippine rendition of this bourgeoisie cannot claim to have ever "frantically [brandished] the notions of nationalization... of the managerial classes"[42] in an attempt to initiate a "takeover of businesses and firms previously held by the colonists,"[43] because the bureaucratic racial logic of U.S. colonial occupation was to facilitate precisely such a "Filipinization" of the proctored Philippine nation-building experiment.

Therefore, if the Philippine national bourgeoisie is understood as both altering and amplifying Fanon's narrative of the neocolonial nationalist "trials and tribulations," then it must also be understood as a template for the postconquest genius of the American neocolonial and white supremacist global formation. The rigorously trained and self-reproducing political coherence of this neocolonial bourgeoisie inscribes a doubled failure: it exists only in the aftermath of a fraudulent "decolonization" granted by colonial decree, and as such, this national bourgeoisie — from its very inception as such — continuously coheres through a devout, protoreligious loyalty to its proctor/emancipator.

> The new Filipino generation learned of the lives of American heroes, sang American songs, and dreamt of snow and Santa Claus. The nationalist resistance leaders... were regarded as brigands and outlaws. The lives of Philippine heroes were taught but their nationalist teachings were glossed over. Spain was the villain, America was the savior.[44]

While Fanon calls upon his neocolonial bourgeoisie "to betray the vocation to which it is destined" in order to undertake the labor of social revolution and authentic national liberation, the Philippine national bourgeoisie has no such alternative destiny toward which it can defect. Unlike Fanon's national bourgeoisie,

which identifies its origins with a mythology of national independence struggle, the Philippine national bourgeoisie articulates its
genesis through a political and cultural allegiance to the post-
1946 United States of America, its national emancipator. The
Philippine Daily Inquirer's commemoration of the 60th anniversary of the U.S. "restoration" of Philippine independence evokes
this political common sense. The July 4, 2006, editorial reads:

> The Philippines and the United States have had a continuing love-hate
> relationship in the 60 years since the U.S. restored the independence
> of the Philippines.
>
>   It has been a love relationship because Filipinos look up to the
> U.S. as Mother America, a teacher and guardian that taught them
> English, laid down the foundation of a modern educational sys-
> tem and set up many of the institutions of democracy. Soon after
> the American colonizers took over in 1898, Filipinos veered away
> from Mother Spain and quickly took a liking to Hollywood, Coca-
> Cola and jazz. Now, the dream of many Filipinos is to emigrate
> to the U.S. and become green card holders, if not naturalized U.S.
> citizens.[45]

This paean to a nurturing maternal American colonialism speaks
to the extended modus operandi of a postconquest (and nominally postgenocidal) white supremacist institutionality: namely,
the Filipino-as-"national"-subject not only cannot escape the
material remnants of white colonial dominance; it is matured and
culturally enlivened by a symbiosis of consumptive desire, white
politicality (proctored "democracy"), and "modern" racial comportment that is constitutive of its very terms of "independence."

The historical present of the U.S. genocidal white supremacist
conquest of the archipelago, marked by the indelibility of a half
century of benevolent colonization that produced the institutional terms and common sensibilities of a Philippine national
bourgeoisie, carries forth a unique cultural and political antagonism: the discursive coherence of this "national" class pivots
on the suspension of the apocalyptic moment of the Philippine–
American encounter, while its political animus orbits around

the labors of white supremacist governmentality — the modern, independent Filipino bourgeois subject's inhabitation of the very institutional apparatuses that genocide and colonialist dominance historically produce and continuously enable. It is within this antagonism that the figure of the Filipino American obtains its currency as a correlate of the national bourgeoisie and vindication of the Filipino's capacity for self-governance.

Rethinking (Post-1965) Immigrant Pedigrees: The Filipino as Colonial Non-Asian

The composite figure of Fanon's national bourgeoisie anticipates the emergence of a "globalized" (or "transnational") Third World and (allegedly) postcolonial[46] petite bourgeoisie, reified in the U.S. context through the symbiotic institutional rhetorics of "diversity" and "multiculturalism." This bloc is significantly schemed and mobilized through the technologies of neoliberalism and, particularly, through the careful enactment of eligibility hierarchies in the 1965 Immigration Act (HR 2580). As summarized in a 1965 edition of *Congressional Quarterly,*

> The new law abolished the existing system of country-by-country quotas which had fixed a legal maximum of about 158,000 persons who could enter annually on a quota basis from non-Western Hemisphere areas, and which, by assigning over two-thirds of all quota numbers to Britain, Ireland and Germany, had sharply limited immigration from Southern Europe, Asia and Africa....
>
> HR 2580 set up a new system, to become fully effective in mid-1968 after a three-year transition period.... Instead of country-by-country quotas, an over-all quota of 170,000 annual immigrants from outside the Western Hemisphere was to be permitted.... Under this system, first preference for immigration (20 percent of the 170,000 total) was to be given to adult, unmarried children of U.S. citizens, in order to unite families. The remaining preferences would go to other categories of relatives of U.S. citizens and residents; *to persons possessing special skills, or needed to fill labor shortages in the United States*; and to displaced persons and refugees from political, religious and racial persecution.[47] [emphasis added]

For the sake of emphasis and clarity, it is worth closely reading the third-ranked preference for the granting of visas under the 1965 Act:

> (3) Visas shall next be made available, in a number not to exceed 10 per centum of the number specified in section 201 (a) (ii), to qualified immigrants *who are members of the professions, or who because of their exceptional ability in the sciences or the arts will substantially benefit prospectively the national economy, cultural interests, or welfare of the United States.*[48] [emphasis added]

It is through such a juridical schema that the "postcolonial" migrations — in spite and because of the political and cultural crises they induce — have orchestrated the historical vindication of the imperial metropoles as the durable sites of the postcolonial native's desire, aspiration, and bodily/economic (upward) mobility. In fact, the 1965 Immigration Act has formed a primary historical and juridical point-of-origin for contemporary "Asian American" discourse, (immigrant) community formation, and political mobilization. Conventional Asian American historical, sociological, and empiricist explanations/narrations of the post-1965 immigrations thus foreground the statecraft of the 1965 Act as the seminal moment of the contemporary Asian and Third World migrant influx to the United States.[49] These Asian Americanist narrations, however, often fail to account for the political genealogy of the Filipino condition, particularly in relation to the specificities of the Filipino's formation as a particular (racial) subject of colonialist white supremacy and genocidal U.S. nation building.

Legal scholar Bill Ong Hing's simplistic depiction of the post-1965 historical period is exemplary of the Asian Americanist academic tendency to compress the Filipino historical experience into the compulsory narrative requirements of a panethnic racial project. Collapsing his discussion of colonialism, immigration policy, and Filipino political desire into several sentences in the introduction to the widely read *Making and Remaking Asian America through Immigration Policy,* Hing writes that the

U.S. conquest of the archipelago "met with violent resistance from many Filipinos who had yearned for independence from colonial domination." Offering no elaboration of this historical moment or its constituting political antagonisms, Hing continues, "If becoming a United States colony *had a positive side*, it was that Filipinos automatically became noncitizen nationals of the United States. They could travel without regard to immigration laws, they were not subject to exclusion or deportation, and requirements for obtaining full citizenship were relaxed" [emphasis added].[50] Putting aside for the moment Hing's careless (if fleeting) stipulation of U.S. colonialism's juridical benevolence, it is precisely his fetishizing of American "nationality" and citizenship, as well as Hing's implicit valorization of the putative Asian/Asian American immigrant as a figure of contested (or denied) juridical "freedom" and contingent mobility in relation to the U.S. national form, that I wish to critically disassemble.

Hing's otherwise informative study of U.S. immigration policy moves from an assumptive structure that is common to Asian American academic, political, and community formations, trading vulgar historical simplifications for the sake of a mystified panethnic coalitional integrity. In this analytical context, Hing's insistent absorption of Filipinos into the rubric of "Asian American immigration" seems to voraciously deflect, rather than seriously engage, the possibility that Filipinos constitute a *dis*articulation of the Asian American rubric. This political and intellectual tendency is actually essential to the coherence of Asian Americanism as a multiculturalist allegation of "community," "collective interest," and "shared identity." Here in a transparent substitution of autobiographical anecdote for rigorous argument and conceptualization, Hing simply demands Filipino (and "Asian Indian") assimilation into the Asian American immigrant bloc:

> Some may take issue with my inclusion of Filipinos and Asian Indians because their unique racial features supposedly set them apart from Chinese, Japanese, and Vietnamese. These critics also note

that the Philippines and India are geographically distanced from the rest of Asia and have distinctive cultures, and that Filipino and Asian Indian experience in the United States disassociates them from others.... *Based on my experiences,* I find such arguments unpersuasive.[51] [emphasis added]

Hing follows his rejection of Filipino "disassociation" from Asian America with a brief narrative of his adolescent memories of an individual Filipino acquaintance, followed by a recounting of the Filipino presence in his Asian American college fraternity and a generalized affirmation of the coalitional impetus guiding Asian American community organizations. I note the analytical sloppiness of Hing's schema in this regard not because it is particularly remarkable or exceptional, but rather because it signifies a pedagogical logic that consistently conflates Filipino historical experience with more familiar multiculturalist narratives. It is worth emphasizing that the coherence of Filipino Americanism as a multiculturalist correlative of parochial Asian Americanist narratives and pedagogies persistently identifies the figurative Filipino's ontology and historical routes with those of immigrant and refugee groups that lack even remotely similar genealogies of conquest, occupation, and colonization by the United States. Such schematizations offer radically insufficient accounts of the Filipino neocolonial and postcolonial migration, and therefore fail to substantively contextualize the conditions of the post-1965 Filipino American community formation. This is to also suggest that the dramaturgy of Fanon's composite national bourgeoisie is profoundly extrapolated by the Filipino example.

Rupturing the generalized notion of a contemporary "Asian immigrant" and "Asian American community" formation, the post-1965 Filipino American national bourgeoisie is more appropriately conceptualized as a late neocolonial constituent of the "post–Civil Rights (movement)" U.S. multiculturalist national project. The production of Filipino Americanism as a collective identity and discursive site of political and psychic identification can and must be traced to the postconquest U.S. colonial project in the Philippines, which was premised on the assimilation and domestication of an undercivilized and racially subjected population into the political, educational, and religious institutionalities of U.S. state and civil society. Such a genealogy stretches the political geography and temporality of American ludic multiculturalism, to the extent that racially and ethnically pathologized subjects become primary to the self-articulations of the nation-state rather than its derivative artifacts, and are thus subjects of selective accommodation into the agential and leadership roles of social reproduction (as the "Filipinized" state officials, cultural and religious leaders, entrepreneurs, educators, and scholars of an independent nation).

This spatial-temporal stretching detaches the Filipino American formation from its alleged Pacific immigrant peer group, the "Asian American" theoretical and political construction, and resituates the Filipino American in a relation of organic continuity to the Philippine national bourgeoisie of the colonial and early neocolonial periods. Here it is worth reflecting on the work of cultural theorist Lisa Lowe, whose important and widely read text *Immigrant Acts: On Asian American Cultural Politics* conceives the antagonism between the "American citizen" and the (alien) "Asian immigrant" as a symptom of the political anxieties and contradictions that constitute American national culture and its racially formed ambitions of "[inspiring] diverse individuals to identify with the national project." While Lowe's is one of the rare texts that exhibits a sensibility to the tensions and disjunctures that sediment in the incorporation of the Filipino American figure within the "Asian Americanist" rubric, a productive moment of theorization remains latent in her work. While Lowe does, somewhat fleetingly, reference the "considerable distortion of social relations in Asian countries affected by U.S. imperialist war and occupation," Lowe's theoretical concerns are anchored in what she calls the structuring *"contradictions* of Asian immigration," which, she argues, simultaneously locate Asians "within" the United States, while marking them as permanent "foreigners" and "outsiders" to the national polity.[52] It is here that the placement of Filipinos and Filipino Americans within Lowe's narrative requires further theorization and perhaps additional conceptualization. ✓

Breaking from the schematic Asian Americanist narrative that tends to foreground the post–World War II (and particularly the post-1965) period as the primary historical moment in which the figure of the Asian immigrant induces and embodies the anxieties and contradictions of American national culture and the U.S. nation-building project, the Filipino condition is marked by the immanence of the U.S. national (cultural) project prior to the definitive, latter twentieth-century emergence of the Asian American immigrant bloc. This is to analytically emphasize two distinguishing features of the Filipino–American relation: (1) the Filipino encounter with the cultural dominion of Pacifica Americana in the first half of the twentieth century historically precedes "post-1965" Asian immigration and geographically distends the proper domain of U.S. national culture as a (racially) disciplining and domesticating force; and (2) the post-nineteenth-century Filipino condition's foundational constitution by the particularities of formal American colonialism — replete with its technologies and apparatuses of cultural dominance and interpellation — distinguishes the figure of the Filipino (pre-1934) "U.S. national" migrant and (post-1934) "alien" immigrant from the rest of its alleged Asian immigrant cohort.

To clarify: the colonization of the archipelago was conceived from its outset, as an experimental racial conquest *form,* a modality or prototyping of dominance that pivoted on the training, enrichment, and political domestication of an indigenous and mestizo population that was notoriously inscribed by American politicos as being racially incapable of self-government. Literary scholar Bienvenido Lumbera, contextualizing the Philippine national historical memory of World War II and the inscription of the American military as putative "liberators" from the brief Japanese occupation, writes:

> For forty years prior to the Japanese invasion, Filipino had been acculturated as Westerners by American popular culture. Movies, magazines, comic books, phonograph records, and even candy bars from the United States freely inundated Philippine society, introducing Filipinos to American customs, food, fashion, and entertainment. The war cut off the flow of culture items from America and the resulting deprivation intensified the fervor of waiting for the return of the Americans. Then the Americans did come back in 1945, and memories of "liberation" later would always include "Babe Ruth," chewing gum, and cigarettes made from aromatic Virginia tobacco.[53]

Crucially, it is this coercive American cultural occupation — coercive not only because of its overbearing material presence but also because its condition of possibility is genocidal white supremacy — that centrally composes, deforms, and transforms the Philippine colonial and (independent) national formations during the twentieth century and beyond. Thus, the alienations and racial antagonisms constituting the body of "American national culture" and the post-1898 Filipino condition are not only fundamentally inseparable, but also complexly, violently symbiotic.

The "post-1965" narration of the Filipino migration to the United States is exceeded and overdetermined by its historical precedents and extra-"national" or transpacific contingencies. Landmarked by a genocidal contact, rearticulated through the comportments of a comprador native governing class, and extenuated by the introduction of white institutionalities such as "democratic" state forms and "public" education, the American conquest, domination, and transpacific dominion over the archipelago traces a genealogy of multiculturalism as a specifically sited technology of white supremacist colonialism. It is precisely the specificity of the U.S. colonial legacy in the Philippines — the putative point of origin for what is now the largest "Asian" immigrant population in the United States — that Lowe's schematic embraces and opens to deeper theorization. Thus, while Lowe suggestively gestures to the deviation of the Filipino and Filipino American historical experience from her Asian Americanist analytic in several crucial moments in her text,[54] and prefaces these gestures with the contention that "Philippine immigration after the period of U.S. colonization animates yet another kind of contradiction,"[55] I am focally concerned with the dense specificity of this other contradiction. Here, the critical utility of Lowe's work is primarily in its development of a *methodological* schema that enables examination of how the particular contradictions constituting the postconquest Filipino condition may disarticulate "Filipino American" social and communal formations as they are conventionally understood within multiple Asian Americanist rubrics.

Lowe's materialist historicization of the Asian immigrant, American national culture, and immigrant act thus provides an opportunity to critically extrapolate and productively disfigure the political structure of the Asian Americanist project, which in its academic, community-based, and activist forms has generally failed to facilitate a substantive historical and cultural inventory of the genesis, presence, and legacies of American colonialism in the Philippines, and has minimized and obscured the Philippine experience with programmatic biological and cultural genocide at the hands of the American nation-state.

E. San Juan Jr. concisely asserts that "the chief distinction of Filipinos from other Asians domiciled here is that their country of origin was the object of violent colonization by U.S. finance capital."[56] I would extend the scope of San Juan's crystallization by specifying that the racial technologies and social logics of this violent colonization encompass a genocidal conquest that has indelibly inscribed American white supremacist dominance on the Filipino condition. This inscription, moreover, is not limited to oppressive subjection to U.S. state and economic power, but is materially imprinted on the collective identity formation of the "Filipino" as a national (racial) subject.

Filipinos, in organic connection with North American indigenous peoples, embody some of the earliest prototyping of U.S.
multiculturalism as it articulates through the genocidal white
supremacist colonial form: the objectives of U.S. (neo)colonialist
multiculturalism in the archipelago — the pedagogical nourish-
ing, economic edification, and political proctorship of a native
bourgeoisie and "little brown brothering" of U.S. political and
social institutionalities — self-enunciate as a national project of
racially progressive social engineering wherein white supremacist
genocide is an assumptive (and perpetual) condition of possibility. In this context, the extravagant fabrications of transpacific
"American national culture" in the Philippine archipelago vis-à-
vis colonization and U.S.-proctored neocolonial multiculturalism
are not only central to the condition of suspended apocalypse,
but also constitute an altered state of nationality, a deformation
of cultural identification, and a racialization of "class" identity
that reinscribe white supremacist hierarchies onto differentiated
Filipino subjects.

Thus, if we theoretically center a transpacific conceptualization of American national culture that accounts for its structured
immanence in the colonial and neocolonial Philippines (and
speaks to its transpacific racist and white supremacist formation), we must also come to terms with the fact that conventional
sociological and empiricist "push-pull" explanations of the post-
1965 Filipino immigrations to the United States are utterly
insufficient. The prototypical rationales for the Asian migrations — enhanced employment and educational opportunities,
escape from martial law and Third World underdevelopment,
and family reunification, to name a few — do not adequately
characterize the animating logic of the contemporary "Filipino
American" formation. Rather, these objective conditions are
overdetermined by a postconquest, protoreligious belief structure that distinguishes the Filipino American formation from all
other "Asian" migrations to the United States. This belief structure — an interpellating and material technology of transpacific

American national culture — is the a priori of the Filipino immigrant political desire, to the extent that it alleges a coherent historical communion within the multiculturalist auspices of the United States national project. \

The continuities between the Philippine national bourgeoisie and Filipino American petite bourgeoisie disarticulate the composition of an "Asian American" immigrant rubric not only because the Filipino is marked by a unique history of U.S. colonization, but also because these continuities mark the peculiarity of a fundamental political allegiance to and religiously articulated faith in the United States as both a cultural imaginary and formal governing entity.

Conclusion: Revelation, Uncovering, and the Colonial *Telos*

"America," for the Filipino national bourgeoisie and its Filipino American derivatives across "class" strata, is a site of redemption and existential progress, an imagined journey that invokes the Catholic ritual of Confirmation, wherein the adolescent subject undergoes an ornamental training in the responsibilities of the adult Christian. Thus, notions of modern civic responsibility, appropriate American mores and comportment, and incessant displays of patriotism install the United States as a kind of religious figure in the Filipino American social imagination. This imagination, which often articulates through vernaculars of Christian reverence, elevates unconditional love of adoptive mother country alongside rituals of loyalty to the Catholic mythologies of Christ and the Virgin Mary herself. Historian Fred Cordova, valorized in some quarters as "the father of Filipino American history" and a cofounder (with his wife, Dorothy Cordova) of the Filipino American National Historical Society (where he is known as "Deacon Fred Cordova"), inscribes his pictorial history *Filipinos: Forgotten Asian Americans* with a multicultural patriotism that explicitly situates the U.S. national project within this presumptive Catholic imaginary. In fact, Cordova's text installs Filipino and Filipino American men as undifferentiated martyrs for the cause of a rather undifferentiated "Americanism," not unlike faithful disciples of a national son of god. A close reading of Cordova's account of World War II is useful here. In addition to its gaping silence on the emergence and empowerment of U.S. imperialism in and through its military campaign in the Pacific theater, Cordova's history self-discloses as a *religiously* nationalist coming-of-age story. He writes near the end of his text:

> It was a terribly long war. Pinoys feared for the fates of their own little brown brothers and sisters under the harsh Japanese Occupation. Then on October 20, 1944, U.S. General of the Army Douglas MacArthur fulfilled his promise of "I Shall Return" by wading ashore at a Leyte beach.... Meanwhile, MacArthur ikons sprang up everywhere. MacArthur statuettes shared places of honor alongside statues of the Blessed Virgin and other religious objects in many Filipino American homes. MacArthur portraits hung in Pinoy pool halls, barbershops and restaurants. Pinoys were not only thankful the war had ended, but they also were grateful for the American liberation. Yet, Filipinos themselves paid the price for freedom and democracy.
>
> An estimated one million innocent Filipino men, women and children died while defending Americanism during World War Two.[57]

Cordova's narrative, long considered a canonical work in Filipino American and Asian American studies, embraces and celebrates what might be called the "perfection of the colonial *telos*," the culmination of which materializes through the patriotic and proto-Catholic idolatry of the venerable General MacArthur. Here also is the reproduction of a familiar redemption story: the United States, earth's most heavenly kingdom, is the site of (biological) *birth* and (naval) *berth* for the idolized MacArthur, and is the destination of infinite promise for the truly devout "Filipino American."

I end this chapter with a closing meditation on the meaning of suspended apocalypse. By invoking apocalypse, I am calling on the term's etymological structure, which reaches across the

Latin expression for "revelation" and the Greek notion of an "uncovering" (*apocalypsis*).[58] While it is best known for its biblical usage bespeaking Judgment Day or the end of the world, I am appropriating the concept to bring attention to the earthly obverse of the *dreamed* United States of America that is inscribed by the Filipino national bourgeoisie, its Filipino American correlates, and the discursive productions of Filipino Americanism. This earthly obverse, profoundly inscribed in both recent and historical events, bespeaks "America" as a global formation that is inextricable from its founding — and current — technologies of gendered white supremacist warfare, genocide, and human exploitation, forms of domination that the Filipino American renaissance can only bear to confront through suspension of the historical present of apocalypse. The Filipino American dream of the United States of America is, in this light, a profound anti-memory, an un-remembering and un-witnessing, of U.S. conquest, colonization, and genocide that is not unlike what other racially pathologized populations have indulged under the seductions of post–civil rights multiculturalism. This is the context of what I have been calling the suspended apocalypse of the Filipino encounter with America, a moment which forms the necessary premises for Filipino arrested raciality in its broadest enunciations, and particularly enables contemporary Filipino American rationalizations of the historical Filipino condition.

Positioned within the discursive logic of suspended apocalypse, Filipino Americanism is a labor of allegation: it is a political imagination that articulates a familiar metropolitan petite bourgeois pretension and anxiety, while asserting conspicuous, amplified avowals of political solidarity with, and visceral protoreligious devotion to, a projected "America." As such, the making of the Filipino American subject and collective identity is essentially a project of allegiance, and the labor is entangled in a genealogy of transpacific American statecraft and social formation that has variously (and often simultaneously) liquidated, domesticated, and incorporated its objects of (neo)colonization.

What, then, might it mean to conceptualize the production of Filipino Americanism as a cultural echo from the historical juncture and material intersection between the "zones of death" constituted by U.S. military conquest and genocide, and the century of colonization and neocolonialism that has followed? What alternative genealogies and political possibilities might enable a different articulation of the Filipino condition, one that recognizes and radically struggles against the conditions of perpetuity marked by white supremacy, colonialism, and genocide? I turn to this kind of political project in the final chapter.

— 5 —

"Death Was Swiftly Running after Us"

Disaster, Evil, and Radical Possibility

> Forgotten places are not outside history.
> — Ruth Wilson Gilmore, 2007

Intimacies with Disaster and the Problem of White Life

There is much to be said of the unnatural relation between one's volcanic eruption and another's Category 5 hurricane.[1] In addition to culturally confirming and materially restoring the ascendancy of white humanity as the essential primacy of this earthly ordering, the technologies of "natural disaster" — particularly, the racial statecraft endemic to disaster's management — refract the lineages of conquest, colonialism, and enslavement that both compose and disorder our/other peoples' identifications. I am not interested in offering a point of closure, prescriptive salve, or discrete political trajectory that "makes sense" of white supremacy's global apparatus of terror through the Filipino condition. The closing pages of this book have no investment in remaking the Filipino as a body of authentically or reliably radical politicality. Instead, it is disaster's decomposition of the Filipino body — both its physical disintegration and dispersal into unfamiliar relationalities — that offers the political possibility with which I am most concerned. Perhaps such decomposition and possibility are more persistently present and accessible than we have come to imagine.

The simultaneities of colonialist genocide and regimented, engulfing, and interpellating white institutionality have produced the Filipino as a semi-illegible figure of the American national project and its global distensions. At odds with the essential political allegations of Filipino American discourse is the material fact of a Filipino subjectivity that is irreducibly linked to the violent and constitutive externalities of U.S. nation building. There can ultimately be no coherent conception of the "Filipino American" because the Filipino is permanently distorted by the most violent and experimental extrapolations of American global ambition. Such a joining of terms requires a fantastic suspension of historical disbelief, to the extent that "Filipino American" subjectivity has not been organically articulated through a critical conception of its origins in — and reproductions through — the profound "national" and epochal technologies of white supremacy as a global social ordering.

This is not to suggest that Filipinos are, or should be, easily analogized or straightforwardly compared to all other peoples who have encountered institutionalized racial subjection under the varying regimes of American state and civil violence. Instead, it is to argue that the Filipino condition can be adequately conceptualized and rigorously located within its determining regimes of dominance and contexts of cultural–political production only when the discursive structure of arrested raciality is critically imploded: only therein can "race" be sufficiently understood — and politically practiced — as a central, indelible, and dynamic historical analytic rather than an isolatable sociological variable, cultural description or signification of marginality, or epiphenomenal formation of power.

Theoretically, this analytical and political work suggests a strategic decentering (though not dismissal) of the broad rubrics of "colonialism," "empire," "diaspora," "globalization," "neoliberalism," and "militarization" (etc.), each of which differently conceptualizes "race" as a theoretical additive to or derivative of other, allegedly more fundamentally determining sets of power relations. Let me be clear: I am not positing that decentering these rubrics is somehow equivalent to denouncing them as obsolete, passé, or less than relevant to a substantive historical diagnosis of the Filipino condition. Rather, I am arguing that they are not sufficient nomenclatures for interrogating the aspect of Filipino social and cultural formation that is arguably the least rigorously conceptualized and, indisputably, among the most blatantly undertheorized by scholars and activists alike.[2] "Race," in the perpetually coercive historical constitution of the Filipino condition during and since the moment of the U.S. encounter, encompasses a nexus of historical transformations and identifications. Hall's elaboration of overdetermination in the context of identification provides a useful framing for what follows in this final chapter:

> In common sense language, identification is constructed on the back of a recognition of some common origin or shared characteristics with another person or group, or with an ideal, and with the natural closure of solidarity and allegiance established on this foundation. In contrast with the "naturalism" of this definition, the discursive approach sees identification as a construction, a process never completed — always "in process...." Though not without its determinate conditions of existence, including the material and symbolic resources required to sustain it, identification is in the end conditional, lodged in contingency. Once secured, it does not obliterate difference. The total merging it suggests is, in fact, a fantasy of incorporation.... Identification is, then, a process of articulation, a suturing, an over-determination not a subsumption. There is always "too much" or "too little" — an over-determination or a lack, but never a proper fit, a totality.... It obeys the logic of more-than-one.... It requires what is left outside, its constitutive outside, to consolidate the process.[3]

To confront the possibilities of identification in the nexus of disaster is to situate the genealogy of the post-nineteenth-century Filipino condition as a tracing of the epochal forms of global white supremacy, from its militarized genocidal logics to the seductions of multiculturalist white institutionality.

This chapter seeks political possibility in a Filipino genealogy and (collective) self-articulation that seeks radical engagement and intimacy with the racial terror, programmatic death, and structured vulnerabilities of white supremacy that form the architecture of historical possibility for both the apparent perpetuity of global white institutionality (and hence white human ascendancy) and its radical undoing. Stated differently, it is precisely the extremities of white nation building — its most profound, nuanced, and institutionally durable mobilizations of racial violence — that reveal the logical coherence and material continuities of white supremacy as a global organization of bodily dominion across localities; at the same time, this white supremacist globality systemically enables — or really, necessitates — kinships of liberationist thought, desire, and praxis that productively reconfigure and disarticulate Filipino subjectivity and politicality. Hence, the convergence of white supremacy, genocide, and the differential local logics of racial dominance on the historical present of apocalypse, disaster, and the statecraft of terror announces the urgency of a liberationist praxis that both disassembles parochial "Filipino" politicalities and disperses them into existing and still-unexplored communities of transformation.

I approach this closing meditation, then, as a reflection on the necessary task of exploding certain varieties of Filipino political narcissism, including and beyond its Filipino Americanist formulations. What possibilities emerge when the perpetual apocalypse of white supremacist globality, hallmarked by its particular and peculiar proctorship over preventable human disaster, comes to form the grounds of political articulation for a Filipino genealogy that does not require an internal coherence — that radically diverges from insistence on the political life and enunciation of the "Filipino" — and instead accelerates confrontation with the scariest and most uncertain social truths of liberationist praxis? This is not to posit an absolutist (or elitist) deferral or refusal of politically formulaic and ideologically self-assured progressive Filipino practices and identifications, but rather to insist on their fundamental inadequacy in not fully recognizing the overdeterminations of white supremacist globality as a social substructure, global way of life, and historically present mobilization of racial subjection.

Filipinos, in other words, are uniquely (though not exclusively) positioned to unravel the mystifications of preventable and programmatic racial death and disaster in a manner that resituates the genealogical, political, and historical connectedness of peoples encompassed by the epochal apocalypse of white supremacist civilizational ordering. Here the genocidal antiblack logic of Hurricane Katrina awakens an accounting of the Filipino condition that dismantles arrested raciality, catalyzing an acute sensibility of the political meanings and social practices of life and evil.

The Time of Katrina: Toward an Epochal Indictment

Spectacular white supremacist violence is conspicuous and normal to the everyday historical functioning of the United States. This is why the racist apocalypse that continues to unfold through the disaster of state-organized and civically proctored social displacement, civil neutralization, and bodily extermination exceeds the already time-contained rendition of Hurricane Katrina as an exceptional episode in U.S. history — as something already invoked in the vernacular of the past tense. Contrary to such sanitizing containments of systemic human suffering, this historical moment signifies — and materially fortifies — the essential and structuring logics of American white civil existence. The transparent universality of white life, fixed through a fabricated immunity to categorical (that is, racial) fragility and constant pronouncements of alienated unfamiliarity with premature death, self-reveals as a structure of racial dominance in times like this. One unavoidable historical truth sits at the heart of this reflection: the technologies of white life as we know it, its means of sustenance and reproduction, have always formulated and mobilized the liquidation (socially, politically, physically) of the white world's durable racial antagonist(s).

Thus, the living time of disaster (here the time of Katrina), which I understand as an ongoing material history of rigorously organized, state-facilitated, and militarized white racial dominion (in this instance focused on, though not limited to, the eviscerated urban geography of New Orleans and the Lower Ninth Ward), presents an acute opportunity to articulate (and for many, to firmly restate) the logic of dominance that constitutes our collective existence. My purpose here is to offer a situated reflection on the circumstances of this logic of dominance in order to elaborate (and perhaps extrapolate) how a radical response to this logic pronounces a social indictment that is epochal rather than individual, that is neither politically unprecedented nor uncommon, and that cannot possibly be adjudicated or "pragmatically" translated into public policy or institutional/state reform, because no such (state or white civil) mediation can bring back the dead. That is, the fundamental purpose of most such pragmatisms is never to seriously attempt a return of the displaced, reparation of unquantifiable damage, redemption of the socially evil, or accountability of radical and transformative social justice.

Thus, the indictment is in many ways unavoidable: the white supremacist animus of the United States of America — more concretely, the everyday modes in which this animus is inhabited and materialized by both hegemonic institutions and ordinary people — created Katrina, fabricated its structure of inevitability ("God has allowed it," according to white Christian nationalist leader Billy Graham),[4] enabled and ensured its maximum deployment as a protogenocidal "tragedy," and celebrated it as an opportunity for nationalist renewal, framed in the language of a sappy, mourning racial sentimentality.[5] Hurricane Katrina has refurbished the multiculturalist pretensions of the American national and global formation and reinserted the sanctity of white existence, white bodies, and white life as the central condition of U.S. racial-national coherence.

While we are living in the early ages of multiculturalist white supremacy, wherein "people of color" are increasingly, selectively, and hierarchically incorporated/empowered by the structures of institutional dominance — government, police, universities, corporations, etc. — that have historically formed the circuits of U.S. apartheid and racist state violence, Katrina reminds us that white America occupies a category of social existence that is without global parallel: the categorical imperative of whiteness as a historical structure of life pivots on the capacity to presume entitlement to things like bodily integrity, communal (read racial) security, and militarized state responsiveness in a manner that no other human category can allege to share in this moment. While certain geographies of white America are exposed to some of the unnatural violence of the white supremacist social formation in the time of globalization, it remains a remarkable racial fact of life that the white body is a permanent object of nationalist sympathy, a durably epidermalized site of (relative though consistent) decriminalization, and a systemically protected currency of exchange within even the most horrific distensions of U.S. nation building. At worst, pathologized white bodies are marginally or contingently exposed to severe systemic exploitation and harsh national discipline, but they systemically avert intimacy — much less genealogical familiarity — with the visceralities of absolute (racial) disposability and the social logic of genocide. Imagine, then, the sheer accumulation of racially organized death, vulnerability, and bodily disintegration that must accrue in order to render these white life entitlements so massively that they can, in fact, be taken for granted by whites *and their racial others.* (That is, "people of color" living in the regime of liberal multiculturalism tacitly assume the sanctity of white life over and above their own.) Herein the particularity of antiblack white supremacy requires some theoretical elaboration for the purposes of clarifying the global circumstances of the Filipino condition and the proximities of the Filipino American communion.

While accountings of indigenous, Latino/a, Asian, and white suffering at the hands of Katrina continue to be written, we ought to be clear that the fundamental economic, cultural, and state/military logic governing the discrete geographic and human drowning of a postsegregation, effectively apartheid New Orleans is animated by the sturdy symbiosis between black disposability and American nation building. This is to say that contemporary black social death[6] is characterized by the seemingly instantaneous social alienation of a delineated category of racially pathologized people whose formal status within the civic body is permanently marked by an irreconcilable — and socially defining — historical tension. The white supremacist social formation of genocidal enslavement not only indelibly marks the national institutionalities of the United States, but also structurally and endemically enables the historical recodifications of black subjection in the nominal (and relatively recent) historical aftermath of racial chattel slavery. The crucial contradiction that surfaces in the living moment of Katrina's wake, in other words, is not limited to the stubborn and almost trite disjuncture between (aspirations toward) fully enfranchised (hence state-protected) African "American"-ism and persistent antiblack state violence and racism. The more important and productive antagonism arises in Hurricane Katrina's reenshrinement of the specificity of American white supremacy — and specifically mass-based black bodily and geographic liquidation — as an epochal articulation of democracy, state building, and nationalist well-being.

Black death and displacement, ordained through the ritualized negligence and organized dysfunctioning of the state during and after the entirely expected destruction of Katrina — a hurricane that, it cannot be overemphasized, was meteorologically well anticipated — can and must be understood as the organized and enforced condition of contemporary multiculturalism across its different political variations: multiculturalism, as the most current and recent political adaptation of white supremacy, feeds and fosters an "antiracist" desire to, in plain words, live as (we imagine) white people do. When located alongside coterminous structures of white supremacist, nationalist, and democratically articulated antiblack violence — from militarized racist policing to the post-1970s burgeoning of the prison industrial complex — Hurricane Katrina is well within the historical conventions of American white civil society itself, amplifying and restoring the sanctity of white bodily integrity (and multicultural aspirations toward the same) through state-sanctioned and popularly consumed productions of black bodily disintegration.

As Clyde Woods, Cheryl Harris, and others have more adequately elaborated,[7] the sanctity of white civil existence continuously resonates through the time of Katrina, fostering a material — and thoroughly theatrical — conceptualization of black life that affirms the alien relation between (1) the material consequences of black racialization — for example, living in a place below sea level, while neighboring obsolete levees that await instantaneous collapse — and (2) the nationalist postulation and posturing around black civil existence, a mythological modality of social being that is produced through the constant evidencing of its basic fraudulence. Thus, if we consider that the popular rhetoric positing the crisis of Katrina's "(black) refugees" actually bespeaks the white supremacist social truth of the United States rather than a stubborn racist refusal to incorporate black life into the vernacular realms of American liberal humanism or "citizenship," then we are collectively obligated to confront white American existence with at least a

minimal, if not singular political agenda: to radically and decisively undo its premises of social and philosophical coherence,
overwhelm it with global displacements of its asserted and presumptive dominion over the lived meanings of race/place/body,
and thoroughly demystify the massive (and massively tolerated)
architecture of violence that constitutes the normative peace and
entitlement of white life itself. After all, what is "peace," really,
in the time of Katrina (et al.)?

A Nexus of Identification: The Global Relevance of Black/Indigenous Common Sense

A reflection on political and philosophical positioning is appropriate here. I arrive at this initial reflection on Hurricane Katrina
through my own particular (though not simply "individual")
Pinoy genealogy, as one born and raised in the United States while
sustaining lifelong affective, immediate and extended familial, as
well as imaginary, connections to another place. For reasons I
cannot fully explain, the time of Katrina resonates with me in
ways that render humanist sympathy and abstracted (or proto-
nationalist) mourning as inappropriate, even offensive reactions
to what has happened (and continues to happen). I do not feel
as if Hurricane Katrina was/is a "tragedy," and I find myself viscerally objecting to its being characterized as such. While there
are unnumbered tragedies — personal and political — composing the mosaic of this historical moment, Katrina strikes me as
something closer to a planned atrocity, and the spectacle of its
becoming sits with me as a scene of white — and white multiculturalist — popular enjoyment, wherein the drowning of black
people provided an opportunity for white Americana to revel
in its entitlement to remain relatively indifferent to this nearby
theater of breathtaking devastation. (The racial dramatization of
Katrina also reminds that the pleasure of charity is significantly
derived from the sense that one is extending assistance to others
despite the absence of any real moral or material obligation to

do so, as if assisting in the survival of an endangered species.) The white world, quite simply, was both politically familiar and viscerally unfamiliar with what it was watching in 2005 — hence the time of Katrina is, and can only be, a living history in which white subjectivity is both spectator and architect. This structure of witnessing and orchestration, perhaps, is what most disorients my autobiographical sensibilities.

The 1991 explosion of Mt. Pinatubo in the Philippines (the second largest volcanic eruption in the twentieth century), an event arguably best known for effectively ruining the massive Clark and Subic Bay U.S. military bases, is a central component of Filipino diasporic consciousness. While the context, geography, and sociopolitical impact of the Pinatubo eruption do not conveniently parallel or sustain easy comparison with the atrocity of Hurricane Katrina, the explosion undoubtedly contributed to the atmospheric and environmental conditions of possibility for the Gulf Coast devastation. The ash, gas, and toxins distributed by the volcano were so massive that they effectively reduced the overall temperature of the earth by 1.5 degrees Celsius, altered global wind circulation, and destroyed a significant portion of the planet's ozone layer.[8] Beyond this mind-numbing environmental consequence, and the eight hundred dead, two hundred thousand displaced by the eruption and subsequent lahars (the thick, hot mud flow that results from volcanic eruption), Mt. Pinatubo is perhaps most significant to the Filipino diaspora for its signification of instant mortality and involuntary, unexpected "evacuation" at the hands of God (or, if you like, diasporic susceptibility to an inaccessible transcendental agency). This lasting impression is undoubtedly enhanced by the fact that Mt. Pinatubo is less than sixty miles away from Metro Manila, the center of Philippine civic life. In the decade after Pinatubo's explosion, the Clark and Subic Bay military bases were nominally shut down as operational sites of U.S. occupation and were, almost immediately, resurfaced as sites for the facilitated influx of neoliberal capital, renovated as places of tourist enjoyment in fulfillment of white militarist nostalgia, and periodically reopened to U.S. military operations after 2001.[9]

At the time of the Pinatubo explosion, I recall feeling that disaster and social upheaval were the modus operandi of that/my other place. During and prior to my senior year of high school — I was seventeen at the time of the eruption — the Philippines had already come to represent a geography of political terror and commonly witnessed mortality: having been raised in a community of Filipino professionals whose primary political orbit revolved around several political exiles of the Marcos martial law regime who lived in the immediate area, casual discussions of political assassination, premature death of loved ones back home, and disappearance of friends and acquaintances was common, even to these ostensible "first-generation Filipino Americans." The first exposed corpses I ever saw and remembered (outside the controlled environment of the funeral home or church) were inscribed in the widely broadcast images of assassinated Marcos opposition leader Ninoy Aquino — the world news media seemed to endlessly circulate images of his mutilated face and bloody *barong* (a Philippine men's shirt worn on formal occasions) in the weeks following his death — and the more intimate memory of a nameless man whose body I watched being dragged from a Philippine beach, a day after having drowned near my paternal grandparents' house. What I have seen, heard, and read of the time of Katrina is condensing as something uncomfortably similar to this kind of extrapolated and extended trauma — that is, a refraction of death that seems to be telling me something essential about the place where I live, move, and come into/from.

Unexpected displacement and premature death are absolutely unremarkable to Filipinos, above and beyond exposure to the worst of naturalized environmental disaster and intensified poverty (although I will not rehearse the socioeconomic, health, or mortality data here). Whether it is due to the reified status of the Philippines as the most underdeveloped and structurally impoverished place in the Asia Pacific, or its colonial and neo-colonial subjection to U.S. hegemony and American-proctored, hyper-militarized domestic state violence, the scene of Katrina is, despite our misrecognitions and labors of (racial) distancing, not altogether alien to us. Members of the Filipino diaspora, across class and regional distinctions, can almost universally state that they are immediately and personally connected to the episodic or systemic fallout from environmental hazard/disaster, assassination, acute government repression, or U.S. military occupation/mobilization.

Mt. Pinatubo's devastation, however, also reveals that this loose diasporic connectedness is neither seamless nor unaltered by its own reinscriptions of localized productions of racial hierarchy and dominance. Rarely invoked in remembrances, commemorations, and (re)narrations of the eruption is the fact that "hardest hit among the casualties were the Negritos who were not immunized from diseases and even shunned the treatment of doctors."[10] The national/racial positioning of the Negrito people reflects the Spanish colonial and Euroamerican anthropological etymology of their naming, and the Negrito ethnoracial categorization serves as a convenient categorical incorporation of a much broader collection of indigenous Philippine groups, including the Aetas (or Aytas), who inhabited the immediate region of Mt. Pinatubo. The colonial, anthropological, and contemporary Philippine national/racial imaginary thus conceptualizes the Negritos through a version of "epidermalized"[11] blackness that articulates with notions of an aboriginal (and quaint) Philippine "tribal" premodern. As historically racialized and conventionally racially pathologized subjects, Aetas self-consciously sustain a rupturing of universalizing notions of Philippine nationalist, diasporic, "racial," and (pan)ethnic identity, condensing in the vernacular delineation between indigenous/Aetas/Negritos and "straight hair"/lowlander Filipinos. Interviewed in the wake of the volcano's explosion, Aetas Victor Villa and Elvie Devillena considered the delineation of (racial) difference in the moment of disaster:

> I believe that Aytas and straight-hairs have certain similarities in thinking and certain differences in behavior. Aytas are just as intelligent as straight-hairs; the only difference is our lack of education. We eat differently, we dress differently. Straight-hairs like wearing shoes and fancy clothes, while Aytas are comfortable with *bahags* (loin cloth).
>
> The lowlanders look down on Aytas. They even sneer at us as if we were direct descendants of monkeys.[12]

> [W]hen people see that you are short, they already know you are an Ayta. They can tell you are Ita by your skin, height, or speech pattern.... No matter how you look, if you are an Ayta, it will always show. People have called me "Ayta, Ayta, Ayta. Kinky hair, kinky hair, kinky hair." They say that with so much derision. Sometimes we are called *beluga* because we have dark skin. People from Manila think that Zambalas is filled with wild, savage Ayta people.[13]

The Aeta people's embodiment and dense signification of Philippine racial formation is further refracted through one Philippine state official's account of the Pinatubo relief efforts.

> Tarlac Governor Mariano Un Ocampo narrated how he was both amazed and amused at the Aetas' refusal to eat the canned goods given to them. "They have no taste at all for the canned goods," he said.
>
> About the only exception is the pork and beans in cans, Ocampo added. "But they would wash away the sauce and just eat the beans."
>
> Slow to adapt themselves to situations... this attitude also contributed to the many deaths among them, particularly children.
>
> ... But Ocampo expressed admiration for their integrity and honesty. "They would return to us the extra relief items given to them," he said, recalling occasions when the Aetas brought back the excess in the number of tents distributed to them for their shelter.
>
> *"I would never expect our straight-haired people to do that,"* he said. [emphasis added][14]

Such a discourse echoes the categorical status of the Negritos as opportune material for anthropological and ethnographic knowledge production during the latter part of the twentieth century. According to German anthropologist Stefan Seitz, writing in 2004:

> The Aeta form part of the Philippines' aboriginal population, the so-called *"Negritos."* Negritos differ from other Filipino groups in their racial phenotype, characterized by curly hair, dark complexion and small stature and by their lifestyle with its strong focus on foraging strategies.[15]

Seitz continues by remarking on the emergence of scholarly interest in "hunter-gatherer studies" during the 1960s and the particular anthropological fixation on "secluded, 'pristine' cultures with as many 'archaic' traits as possible." He contextualizes the current location of the Aeta people in the anthropological imaginary by considering the acceleration of ethnographic studies in the 1970s and 1980s, asserting that "as a result of this renewed interest, the Negritos of northeastern Luzon joined the San of southern and the Pygmies of central Africa as the hunter-gatherer societies most intensely studied by anthropologists."[16] In fact, Villa's and Devillena's self-narrations of Aeta difference, read alongside Ocampo's state paternalism and Seitz's academic description of Aeta/Negrito phenotype (etc.), constitute differently positioned reinscriptions of the vague, though still overdetermined, cultural and anthropomorphic/"racial" distinctions that distinguish particular Philippine ethnic and aboriginal populations and geographies from those of commonly identified (and nationally authenticated) "Filipinos."

The Aeta/Negrito condition — and its "official" representation through state and academic discourse — in this moment of Philippine national crisis compels a rereading of Mt. Pinatubo's eruption and a reconsideration of how this moment might alter our understanding of the larger genealogy of Filipino familiarity with disaster (etc.), especially in relation to the naturalized global linkages between "blackness" (Negritoness), social liquidation, racial subjection, and historical obsolescence (aboriginalness). A central political and theoretical problem defining the global and historical structure of Filipino intimacy with death and terror is its relative alienation from a common sense of white supremacy that sees, analyzes, and viscerally experiences mortal Filipino suffering as the logical global and historical condition of white (American) life.

There are people in the town of Bacolor, in the province of Pampanga, who articulate a historical memory of disaster that usefully extends the geography and temporality of Mt. Pinatubo's eruption, evincing the possibility of a critical social sensibility that relocates Filipino intimacies with disaster, death, and terror. Having experienced the massive lahars that traveled over twenty miles from Mt. Pinatubo before converging on Bacolor more than four years after the actual volcanic explosion, and having survived Bacolor's drowning in about twenty feet of hot mud and ash, surviving residents Eck, Michael, and Mercy delineate a site and time that escapes compartmentalizing notions of natural disaster. In fact, I would argue that theirs is a profoundly conceptual and narrative insight into precisely the terms of engagement that might enable radical and global identifications, over and against any compulsory "Filipino" national or diasporic identity.

I spoke (in Tagalog) with all three at the San Guillermo Parish Church,[17] the landmark of Bacolor, in December 2006. The church, once almost forty feet tall, was buried to half its height by the 1995 lahars, and the second story archway has been converted into the church's main entrance. To this day, numerous surrounding structures, including small residences, a mausoleum, and numerous cemetery monuments, are visible only by their roofs or pillars, and the eeriness of recent, avoidable human mortality is dense and unavoidable. Eck, Michael, and Mercy's accounting of the lahars, literally the disaster after the disaster, illuminates the social and political logics that condition this living apocalypse:

ECK: The flow of the lahar was fast and hot.

DR: You stayed here? Where did you live?

ECK: We didn't bother leaving, we stayed in the evacuation centers.

DR: Did the Philippine government set the evacuation centers up?

ECK: No, we put them together ourselves. The government helped a little bit. But if we hadn't put them up ourselves, we'd have all died.

DR: If you hadn't built the shelters, then that would have been it.

ECK: Yes. We'd have all been dead. The lahars came, fast and early, and we had to wake up all the children to evacuate their houses. There was an elderly person who used to live right over there who died. They got buried. When it got hot, that was it. The rich ones, they left, they just went to higher ground because they had money to live in another house.

DR: And did they ever come back?

ECK: They did come back, once the lahars had stopped.

DR: They built new houses?

ECK: Yes, the ones with money, like those people over there, the rich ones. The ones without money, we just lived in shacks after the lahars were over.[18]

MICHAEL: The rich people just ran away. They just ran away.

DR: That's what I heard.

MICHAEL: Of course. They had a place to go. We had no place to go. When the lahars came, we just tried to go up to the highest ground we could find. Once the lahars eased up, we would go back down.

DR: Did a lot of people die?

MICHAEL: The ones who lived over there, on that side, a lot of them died. We tried to get them to leave, but they wouldn't. We were already on higher ground, so when the lahar came, it drowned everyone really fast. The lahars moved faster than we imagined they would.

DR: Do you know how many people died?

MICHAEL: I'm not sure, but it was a lot.

DR: So you could really see that the lahars were coming on?

MICHAEL: Oh yes. It was fast, it was hot, and it stunk.

DR: It must've been hard to breathe.

MICHAEL: Yes. The flow of the first lahar was a lot slower. But the second one was much faster and more massive. The rich people had already left town. But us poor people, we were stuck here.

DR: So the government didn't help much.

MICHAEL: Really, all the government sent us was the kind of food they usually feed to dogs.[19]

MERCY: : We couldn't eat the rice the government sent us. It stunk. And we had nothing else to eat because, obviously, the *palenke* (market) was drowned, there was no water, everything was gone.[20]

Here, on the one hand, is a renarration of the Philippine national bourgeoisie that was examined in the previous chapter: the rich who abandon big houses for higher ground, leaving the rest for dead, then return at disaster's end to rebuild even grander provincial homes on top of the bodies of those who were not meant to survive. On the other hand, herein is a short depiction of a disaster-making state, condensing in a government of limited capacity that seems to actively invest in strategies of negligence: consider that the state must *mobilize* to distribute rotting rice and dog food to survivors; hence these must be seen as labor-intensive rather than passively negligent acts. Bacolor, post-1995, is defined by the multiple rearticulations of white institutionality as an apparatus of systemic environmental exposure, human dispersal, and bodily disintegration.

It is white civil existence and its analogues (including elitist versions of Philippine cosmopolitanism and diaspora), in other words, that create and circulate the "racial" and aboriginal existence of the Negrito people and their local/global cohorts, and install them as the durable center of gravity for precisely the forms of civil, social, and biological death rendered so immediately accessible in the United States through the racial atrocity of Hurricane Katrina, and in the Philippines through the planned disaster(s) of Mt. Pinatubo. Such a racial common sense is precisely what black and indigenous people in the United States have

Rear of San Guillermo Parish Church, Bacolor, December 2006.

involuntarily obtained and rigorously, commonly theorized over the last several centuries of national formation.

This critical black and indigenous common sense — the notion, consistently sustained as a Fanonist "historical truth,"[21] that black and indigenous peoples' intimacy with death and terror is the fundamental purpose of white civil existence, and, perhaps, of global white life itself — is (again) being stunningly vindicated as plans are made to "reconstruct" New Orleans in the image of a gentrified white metropolis.[22] Perhaps it is the latent possibility of manifesting an authentically global and translocal significance to this racial common sense that most resonates with my own subjective and political–intellectual positionality. The time of Katrina amplifies the necessity for a political articulation of white supremacy that is "radical" in the most historically contextualized sense of the term. We can understand the planning of Katrina in its geographic and political specificity as antiblack state violence and orchestrated, "natural" population control, while also situating it in relation to the global material structuring, and material genealogy, of white Americana as a perpetual state of warfare that is fundamentally racial in its historical architecture, social vision, and militarized ordering of human disposability.

I am suggesting that the significance of black death and displacement in the living time of Katrina is reflected in the creative possibility for black common sense to resonate with, and provide substantial political–theoretical premises for, other (neo)colonized, underdeveloped, and racially pathologized peoples' self-conceptualizations and global political identifications in relation to things like U.S. (and U.S.-proctored) state violence, "natural" disaster, poverty, disease, and bodily disintegration. Perhaps most importantly, this political possibility suggests the global rather than narrowly "national" or even "regional" significance of U.S.-based antiblack violence as a modality of white supremacist social ordering, at times parallel and other times overlapping with the genealogy of genocidal anti-indigenous violence examined in chapter 3. A radical racial genealogy of the Filipino condition, in this sense, enables a conceptualization of how naturalized American antiblackness forms a material regime through which other circuits of global dominance — including neocolonialism, nationalism, globalization and empire — elaborate autonomous matrices of warmaking, racial subjection, and hierarchized material and ideological structures of human mortality. *Redness 2,*

Mt. Pinatubo's eruption did not merely contribute to the global climatic condition for Katrina; it also marked the deep connection between apparently disparate "natural" occurrences which, in turn, resurface as linked formations of global racism, which Ruth Wilson Gilmore conceptualizes as "the state sanctioned and/or extra-legal production and exploitation of group-differentiated vulnerabilities to premature death."[23] By way of example: most journalistic, state, "relief aid," and academic commentary on the postdisaster conduct of the Aeta people emphasizes (in patronizing vernacular) their "irrational" refusal to accept medical aid, naïve hesitance to pursue government assistance, and quaint adherence to spiritual and "animistic" rather than pragmatic conceptualizations of life and survival. In direct opposition to this narrative of noble and naïve savagery, Aeta testimonials in the aftermath of the Pinatubo eruption suggest a firsthand, organic accounting of the Philippine state that more clearly renders its relation to the American white supremacist/racist state. It is within such testimonials that we encounter traces of precisely the critical common sense that (1) formulates a fundamental *dis*identification with the social and political logic of the Philippine national/racial formation, and (2) reflects the latent possibility of a rearticulation of cosmology, history, and identity that can think alongside the critical black common sense of the Katrina moment:

> I think all [this] happened because God is testing us.
> According to the elders, they have always taken care of Pinatubo. The word *pinatubo* in our language means "nurtured with care." Since long ago our ancestors have taken care of the mountain. But, perhaps in time, our leaders' minds had been tainted with a destructive nature. Thus, they allowed the Philippine National Oil Company, which had no right to disturb the mountain, to get in.... [S]ince it was the government that ordered the operation, the Aytas couldn't do anything about it.[24]

> We wanted the government to know that the Philippine National Oil Company [PNOC] promised our people many good things, like schools and employment for the Aytas. Many of us liked the idea. But not everyone thought it wise to drill into Pinatubo. The Ayta leaders thought that these operations would affect our way of living, the environment, the water, and our resources.... We didn't want PNOC to endanger these basic needs. But we were betrayed.... That was when Pinatubo started to emit smoke. It was around April.[25]

> "We were provided with multicolored plastic tents for shelter. We were told that they were the best possible solution to our problem," said Nestor Solomon. However, the Aeta added, "We know that tents are hardly suitable for the summer or the rainy season. It was hardly

a home. It never gave us warmth.... Whenever the sun shines, it becomes unbearably hot inside a tent. When it rains, it becomes too cold for comfort because the ground gets damp.... For many months, we had to endure sleeping close to the cold and damp earth," he added. Comparing his life before and during the Pinatubo eruption, he said, "I always slept well up in the mountain."[26]

Many died at the evacuation center at Cabalan. It's so painful that many were claimed by diseases like measles, diarrhea, bronchopneumonia.... Everyday, from June to July, August, September, people died. The fact that many Aytas in Cabalan died makes me cry. There were a lot of medicines, but most were useless, like paracetamol. There were also hospitals, like the two converted rooms in the school, but people died anyway. This is the sad plight of the Aytas.[27]

The relief operations weren't any better either. The sardines were old and already expired.... Many died in Cabalan because of flies. The flies were on our food, in our coffee. These flies caused diarrhea.

And the sardines — the cans were rusted inside. That is why I did not eat sardines. I showed them to Mrs. Gordon [wife of Kakilingan mayor Dick Gordon] and I asked her why we got expired sardines. All she said was, "Just throw it away, Son." So I did. And when I did, the cans exploded. I found out that the sardines were over five years old.[28]

When we relocated to Iram, the government constructed the road. However, the bridge they built was weak, and it gave way during Typhoon Kadiang.... In Iram, the Department of Environment and Natural Resources allotted 70 hectares for our farm lots and 30 hectares for our home lots. But it's already 1994, and we still haven't received our farm lots. That's why a lot of Aytas still don't have a decent means of livelihood.[29]

An Ayta without land is a fish out of water. Bring him to the city and he will wither away. Government projects do not address this very important issue
We need funds for land. The government gives us funds for electricity and facilities. They give us roads, schools, hospitals, and comfort rooms. But what they don't give us are the means to feed ourselves. A home without anything to eat is worthless....

The government is not solving anything. Many Aytas are now becoming domestic workers, cowhands, and beggars. If the government acted quickly after the eruption, this would not have happened.[30]

This series of reflections from displaced Aetas implicates a structure of planned social obsolescence[31] — "We native Aytas feel that our culture is slowly being erased as we become more civilized"[32] — as well as semipermanent subjection to "client" status under the hegemonic Philippine state. It also provides the basis for elaborating a far deeper set of political, cultural, and philosophical linkages between differently located black/indigenous people, weaved through politically constitutive scenes of disaster. This is how the Aeta retrospective on the Philippine neoliberal state's tampering with the ecology of the mountain politically resonates with the common, longstanding suspicion shared among black Louisianans (and many others) that the U.S. state was largely responsible for manufacturing and (urban) planning the human casualties of Katrina (e.g., the decades of refusal to address the obsolescence of levees adjoining the Lower Ninth Ward, and the generalized withholding of response/relief capacities as the atrocity unfolded).

My momentary reflection on Mt. Pinatubo is here intended as an amplification of the time of Katrina, and rather than displacing or diluting the gravity that Katrina brings to discussions of black life, survival, struggle, and liberation, I am suggesting that movements, activists, and intellectuals inhabiting different genealogies and heritages of subjection to white supremacist violence are called upon, in such moments of racial apocalypse, to accelerate their different modalities of struggle against global white civil existence and its conditions of possibility. This is to also foreground the potential for a global political resonance of critical black common sense that forms at least one philosophical and pragmatic basis for history's rewriting in the sense of both scholarly vocation and living, radical praxis.

If the structuring dominance of white life is to be displaced or obliterated, and the cultural-material possibility of an authentic human existence somehow vindicated, then those whose death and displacement are taken for granted truly encompass a state of emergency for the white world. Natural disaster, as a modality of human elimination, coercive "modernization" (in the case of the Aetas), strategic urban population control (in the case of black New Orleans), and racist state violence is simultaneously a radical narrative moment in the elaboration of global hierarchies of life and death, and a radical political moment for comprehending the productive necessity of massive, collective, transformative struggle against white civil existence, which literally watches in tragic delight as disaster renders new opportunities for expanding its spheres of dominion and domination.

For many Filipinos across the global diaspora, the explosion of Mt. Pinatubo may always in some sense signify humility before the hand of God, but it can also be renarrated as a moment of profound intimacy with the mortal logic of living a century under white Americanist dominion: What does it mean for one's alleged kin to live at the base of an active volcano, nearby two active U.S. military bases? What of the Aeta/Negrito sensibility that posits fundamental suspicion with Philippine state and civil attempts to offer (and, in places, coerce) "relief" of their disfranchisement, displacement, and exposure to preventable illness? If some form of war, evacuation, human disaster, and collective death are "built in" as the virtual inevitability of such a (racial) geography, then how should Filipinos (in and beyond the United States) understand themselves, in relation to black people, in the time of Katrina?

Strident and open Filipino negrophobic racism notwithstanding, it may well be that the only possibility for serious political kinship between blacks and Pinoys (locally and diasporically, beyond liberal, culturalist, or compensatory Filipino negrophilia) exists in the space of proximity and familiarity that can be shared only as we approach our differently produced — though somehow still stubbornly common — identifications with the horror of a collective vulnerability to sudden mortality and bodily subjection to higher forces (whether "god," "nature," the U.S. state, or officially sanctioned white supremacist violence). What if we understood the death and destruction of Mt. Pinatubo's eruption, and the genealogy of Filipino suffering and disaster itself, as mutually and materially articulating with black death and displacement before, during, and beyond the time of Katrina?

The statement issued a year after Mt. Pinatubo's eruption by the Central Luzon Ayta Association, part of a Philippine umbrella network of indigenous peoples' organizations, complexly echoes and differently locates a black critical common sense of the state in moments of disaster.

> One Year Has Passed. Slowly and Swiftly.
> Slowly. The promises were slowly fulfilled. Medicines and food were slowly delivered. Rescue slowly reached us.
> Swiftly children and elders got sick. Death was swiftly running after us. We were soon forgotten, and our problems quickly passed from one government agency to another.[33]

I am not pleading for another modality of multicultural coalition or even black–Filipino solidarity here. Instead, I am asking for a different paradigm of identification — encompassing the realms of spirituality, cosmology, (racial) identity, cultural imagination, and political fantasy — one that precedes and perhaps generates a different kind of praxis, across the localized global sites of U.S. white supremacy. I am also openly wondering if this semiautobiographical reflection is really an extended articulation of a political desire to instigate and participate in a radically collective global communion of people who are capable of mustering the voice to (at least) accuse the white world of conspiring and reveling in the death of others. It is in the act of making such an accusation that we might see the genesis of political labors that push and break the limits of rationalistic, formulaic, and pragmatist agendas challenging white supremacist American hegemony and neoliberal capital. Of course, such an accumulation of identification and bonding, alongside others, could well contribute to the end of white life as we know it.

Conclusion: Empire, Evil, and Humanism

Of our contemporary global ordering Antonio Negri and Michael Hardt write in their widely read text *Empire*:

> Empire is emerging today as the center that supports the globaliza-
> tion of productive networks and casts its widely inclusive net to try
> to envelop all power relations within its world order — and yet at the
> same time it deploys a powerful police function against the new bar-
> barians and the rebellious slaves who threaten its order. The power of
> Empire appears to be subordinated to the fluctuations of local power
> dynamics and to the shifting, partial juridical orderings that attempt,
> but never fully succeed, to lead back to a state of normalcy in the
> name of the "exceptionality" of the administrative procedures.[34]

Surely there is a "juridical ordering" that shapes the actual administration of "disaster" — such is seen in the popular tendency to overfocus on the bureaucratic fumblings of FEMA in the case of Katrina. What I find more significant here, however, is the manner in which "natural" disaster itself, as a normalization of profound bodily violence against "slaves and barbarians," most often escapes the critical lens of critical theorists, activists, and even human rights advocates. This is to demystify the notion of "natural disaster" as something that naturally kills the abject of Negri and Hardt's Empire. The apparent unavoidability of things like volcanic eruptions and Category 5 hurricanes must be theoretically and politically distinguished from the proctored processes and architectures of mass-scale death that are manufactured in the midst of natural disaster's presumed inevitability. Perhaps the targeted chaos, socially planned displacement, and flexible (non)administration of "relief" and fatality in moments of disaster illuminate the global dominion of white civic life as the fundamental collective project that simultaneously precedes, constitutes, and overdetermines empire, globalization, neoliberalism, and so forth.

What concerns me here is the kind of gravity that "barbarians and rebellious slaves" embody in the crafting of global white supremacy, a technology of violence and social architecture of dominance that somewhat dis-/relocates the machinery of Negri and Hardt's conceptualization of empire as "world order." Arguably, what is manifest as amplified police power within the global operations of white supremacy — neocolonial rule, militarized occupation, perpetual domestic and global war — is the ongoing condition of possibility for empire itself. Unless there are constant deployments of racist violence that consolidate the capacity to presume the earthly integrity and transcendence (universality) of white life, the apparatus of empire — its structures of governmentality, disciplined bodily mobility, and coercive orderings of local and global "peace" — would implode.

To be clear: the allegedly encompassing and globally integrating constitution of Empire as an arrangement of power *does not* subsume or supersede the apartheid and disintegrating genocidal logic of white supremacy. Thus, the state violence that Hardt and Negri relegate to the realm of "police" power is actually much more than a state of exception to the "normalcy" of empire's arrangement of power. While their notion of world order usefully offers the notion that "Empire is born and shows itself as crisis," and suggests that mobilizations of police power speak to the embedded "contradictions" of Empire — "the question of the definition of justice and peace will find no real resolution" — the time of Katrina, Pinatubo, et al. suggests the existence of entire categories of people for whom the civic discourse of "justice and peace" is entirely irrelevant. ⌐

This structured irrelevance helps make sense of why such scenes of racial apocalypse bring forward eerie (and usually undertheorized) resonances between black American premature death and Third World mass suffering and normalized population liquidation. |Unnatural black death, alongside indigenous planned obsolescence, is constitutive of U.S. nation building across historical moments, while (undeclared) war, disaster, and protogenocide (sometimes referenced as "overpopulation") are central to the global formation of contemporary white supremacy in the neocolonial and postcolonial worlds. Imagine, then, the intensity of state, cultural, and (para)military labor required to expose a racially identifiable urban "civil"/"citizen" population and discretely racial geography to the front lines of preventable mass displacement and death, and to then successfully fortify this exposure with multiple mobilizations of domestic police and civil forces that focus and contain the fallout of such a scene.

Finally, disaster, conceived in the present-tense regimes of white supremacy, definitively and conclusively means the end of any viable, much less rational, possibility for the future of white liberal humanism. Something that many survivors of European and Euroamerican colonialism, slavery, and genocide share is a durable belief in the existence of evil, a basic conception that its force of possibility is always lurking in the overlapping spiritual and material worlds, and a powerful (though often understated) conviction that evil inhabits and possesses the white world, its way of life, and its relationality to "others." Liberal white humanism, which constantly circulates and rearticulates notions of a shared universal "human" character, while morbidly militarizing against manifest human threats to the integrity of the coercively universalized white body, cannot authentically survive the white supremacist time of disaster. In fact, white humanism can survive at all only if it is capable of persistently reconstructing its apparatus of meaning to accommodate the materialization of white evil in the face of black New Orleans, Aeta Mt. Pinatubo, and so forth. Perhaps, then, another question we might visit is, What does disaster tell us of evil? What happens when we look up and evil is armed absence and militarized neglect, intentional and institutional without a doubt, but materialized through the white world's persistent festival of health, happiness, and physical integrity in the face of such incredible suffering?

Notes

I. Filipino American Communion

1. By way of example, Rick Bonus, *Locating Filipino Americans: Ethnicity and the Cultural Politics of Space* (Philadelphia: Temple University Press, 2000); Martin F. Manalansan, *Global Divas: Filipino Gay Men in the Diaspora* (Durham, N.C.: Duke University Press, 2003); and Antonio T. Tiongson Jr., Edgardo V. Gutierrez, and Ricardo V. Gutierrez, eds., *Positively No Filipinos Allowed: Building Communities and Discourse* (Philadelphia: Temple University Press, 2006) pursue multiple lines of ethnographic, historical, sociological, and interdisciplinary–humanistic inquiry into the sociocultural materiality of putative "Filipino American" communities. While this book relies on such studies as examples of thoughtful, rigorously researched examinations of Filipino American community and identity formations, it also attempts to provide a conceptual disarticulation of the "Filipino Americanist" rubric through a theoretical centering of its conditions of possibility.

2. See Stuart Hall, "Race, Articulation, and Societies Structured in Dominance," in *Black British Cultural Studies: A Reader,* ed. Houston A. Baker Jr., Manthia Diawara, and Ruth Lindeborg (Chicago: University of Chicago Press, 1996), 16–60; the article originally appeared under the same title in *Sociological Theories: Race and Colonialism* (Paris: UNESCO, 1980), 305–45.

3. Denise Ferreira da Silva, *Toward a Global Idea of Race* (Minneapolis: University of Minnesota Press, 2007), 116–17.

4. Ibid.

5. Albert J. Beveridge, *Congressional Record,* 56th Congress, First Session, vol. 33 (1900): 704–8.

6. Ibid., 709.

7. See generally Reginald Horsman, *Race and Manifest Destiny: The Origins of American Racial Anglo-Saxonism* (Cambridge, Mass.: Harvard University Press, 1981).

8. Beveridge, *Congressional Record,* 709.

9. Silva, *Toward a Global Idea of Race,* 217–18.

10. Ibid., 218.

11. Daniel B. Schirmer and Stephen Rosskamm Shalom, eds., Introduction to chapter 2: "Colonization," in *The Philippines Reader: A History of Colonialism, Neocolonialism, Dictatorship, and Resistance* (Boston: South End Press, 1987), 35.

12. For historical overviews of Filipino migration to Hawaii and the mainland United States during the twentieth century, see generally Jonathan Y. Okamura, *Imagining the Filipino American Diaspora: Transnational Relations, Identities, and Communities* (New York: Garland Publishing, 1998), 36–44; Barbara M. Posadas, *The Filipino Americans* (Westport, Conn.: Greenwood Press, 1999); Antonio J. A. Pido, *The Pilipinos in America: Macro/Micro Dimensions of Immigration and Integration* (New York: Center for Migration Studies, 1986); Benjamin V. Cariño, James T. Fawcett, Robert W. Gardner, and Fred Arnold, *The New Filipino Immigrants to the United States: Increasing Diversity and Change* (Honolulu: East–West Center, 1990), Papers of the East-West Population Institute, no. 115; and John M. Liu, Paul M. Ong, and Carolyn Rosenstein, "Dual Chain Migration: Post-1965 Filipino Immigration to the United States," *International Migration Review* 35, no. 3 (Fall 1991): 487–513.

13. Silva, *Toward a Global Idea of Race,* 206.

14. For a full conceptualization of "racial projects" see chapter 4, "Racial Formation," in *Racial Formation in the United States: From the 1960s to the 1990s,* ed. Michael Omi and Howard Winant (New York: Routledge, 1994). While my overarching theoretical centering of "white supremacy" in this book constitutes an implicit critique of Omi and Winant's more specific definition of a "racist project," their broader focus on the material and hence socially formative connections between the discourses and social institutionalities of race remains a useful premise from which to begin.

15. In addition to thoughtful and critical scholarly work by Theodore S. Gonzalves and Barbara Gaerlan (see citations in subsequent endnotes), see also S. Lily Mendoza, *Between the Homeland and the Diaspora: The Politics of Theorizing Filipino and Filipino American Identities* (New York: Routledge, 2002).

16. Theodore S. Gonzalves, "Dancing into Oblivion: The Pilipino Cultural Night and the Narration of Contemporary Filipina/o America," *Kritika Kultura* no. 6 (2005): 52.

17. See Dana Y. Takagi, *The Retreat from Race: Asian-American Admissions and Racial Politics* (New Brunswick, N.J.: Rutgers University Press, 1992); and Angelo N. Ancheta, *Race, Rights, and the Asian American Experience* (New Brunswick, N.J.: Rutgers University Press, 1998).

18. The University of Chicago anthropologist and University of California president David P. Barrows, after whom a prominent building at U.C. Berkeley is named, is perhaps best known for his role in reorganizing the Philippine educational system during his tenure as the "general superintendent of education" appointed by President William H. Taft during the earliest phase of the American colonial occupation. Barrows also authored a number of books, including *A History of the Philippines* (Indianapolis: Bobbs Merrill, 1903) and *A Decade of American Government in the Philippines* (Yonkers-on-Hudson, N.Y.: World Book Company, 1915).

19. California's Proposition 209, cynically titled the "California Civil Rights Initiative," was fronted by University of California Regent Ward Connerly and was overwhelmingly approved by the California electorate in November 1996. Connerly, who became a nationally recognized black neoconservative (a political identity he occupied in spite of his own incessant insistence on the compulsory nationalist requirement for a race-blind "American" identity), executed a rather stunning and deforming appropriation of the progressive civil rights rhetorics of the 1950s and 1960s, arguing that the withdrawal of state intervention on racial inequalities (the initiation of the truly "colorblind" state) was the culmination of Martin Luther King Jr.'s venerable "Dream." The text of the proposition reads, in part, "The state shall not discriminate against, or grant preferential treatment to, any individual or group on the basis of race, sex, color, ethnicity, or national origin in the operation of public employment, public education, or public contracting."

20. Loida Nicolas Lewis, National Federation of Filipino American Associations (NaFFAA) Region 1 Chair Emeritus, "Welcome to NaFFAA Region 1," 2004, http://naffaa.net/r1/.

21. Barbara Gaerlan, "In the Court of the Sultan: Orientalism, Nationalism, and Modernity in Philippine and Filipino American Dance," *Journal of Asian American Studies* 2, no. 3 (1999): 257.

22. Frantz Fanon, *The Wretched of the Earth* (1963), trans. Richard Philcox (New York: Grove Press, 2004), 149.

23. Luis H. Francia, "The Other Side of the American Coin," *Flippin': Filipinos on America* (New York: Asian American Writers' Workshop, 1996), 7.

24. Daniel B. Schirmer, "The Conception and Gestation of a Neocolony," *The Philippines Reader,* ed. Schirmer and Shalom, 43.

25. Renato Constantino, "The Miseducation of the Filipino," *Journal of Contemporary Asia* 1, no. 1 (1970): 22–23.

26. Ibid., 29.

27. Benedict Anderson, *Imagined Communities: Reflections on the Origin and Spread of Nationalism* (London: Verso, 1991), 142.

28. Theodore S. Gonzalves, "The Day the Dancers Stayed: Expressive Forms of Culture in the United States," in *Filipino Americans: Transformations and Identity,* ed. Maria Root (Thousand Oaks, Calif.: Sage Publications, 1997), 163–82.

29. Lisa Lowe, *Immigrant Acts: On Asian American Cultural Politics* (Durham, N.C.: Duke University Press, 1996), 2–3.

30. Allan Punzalan Isaac, *American Tropics: Articulating Filipino America* (Minneapolis: University of Minnesota Press, 2006), xxiv.

2. Deformed Nationalism and Arrested Raciality

1. *Oxford English Dictionary,* 2nd ed. (1989), s.v. "Renaissance."

2. See generally Ruth Wilson Gilmore, *Golden Gulag: Prisons, Surplus, Crisis, and Opposition in Globalizing California* (Berkeley: University of California Press, 2007); David Theo Goldberg, *The Racial State* (Malden, Mass.: Blackwell Publishers, 2002); and Omi and Winant, eds., *Racial Formation in the United States.*

3. See Louis Althusser, "The Humanist Controversy" (1967), in *The Humanist Controversy and Other Writings, 1966–1967,* ed. François Matheron, trans. G. M. Goshgarian (London: Verso, 2003), 221–305. I am grateful to my brilliant friend and colleague Prof. Keith Harris (Media and Cultural Studies, University of California, Riverside) for directing my attention to this essay.

4. This strain of theorization in relation to Filipino subjectivities is most rigorously elaborated in Neferti X. M. Tadiar's groundbreaking book *Fantasy Production: Sexual Economies and Other Philippine Consequences for the New World Order* (Hong Kong: Hong Kong University Press, 2004).

5. Anderson, *Imagined Communities,* 6.

6. Among numerous texts, including community-based publications, academic journal articles, student newspapers, and visual media, the following books and essays have proved especially useful as reference points for progressive and counterhegemonic articulations of Filipino and "Filipino American" "community," "politics," and "(collective) identity." Regarding Filipino involvement in U.S.-based union and labor organizing, see Dorothy B. Fujita-Rony's *American Workers, Colonial Power: Philippine Seattle and the Transpacific West, 1919–1941* (Berkeley: University of California Press, 2003) and her essay "Coalitions, Race, and Labor: Rereading Philip Vera Cruz," *Journal of Asian American Studies* 3, no. 2 (2000): 139–62. See also Craig Scharlin and Lilia V. Villanueva's classic text *Philip Vera Cruz: A Personal History of Filipino Immigrants*

and the Farmworkers Movement, ed. Glenn Omatsu and Augusto Espiritu (Los Angeles: UCLA Labor Center, Institute of Industrial Relations & UCLA Asian American Studies Center, 1992). For examinations of gay and queer Filipino diasporic formations in the United States, see Manalansan IV, *Global Divas.* See also articles by Manalansan, Reyes, Mangaoang, Tan, and others in *Asian American Sexualities: Dimensions of the Gay and Lesbian Experience,* ed. Russell Leong (New York: Routledge, 1996). These latter texts foreground the historical experiences of Filipino gay men, and there has been a noticeable gap in the scholarly attention devoted to queer Filipina/Pinay subjectivities. A partial response to this absence was the publication of the collection *Dragon Ladies: Asian American Feminists Breathe Fire,* ed. Sonia Shah (Boston: South End Press, 1997), which includes a foreword by Karin Aguilar–San Juan and a roundtable interview that includes Margarita Alcantara. Both pieces, however, inaugurate a discourse of "Asian American" feminism and queer identity that occludes the specificity of a putative Filipina/Pilipina/Pinay subjectivity. Three recent texts that deal substantively with the political economies of (Filipina) migration, U.S. public policy, and immigrant rights advocacy are Grace Chang, *Disposable Domestics: Immigrant Women Workers in the Global Economy* (Boston: South End Press, 2000); Catherine Ceniza Choy, *Empire of Care: Nursing and Migration in Filipino American History* (Durham, N.C.: Duke University Press, 2003); and Rhacel Parreñas' *Servants of Globalization: Women, Migration, and Domestic Work* (Stanford, Calif.: Stanford University Press, 2001). Three essays offer particularly lucid overviews and historical narrations of the U.S.- based anti–martial law movements and the nuances of the organizing processes that elaborated their critical transnational political rubrics: David Takami, "Marcoses Found Liable for Seattle Cannery Workers Union Murders" (reprinted from *International Examiner,* March 6, 1991), *Amerasia Journal* 18, no. 1 (1992): 125; Madge Bello and Vince Reyes, "Filipino Americans and the Marcos Overthrow: The Transformation of Political Consciousness," *Amerasia Journal* 13, no. 1 (1986): 73–83; and Helen C. Toribio, "We Are Revolution: A Reflective History of the Union of Democratic Filipinos (KDP)," *Amerasia Journal* 24, no. 2 (1998): 155–77. Toribio's scholarship on the U.S.-based KDP is widely recognized and has appeared in numerous popular and academic as well as journalistic forums.

7. Manalansan, *Global Divas,* 13–14.

8. While examples of such texts abound, it is worth mentioning several that are particularly relevant to this critique. I will specifically address elements of Fred Cordova's *Filipinos, Forgotten Asian Americans: A Pictorial Essay* (Dubuque, Iowa: Kendall/Hunt, 1983) later in the book, in

part because Cordova's status as the alleged patriarch of Filipino American history and his central role in the academic field as the founder and president of the Filipino American National Historical Society (FANHS), have arguably elevated this 1983 text to a status of foundational Filipino American intellectual artifact. Ronald Takaki's widely read *Strangers from a Different Shore: A History of Asian Americans* (Boston: Little, Brown, 1989), and *A Different Mirror: A History of Multicultural America* (London: Little, Brown, 1993), as well as the less acclaimed *In the Heart of Filipino America: Immigrants from the Pacific Isles* (Philadelphia: Charles House Publishers, 1995), are paradigmatic historical narratives of late twentieth-century multiculturalist patriotism, and the first two books are often included in introductory and compulsory college (and some high school) courses in American history and/or ethnic/Asian American studies. Lesser known examples, which no less powerfully crystallize a proto-Bildungsroman of the Filipino American immigrant experience, include Estrella Ravelo Alamar and Willi Red Buhay, *Filipinos in Chicago* (Chicago: Arcadia Publishing, 2001); Dorothy Cordova, *Distinguished Asian Americans: A Biographical Dictionary* (Westport, Conn.: Greenwood Press, 1999); and the children's book *Filipino Americans (We Are America)*, by Carolyn Yoder (Chicago: Heinemann Library, 2002).

9. E. San Juan Jr., "One Hundred Years of Producing and Reproducing the 'Filipino,'" *Amerasia Journal* 24, no. 2 (1998): 21

10. Bonus, *Locating Filipino Americans*, 1.

11. Ibid., 3.

12. Gramsci's outline of the highly complex and massively scaled relations of cultural and political power initiated by the proliferation of industrial capitalism as an economic *and social* order also generates a conception of social formation that abandons models of the parochial, singularly coercive state as the primary apparatus of political rule and societal coherence. His extended discussion of the transformation of the state into a *pedagogical* apparatus that wins the consent and allegiance of its constituency ("In reality, the State must be conceived of as an 'educator,' in as much as it tends precisely to create a new type or level of civilisation" [247]), and Gramsci's subsequent situation of the "ethical" or "cultural" state (258) within a socially generative relation to emerging "civil societies," form the most durable strain in his theorization of hegemony. One of the most useful sets of Gramsci's writings on this topic is in part 2, chapter 2, "State and Civil Society," *Selections from the Prison Notebooks of Antonio Gramsci*, ed. and trans. Quintin Hoare and Geoffrey Nowell Smith (New York: International Publishers, 1971), 206–76.

13. Stuart Hall, "Gramsci's Relevance for the Study of Race and Ethnicity," *Stuart Hall: Critical Dialogues in Cultural Studies,* ed. David Morley and Kuan-Hsing Chen (London: Routledge, 1996), 440.

14. Here I am referencing Ruthie Gilmore's widely acknowledged conceptualization of "racism" as "the state-sanctioned and/or extralegal production and exploitation of group-differentiated vulnerabilities to premature death." Her first publication of this definition appears in "Race and Globalization," *Geographies of Global Change: Remapping the World,* 2nd ed., ed. P. J. Taylor, R. L. Johnston, and M. J. Watts (Oxford: Blackwell, 2002), 261.

15. Linda Revilla, "Filipino American Identity: Transcending the Crisis," in *Filipino Americans: Transformation and Identity,* ed. Maria Root (Thousand Oaks, Calif.: Sage, 1997), 96.

16. Leny Mendoza Strobel, *Coming Full Circle: The Process of Decolonization among Post-1965 Filipino Americans* (Quezon City, Philippines: Giraffe Books, 2000), 118.

17. See generally Syed Serajul Islam, "The Islamic Independence Movements in Patani of Thailand and Mindanao of the Philippines," *Asian Survey* 38, no. 5 (1998): 441–56; David Hyndman and Levy Duhaylungsod, "Political Movements and Indigenous Struggles in the Philippines," *Fourth World Bulletin* 3, no. 1 (1993), http://carbon.cudenver.edu/fwc/Issue6/philippines-1.html; Antoinette G. Royo, "The Philippines: Against the People's Wishes, the Mt. Apo Story," in *The Struggle for Accountability: The World Bank, NGOs, and Grassroots Movements,* ed. Jonathan A. Fox and L. David Brown (Cambridge, Mass.: MIT Press, 1998), 151–80; Alexandra Xanthaki, *Indigenous Peoples and United Nations Standards: Self-determination, Culture, Land* (Cambridge: Cambridge University Press, 2007) and "Land Rights of Indigenous Peoples in Southeast Asia," *Melbourne Journal of International Law* 2, no. 4 (2003): 4467–96; At Bengwayan, "6th UNPF Sessions to Focus on Indigenous Peoples' Land Rights," *Bulatlat* 7, no. 14 (2007), www.bulatlat.com/2007/05/6th-unpf-session-focus-ip-land-rights-1; see too the short piece "Summary/Strategies/Recommendations" authored by the head of the Cordillera People's Alliance (and Kankanaey tribe member) Joan Carling, in *Challenging Politics: Indigenous People's Experiences with Political Parties and Elections,* ed. Kathrin Wessendorf (Copenhagen: International Work Group for Indigenous Affairs, 2001); G. Sidney Silliman and Lela Garner Noble, eds., *Organizing for Democracy: NGOs, Civil Society, and the Philippine State* (Honolulu: University of Hawai'i Press, 1998); Kathleen Nadeau, "Liberation Theology in a Post-Marxist Era: The Philippine Context," *East Asian Pastoral Review* 41, no. 4 (2004),

http://eapi.admu.edu.ph/eapr004/nadeau.htm; Frank Hirtz, "It Takes Modern Means to Be Traditional: On Recognizing Indigenous Cultural Communities in the Philippines," *Development and Change* 34, no. 5 (2003): 887–914.

18. Ibid.

19. See generally Douglas S. Massey and Nancy A. Denton, *American Apartheid: Segregation and the Making of the Underclass* (Cambridge, Mass.: Harvard University Press, 1993).

20. Gramsci, *Selections from the Prison Notebooks*, 13.

21. Benjamin Pimentel and Pueng Vongs, "*Philippine News*: Child of Historical Events," *New American Media: Expanding the News Lens through Ethnic Media*, September 25, 2003, http://news.newamericamedia.org/news/view_alt_category.html?page=8&first=70&last=79&category_id=54. Established by Pacific News Service in 1996, *New American Media* is a national collaboration of "ethnic news organizations" that primarily intends to service the "new ethnic majority" of California.

22. For a summation of the newspaper's shifts in focus, ownership, and institutional scale since its 1961 founding, see Beting Laygo Dolor, "*Philippine News* through the Decades," *Philippine News* (online version), August 23, 2005, www.philippinenews.com/news/view_article.html?article_id=1498b1cce8d05eb4499be1d4dafd293d.

23. Stuart Hall, Chas Critcher, Tony Jefferson, John Clarke, and Brian Roberts, *Policing the Crisis: Mugging, the State, and Law and Order* (New York: Palgrave Macmillan, 1978), 54–55.

24. See "About *Philippine News*," www.philippinenews.com (*Philippine News Online*).

25. *Balikbayan*, literally "those returning home," was a term incorporated and widely circulated by the Philippine government after the 1970s for the purpose of fostering a naturalized, affective connection between diasporic Filipinos in the United States and their Philippine "homeland." The word invokes a semiotics of prodigality, and further suggests that the balikbayan has "returned home" to deposit or share social and cultural capital — as well as expendable income — with Philippine "kin" generally and tourist facilities (resorts, malls, clubs, hotels) more specifically.

26. "American Tourists Laud Filipino Hospitality," *Philippine News*, March 19–25, 1997, B-8.

27. See generally Robyn Rodriguez, "Migrant Heroes: Nationalism, Citizenship and the Politics of Filipino Migrant Labor Source," *Citizenship Studies* 6, no. 3 (2002): 341–56; Ligaya Lindio-McGovern, "Labor Export in the Context of Globalization," *International Sociology* 18, no. 3 (2003): 513–34; Dilip Ratha, "Workers' Remittances: An Important and Stable Source of External Development Finance," *Global Development*

Finance 2003, World Bank report #27750 (Washington, D.C.: World Bank, 2004), 157–75; James A. Tyner, "The Gendering of Philippine International Labor Migration," *Professional Geographer* 48, no. 4 (1996): 405–16, and "Global Cities and Circuits of Global Labor: The Case of Manila, Philippines," *Professional Geographer* 52, no. 1 (2000): 61–74; Joaquin L. Gonzalez III, *Philippine Labour Migration: Critical Dimensions of Public Policy* (Singapore: Institute of Southeast Asian Studies, 1998); and Charles W. Stahl and Fred Arnold, "Overseas Workers' Remittances in Asian Develoment," *International Migration Review* 20, no. 4 (1986): 899–925.

28. "GMA Signs New Balikbayan Law, 4 Other Bills," Philippine Government news release, November 13, 2002.

29. "Karilagan Promotes Filipino Heritage," *Philippine News*, February 19–25, 1997, A-8.

30. See especially Paul A. Kramer, *The Blood of Government: Race, Empire, the United States, and the Philippines* (Chapel Hill: University of North Carolina Press, 2006); Jose D. Fermin, *1904 World's Fair: The Filipino Experience* (Diliman, Quezon City: University of the Philippines Press, 2004); Vicente L. Rafael, *White Love and Other Events in Filipino History* (Durham, N.C.: Duke University Press, 2000); and Sharra L. Vostral, "Imperialism on Display: The Philippine Exhibition at the 1904 World's Fair," *Gateway Heritage* (Spring 1993): 18–31.

31. "Philippine Float Bags International Trophy at Rose Parade," *Philippine News*, January 8–14, 1997, A-1, A-11.

32. "OCPS Preserves Family Values," *Philippine News*, February 12–18, 1997, B-3.

33. "Women as Head of Families," *Philippine News*, March 12–18, 1997, A-5.

34. "Worth Its Weight in Gold," *Philippine News*, March 5–11, 1997, A-5.

35. Michel Foucault, *The History of Sexuality*, vol. 1: *An Introduction* (New York: Vintage Books, 1990), 108.

36. See Takagi, *The Retreat from Race*.

37. "The Filipino Americans' Success in the Social and Cultural Aspects," *Philippine News*, February 5–11, 1997, A-5.

38. See especially the paradigmatic piece "Success Story of One Minority Group in U.S.," *U.S. News & World Report*, December 26, 1966, 73.

39. See generally Daniel Patrick Moynihan, *The Negro Family: The Case for National Action* (Washington D.C.: Office of Policy Planning and Research, United States Department of Labor, 1965), and Oscar Lewis, *La Vida: A Puerto Rican Family in the Culture of Poverty — San Juan and*

New York (New York: Random House, 1966), xlv. See also Lewis's *Five Families: Mexican Case Studies in the Culture of Poverty* (New York: Basic Books, 1959), and "The Culture of Poverty," *Scientific American* (October 1966).

40. Diane L. Wolf, "Family Secrets: Transnational Struggles among Children of Filipino Immigrants," *Sociological Perspectives* 40, no. 3 (1997), 458.

41. Yen Le Espiritu, " 'We Don't Sleep Around Like White Girls Do': Family, Culture, and Gender in Filipina American Lives," *Signs* 26, no. 2 (2001): 431.

42. Wolf, "Family Secrets," 463.

43. Ibid., 467.

44. Ibid., 468.

45. Ibid.

46. Ibid., 469–70.

47. Ibid., 471.

48. Espiritu, " 'We Don't Sleep Around Like White Girls Do,' "432.

49. Ibid., 434.

50. San Juan Jr., "One Hundred Years of Producing and Reproducing the 'Filipino,' " 7.

51. Ibid., 14.

52. See, among their other works, Charles Murray, *Losing Ground: American Social Policy, 1950–1980,* 2nd ed. (New York: Basic Books, 1994), and Murray and Richard Herrnstein, *Bell Curve: Intelligence and Class Structure in American Life* (New York: Free Press Paperbacks, 1994). The rigorous, critical responses to Murray and Herrnstein include Steven Fraser, ed., *The Bell Curve Wars: Race, Intelligence, and the Future of America* (New York: Basic Books, 1995); Stephen Jay Gould, *The Mismeasure of Man* (New York: W. W. Norton, 1996); and Troy Duster, *Backdoor to Eugenics,* 2nd ed. (New York: Routledge, 2003).

53. Here I am referencing Michael Omi and Howard Winant's conception of the "racial project" as a struggle for power and social resources through the production of politicized meanings and mobilizations around categories of "race." See Omi and Winant, *Racial Formation in the United States.*

54. Ronald Reagan, "Remarks at a Meeting with Asian and Pacific-American Leaders," February 23, 1984, Public Papers of Ronald Reagan, Ronald Reagan Presidential Library (Simi Valley, Calif.). Text available online through the Ronald Reagan Presidential Library Web site: www.reagan.utexas.edu.

55. While the "panethnic" rubric fails to account for the persistence of various political antagonisms that necessarily fracture alleged "Asian American" organizing practices (particularly along the lines of nationality, citizenship, gender, sexuality, and class), the term nonetheless signifies a hegemonic logic for the emergence of various community organizations, grassroots campaigns, academic initiatives, cultural/artistic productions, and entrepreneurial efforts. See Yen Le Espiritu, *Asian American Panethnicity: Bridging Institutions and Identities* (Philadelphia: Temple University Press, 1992), and Espiritu and Lopez, "Panethnicity in the United States: A Theoretical Framework," *Ethnic and Racial Studies* no. 13 (1990).

56. "Regal Beauties and Leaders," *Philippine News*, January 1–7, 1997, B-6.

57. "Youth Pageantry for Scholarships," *Philippine News*, January 1–7, 1997.

58. Ludy Astraquillo Ongkeko, Ph.D., "When Being Filipino Is a Plus," *Philippine News*, February 19–25, 1997, A-5.

59. Ibid.

60. See Hall, "Race, Articulation, and Societies Structured in Dominance."

61. Jason P. Pugay, "Brothers Charged with Vandalism," *Philippine News*, February 19–25, 1997, A-11.

62. Jason P. Pugay, "Filipino Suspect, Five Others Charged in Vallejo Bombings," *Philippine News*, February 12–18, 1997, A-1.

63. Hall et al., *Policing the Crisis*, 66–67.

64. National Federation of Filipino American Associations, "Preamble," *NaFFAA Constitution*, September 11, 2004, www.naffaa.org/2005naffaa/constitution.html.

65. Anita L. Panganiban, "Pitak Pilipino," *Philippine Mabuhay News*, October 1–15, 2004, 14.

66. "The Filipino Vote: Why Filipina Women Must Help Run U.S. and the World," *Filipino Press*, October 2–8, 2004, 1, 19.

67. Filipina Women's Network, "About FWN," www.ffwn.org/about/index.htm.

68. National Federation of Filipino American Associations, "NaFFAA's Objectives" (2004), http://naffaa.org/about/index.htm.

69. See Omi and Winant's discussion of this concept in chapter 4 of *Racial Formation in the United States*.

70. Eduardo Bonilla-Silva, *Racism without Racists*, 2nd ed. (New York: Rowman & Littlefield, 2006), 10.

71. Ibid., 28.

72. Interview with DJ Q-Bert, conducted by David Mesa, Jose Rivera, and Monica Sagullo under supervision of the author, U.C. Berkeley, Spring semester 1999.

73. Antonio Tiongson Jr.'s work is groundbreaking in this area. His manuscript "Claiming Hip Hop: Authenticity Debates, Filipino DJs, and Contemporary U.S. Racial and Global Diasporic Formations" establishes a critical historical lens through which to conceptualize Filipino American engagements with (and appropriations of) hip-hop as a political–cultural formation.

74. Among other projects, Q-Bert conceived the storyline for the 2001 film *Wave Twisters,* an animated "skratch saga" based on his album of the same name. He has also appeared in several films, including *Scratch* and *Tagumpay.* Among other published interviews, see "Sundance Interview with DJ Q-Bert," Marie K. Lee, National Asian American Telecommunications Association (available online at www.naatanet.org/forumarchive/q_bert.html).

75. See generally Brian Currid, "We Are Family: House Music and Queer Performativity," in *Cruising the Performative: Interventions into the Representation of Ethnicity, Nationality, and Sexuality,* ed. Sue-Ellen Case, Philip Brett, and Susan Leigh Foster (Bloomington: Indiana University Press, 1995), 165–96; Jared Sexton, "Racial Profiling and the Societies of Control," in *Warfare in the American Homeland: Policing and Prison in a Penal Democracy,* ed. Joy James (Durham, N.C.: Duke University Press, 2007), 197–218; Tricia Rose, *Black Noise: Rap Music and Black Culture in Contemporary America* (Hanover, N.H.: University Press of New England, 1994); Gayatri Gopinath, "'Bombay, U.K., Yuba City': Bhangra Music and the Engendering of Diaspora," *Diaspora* 4, no. 3 (1995): 303–11; and Paul Gilroy, *The Black Atlantic: Modernity and Double Consciousness* (Cambridge, Mass.: Harvard University Press, 1993).

76. "I Am Filipino-American," www.epilipinas.com/IamFil-Am.htm.

77. Maria P. P. Root, "Contemporary Mixed-Heritage Filipino Americans: Fighting Colonized Identities," in *Filipino Americans: Transformation and Identity,* 80.

78. Reuben S. Seguritan, *We Didn't Pass through the Golden Door: The Filipino American Experience* (Institute for Filipino American Research, 1997), 53–54.

79. Ibid., 156.

80. Ibid., 156–58.

81. Ibid., 103.

82. Ibid., 112–13.

83. Ibid., 113.

84. Ibid., 174.

85. While there are a number of texts echoing Seguritan's narrative structure of the Filipino American telos, a few notable and perhaps lesser known examples include Cecilia Manguerra Brainard, ed., *Growing Up Filipino: Stories for Young Adults* (Santa Monica, Calif.: PALH, 2003); Peter Jamero, *Growing Up Brown: Memoirs of a Filipino American* (Seattle: University of Washington Press, 2006); Norman Reyes, *Child of Two Worlds: An Autobiography of a Filipino-American — or Vice Versa* (Colorado Springs, Colo.: Three Continents Press, 1995); and Patricia Justiniani McReynolds, *Almost Americans: A Quest for Dignity* (Santa Fe: Red Crane Brooks, 1997).

86. Alex A. Esclamado, "The Future Leaders," *The Philippine News,* March 19–25, 1997, A-4.

87. Gramsci, *Selections from the Prison Notebooks*, 326, n. 5.

3. "Its Very Familiarity Disguises Its Horror"

1. Mahmood Mamdani, *When Victims Become Killers: Colonialism, Nativism, and the Genocide in Rwanda* (Princeton, N.J.: Princeton University Press, 2001), 9.

2. Horsman, *Race and Manifest Destiny,* 297.

3. Ibid., 303.

4. Stanley Karnow, *In Our Image: America's Empire in the Philippines* (New York: Ballantine Books, 1989), 3–4.

5. Discussing such a shift in the political–economic modality of U.S. hegemony in the Philippines, E. San Juan Jr. considers the aftermath of the much valorized "People's Power" insurrection of 1986 as a contingent opportunity for a more effective assimilation into the emergent global structures of neoliberalism: "Scenes of this uprising were televised throughout the world, images exuding an aura of the miraculous. Few know that the restoration of neocolonial democracy — rule of transnationals through the comprador/oligarchic elite — after that event ushered a new stage for the revival of neocolonial apparatuses of domination, agencies of hegemonic rule designed to protract the nation's subservience to transnational corporations and the IMF/World Bank" ("One Hundred Years of Producing and Reproducing the 'Filipino,' " 3).

6. Cordova, *Filipinos, Forgotten Asian Americans,* 217.

7. Ibid., 220.

8. Maria P. P. Root, "Introduction," in *Filipino Americans: Transformation and Identity,* ed. Maria P. P. Root (Thousand Oaks, Calif.: Sage Publications, 1997), xiv.

9. Root, "Contemporary Mixed-Heritage Filipino Americans," *Filipino Americans*, 80.

10. Revilla, "Filipino American Identity," 96.

11. For an extended critical examination of the discourses of multiracialism, multiculturalism, and racial hybridity, see Jared Sexton, *Amalgamation Schemes: Antiblackness and the Critique of Multiracialism* (Minneapolis: University of Minnesota Press, 2008).

12. Nerissa S. Balce, "Filipino Bodies, Lynching, and the Language of Empire," in *Positively No Filipinos Allowed: Building Communities and Discourse*, ed. Antonio T. Tiongson Jr., Edgardo V. Gutierrez, and Ricardo V. Gutierrez (Philadelphia: Temple University Press, 2006), 45.

13. See Avery Gordon's daring meditation on the political and social materiality of haunting in *Ghostly Matters: Haunting and the Sociological Imagination* (Minneapolis: University of Minnesota Press, 1997).

14. Silva, *Toward a Global Idea of Race*, 117.

15. Omer Bartov, *Murder in Our Midst: The Holocaust, Industrial Killing, and Representation* (New York: Oxford University Press, 1996), 53, 70.

16. Fanon, *The Wretched of the Earth*, 150.

17. See generally Bartov, *Murder in Our Midst*; Alan S. Rosenbaum, ed., *Is the Holocaust Unique? Perspectives on Comparative Genocide* (Boulder, Colo.: Westview Press, 2001).

18. Ward Churchill, *A Little Matter of Genocide: Holocaust and Denial in the Americas, 1492 to the Present* (San Francisco: City Lights Books, 1997), 410. It should be emphasized that Rafaël Lemkin, the legal scholar retained by the U.N. Secretariat whose text *Axis Rule in Occupied Europe* (1944) greatly influenced the earlier formulations of the UN Genocide Convention, actually opposed the inclusion of "political groups" in the Secretariat's draft. I am indebted to activist, doctoral student, and legal scholar Darryl Li for generously sharing this insight, which provides a corrective to Churchill's conflation of Lemkin's own political position with the content of the U.N. Secretariat's draft. While Lemkin played a central role in the Secretariat's draft, he was overruled on the inclusion of "political groups" by other participating scholars and experts. I should also note that much of the historical summary and concise legal analysis that follows stems directly or indirectly from Churchill's text, particularly the final two chapters, "The United States and the Genocide Convention: The Saga of an Outlaw State, 1948–1988," and "Defining the Unthinkable: Towards a Viable Understanding of Genocide," 363–437.

19. In addition to his *Axis Rule in Occupied Europe*, see Raphaël Lemkin, "Genocide as a Crime under International Law," *American Journal of International Law* 41, no. 1 (1947): 145–51.

20. Raphaël Lemkin, *Axis Rule in Occupied Europe* (Washington, D.C.: Carnegie Endowment for International Peace, 1944), 92–94.

21. Darryl Li, "The Idea of Mass Atrocity," M.Phil. thesis, University of Cambridge Centre for International Studies, 2003, 32–33.

22. In addition to Churchill's book, Frank Chalk and Kurt Jonassohn's text *The History and Sociology of Genocide: Analyses and Case Studies* (New Haven: Yale University Press, 1990) offers a rigorously researched and frequently incisive critique of the U.N. Genocide Convention's fruition. See especially the subsection "Genocide: Origins of a Concept," contained in "Part I: The Conceptual Framework," 8–12.

23. Quoted in Churchill, *A Little Matter of Genocide,* 411.

24. See generally David E. Stannard's short essay "On Racism and Genocide," in appendix 2 of his text *American Holocaust: The Conquest of the New World* (New York: Oxford University Press, 1992), 269–81.

25. "Convention on the Prevention and Punishment of the Crime of Genocide," United Nations, December 9, 1948. Full document accessed through the United Nations Web site: www.un.org/millennium/law/iv-1.htm.

26. Chalk and Jonassohn, *The History and Sociology of Genocide,* 10.

27. Ibid., 11.

28. See Jean-Paul Sartre, *On Genocide: And a Summary of the Evidence and the Judgments of the International War Crimes Tribunal by Arlette El Kaïm-Sartre* (Boston: Beacon Press, 1968).

29. Leo Kuper, *Genocide: Its Political Use in the Twentieth Century* (New Haven, Conn.: Yale University Press, 1981), 32–33.

30. Chalk and Jonassohn, *The History and Sociology of Genocide,* 11.

31. Churchill, *A Little Matter of Genocide,* 431–32.

32. See Churchill's "Proposed Convention on Prevention and Punishment of the Crime of Genocide (1997)," in *A Little Matter of Genocide,* 431–36.

33. Lemkin, *Axis Rule in Occupied Europe,* 82–85.

34. Civil Rights Congress, *We Charge Genocide: The Historic Petition to the United Nations for Relief from a Crime of the United States Government Against the Negro People,* ed. William L. Patterson (New York: Civil Rights Congress, 1951), 3.

35. Ibid., 3–4.

36. Ibid., 4–7.

37. Ibid., 126.

38. Ibid., 19.

39. Ibid., 132–34.

40. See João Costa Vargas, *Never Meant to Survive: Genocide and Utopias in Black Diasporic Communities* (New York: Rowman & Littlefield, 2008).

41. See Andrea Smith, *Conquest: Sexual Violence and American Indian Genocide* (Cambridge, Mass.: South End Press, 2005).

42. Luzviminda Francisco, "The First Vietnam: The U.S.–Philippine War of 1899," *Bulletin of Concerned Asian Scholars* 5, no. 4 (December 1973): 7.

43. Julian Go, "Introduction: Global Perspectives on the U.S. Colonial State in the Philippines," in *The American Colonial State in the Philippines: Global Perspectives*, ed. Julian Go and Anne L. Foster (Durham, N.C.: Duke University Press, 2003), 8–9.

44. Stuart Creighton Miller, *"Benevolent Assimilation": The American Conquest of the Philippines, 1899–1903* (New Haven, Conn.: Yale University Press, 1982), 179–80.

45. Lenore A. Stiffarm with Phil Lane Jr., "The Demography of Native North America: A Question of American Indian Survival," in *The State of Native America: Genocide, Colonization, and Resistance*, ed. M. Annette Jaimes (Boston: South End Press, 1992), 34.

46. *Congressional Record*, 57th Congress, First Session (1902), vol. 35, part 2, 1904.

47. Ibid.

48. *Congressional Record*, 57th Congress, First Session (1902), vol. 35, part 6, 5788.

49. See generally George F. Hoar, *Autobiography of Seventy Years*, vols. 1 and 2 (New York: Scribner's Sons, 1903); and Richard E. Welch Jr., *George F. Hoar and the Half-Breed Republicans* (Cambridge, Mass.: Harvard University Press, 1971).

50. *Congressional Record*, 57th Congress, First Session (1902), vol. 35, part 6, 5789.

51. Ibid.

52. "Issuance of Certain Military Orders in the Philippines (telegraphic circular no. 3, Batangas, December 9, 1901)," *Senate Document 347*, 57th Congress, First Session (1902), 8.

53. Ibid., 8.

54. The full three volumes of the testimonies can be found in *Senate Document 331*, 57th Congress, First Session (1903) (serial numbers 4242–44). For the sake of offering a more reader-friendly discussion of key points from this extensive document, the passages from the Hearings that follow are gathered from Henry F. Graff's more selective and accessible compilation of the testimonies in the valuable text *American Imperialism and the Philippine Insurrection: Testimony Taken from Hearings on Affairs in the Philippine Islands before the Senate Committee on the Philippines — 1902* (Boston: Little, Brown, 1969).

55. "Testimony of William Howard Taft," *American Imperialism and the Philippine Insurrection,* ed. Graff, 95.

56. "Testimony of Brig. General Robert P. Hughes," *American Imperialism and the Philippine Insurrection,* ed. Graff, 68.

57. Ibid., 117–18.

58. See especially *Senate Document 205* ("Charges of Cruelty, Etc. to the Natives of the Philippines"), Part I, 57th Congress, First Session (1902); and Richard E. Welch Jr., "American Atrocities in the Philippines: The Indictment and the Response," *Pacific Historical Review* 43, no. 2 (1974): 233–53.

59. "Testimony of Sgt. Leroy E. Hallock," *American Imperialism and the Philippine Insurrection,* ed. Graff, 106.

60. "Testimony of Major General Arthur MacArthur," *American Imperialism and the Philippine Insurrection,* ed. Graff, 114.

61. Leon Wolff, *Little Brown Brother: How the United States Purchased and Pacified the Philippine Islands at the Century's Turn* (New York: Doubleday, 1961), 317–18.

62. Smith, *Conquest,* 122.

63. "Testimony of Corp. Daniel J. Evans," *American Imperialism and the Philippine Insurrection,* ed. Graff, 83–84.

64. "Issuance of Certain Military Orders in the Philippines (telegraphic circular no. 3, Batangas, December 9, 1901)," *Senate Document 347,* 57th Congress, First Session (1902), 9.

65. See generally Luana Ross, *Inventing the Savage: The Social Construction of Native American Criminality* (Austin: University of Texas Press, 1998).

66. Full text of this memorandum is in the appendix to *Senate Document 331,* 57th Congress, First Session (1903), 2073–96.

67. The entirety of this memorandum is also in the appendix to *Senate Document 331,* 57th Congress, First Session (1903), 2070–72.

68. *Congressional Record,* 57th Congress, First Session (1902), vol. 35, part 6, 5796.

69. In addition to the sources that follow, see generally *Senate Document 213,* 57th Congress, Second Session (1903).

70. "Issuance of Certain Military Orders in the Philippines," *Senate Document 347,* 57th Congress, First Session (1902), 6.

71. "Major Waller Has Returned," *New York Times,* June 14, 1902, 8.

72. "Gen. Smith's Orders," *New York Times,* April 27, 1902, 6.

73. See David L. Fritz, "Before the 'Howling Wilderness': The Military Career of Jacob Hurd Smith, 1862–1902," *Military Affairs* 43, no. 4 (1979): 186–90. While Fritz's short piece offers a rather onerous defense

and valorization of Smith's military career and even opens with a curt denial of Smith's complicity in genocide, it provides a useful and concise outline of the context surrounding Smith's court-martial. See also "Gen. Jacob H. Smith Dead," *New York Times*, March 3, 1918, 23.

74. "President Retires Gen. Jacob H. Smith; Philippine Officer Reprimanded for 'Kill and Burn' Order," *New York Times*, July 17, 1902, 1.

75. Brian McAllister Linn, *The U.S. Army and Counterinsurgency in the Philippine War, 1899–1902* (Chapel Hill: University of North Carolina Press, 1989), 169.

76. Linn writes in the preface, "Since this work relies heavily on Army operational records and personal papers, it is possible that the views of the officers and men serving in the provinces may have colored my own perceptions."

77. Linn, *The U.S. Army and Counterinsurgency in the Philippine War, 1899–1902*, 170.

78. Arthur Kleinman, "The Violences of Everyday Life: The Multiple Forms and Dynamics of Social Violence," in *Violence and Subjectivity*, ed. Veena Das, Arthur Kleinman, Mamphela Ramphele, and Pamela Reynolds (Berkeley: University of California Press, 2000), 239.

79. Frantz Fanon, "The Negro and Language," chapter 1 of *Black Skin, White Masks* (New York: Grove Press, 1967), 17–18.

80. Ibid., 18.

81. David Theo Goldberg, *Racist Culture: Philosophy and the Politics of Meaning* (Cambridge, Mass.: Blackwell, 1993), 4.

82. See generally Goldberg, *Racist Culture*.

83. Graff, *American Imperialism and the Philippine Insurrection*, 64–65.

84. See especially Orlando Patterson, "Authority, Alienation, and Social Death," chapter 2, or *Slavery and Social Death: A Comparative Study* (Cambridge, Mass.: Harvard University Press, 1982), 35–76.

85. Nerissa Balce's incisive analysis of the entanglements between the racialization of Filipinos and contemporaneous anti-black and anti-Indian racial ideologies further resonates the context of American modernity's racialized conquest. See "Filipino Bodies, Lynching, and the Language of Empire," 43–60.

86. Francisco, "The First Vietnam," 4.

87. Ibid., 10.

88. Miller, *"Benevolent Assimilation,"* 208.

89. See Silva, "Transcendental Poesis," chapter 4 of *Toward a Global Idea of Race*, 69–89.

90. "Telegraphic Circular No. 2 (Batangas, December 8, 1901)," *Senate Document 347,* 57th Congress, First Session (1902), 8–9.

4. Suspended Apocalypse

1. Michel Foucault, *"Society Must Be Defended": Lectures at the Collége de France, 1975–1976,* trans. David Macey (New York: Picador, 2003), 265.

2. Warwick Anderson, *Colonial Pathologies: American Tropical Medicine, Race, and Hygiene in the Philippines* (Durham, N.C.: Duke University Press, 2006), 3.

3. Resil Mojares, "The Hills Are Still There," *Vestiges of War: The Philippine–American War and the Aftermath of an Imperial Dream, 1899–1999,* ed. Angel Velasco Shaw and Luis H. Francia (New York: New York University Press, 2002), 81–83. Mojares provides an extended discussion of the complexities of "class" in his examination of the Cebu province on pp. 81–85.

4. Teodoro A. Agoncillo, *History of the Filipino People,* 8th ed. (Quezon City, Philippines: Garotech Publishing, 1990), 382.

5. See Espiritu, *Asian American Panethnicity.*

6. Michael Salman, *The Embarrassment of Slavery: Controversies over Bondage and Nationalism in the American Colonial Philippines* (Berkeley: University of California Press, 2001), 5.

7. Fanon, *The Wretched of the Earth,* 97.

8. Ibid., 98.

9. Ibid.

10. Ibid.

11. My use of this phrase in the context of engaging the nominal "aftermath" of U.S. conquest directly resonates the aptly titled anthology edited by Angel Velasco Shaw and Luis H. Francia, *Vestiges of War: The Philippine-American War and the Aftermath of an Imperial Dream, 1899–1999* (New York: New York University Press, 2002).

12. According to Brian Massumi's reading of Deleuze, a simulacrum "bears only an external and deceptive resemblance to a putative model. The process of its production, its inner dynamism, is entirely different from that of its supposed model; its resemblance to it is merely a surface effect, an illusion." Brian Massumi, "Realer Than Real: The Simulacrum according to Deleuze and Guattari," *Copyright* no. 1 (1987).

13. Reynaldo Ileto, "The Philippine–American War: Friendship and Forgetting," in *Vestiges of War,* 3.

14. See Bienvenido Lumbera, "From Colonizer to Liberator: How U.S. Colonialism Succeeded in Reinventing Itself after the Pacific War," in *Vestiges of War*, 198–99.

15. Renato Constantino, *The Making of a Filipino: A Story of Philippine Colonial Politics* (Quezon City, Philippines: Malaya Books, 1991), 118.

16. See Constantino, "The Mis-Education of the Filipino," 20–36.

17. Carter G. Woodson, *The Miseducation of the Negro* (Trenton, N.J.: Africa World Press, 1998).

18. Constantino, "The Mis-Education of the Filipino," 24.

19. Fanon, *The Wretched of the Earth*, 98–99.

20. Ibid., 99.

21. Ibid.

22. Ibid., 101.

23. According to then-Secretary of Defense Dick Cheney, the rehabilitation and continued use of Clark Air Force Base was "just not a viable prospect" in the wake of the eruption. See Eileen Guerrero, Associated Press, "Cheney Says Clark to Be Closed," July 16, 1991.

24. See Clifford Krauss, "Volcano Is Unforeseen Third Party in Talks on Bases in Philippines," *New York Times*, July 11, 1991; Philip Shenon,"U.S. Will Abandon Volcano-Ravaged Air Base, Manila Is Told," *New York Times*, July 16, 1991.

25. Don Oberdorfer, "U.S. Base Rejected in Philippines," *Washington Post*, September 10, 1991.

26. "Implications of the U.S. Withdrawal from Clark and Subic Bases," Hearing before the Subcommittee on Asian and Pacific Affairs of the Committee on Foreign Affairs (House of Representatives), 102nd Congress, March 5, 1992 (Washington, D.C.: U.S. Government Printing Office, 1992), 19.

27. Ibid., 29.

28. Ibid., 32.

29. Philip Shenon, "How Subic Bay Became a Rallying Cry for Philippine Nationalism," *New York Times*, September 15, 1991.

30. Keith W. Eirinberg, "Preserve U.S.–Philippines Ties," *Christian Science Monitor*, September 12, 1991, 19.

31. "Subic Rises from the Ashes a Year After the U.S. Pullout," *Japan Economic Newswire*, November 23, 1993.

32. Floyd Whaley, "U.S. Navy Returns to the Philippines; Submarine Santa Fe Makes Quiet Visit," *Washington Times*, December 31, 1999.

33. "After 2 US Warships, Comes a Spy Plane," *Manila Standard*, September 16, 2003. The article reads, "Two days after three warships docked

with 1,500 US marines at the Subic Bay naval base for a joint military exercise, a US spy plane is expected to arrive today with a smaller contingent of American troops for surveillance training."

34. Gabriela Network Publishing Center, "Action Analysis: On the Intensifying Sex Trade in the Philippines," *KaWOMENan* (Spring 1998).

35. See for example, Margo Okazawa-Rey and Gwyn Kirk, "Women Opposing U.S. Militarism in East Asia," *Peace Review* 16, no. 1 (2004): 59–64; Ilene Rose Feinman, *Citizenship Rites: Feminist Soldiers and Feminist Antimilitarists* (New York: New York University Press, 2000); Setsu Shigematsu and Keith Camacho, eds., *Militarized Currents: Toward a Decolonized Future in Asia and the Pacific* (Minneapolis: University of Minnesota Press, 2010); Cynthia Enloe, *Bananas, Beaches and Bases: Making Feminist Sense of International Politics* (Berkeley: University of California Press, 2000); and Winona LaDuke, *All Our Relations: Native Struggles for Land and Life* (Cambridge, Mass.: South End Press, 1999).

36. Constantino, "The Mis-Education of the Filipino," 25.

37. Fanon, *The Wretched of the Earth*, 98.

38. Rafael, *White Love and Other Events in Filipino History,* 23.

39. Agoncillo, *History of the Filipino People,* 436.

40. One excellent example may be found in the discursive production of the Philippine Consulate General in New York, whose Philippine Independence Day Committee organizes an annual celebration based on three linked objectives: (1) to celebrate Philippine Independence in the Northeast U.S.A.; (2) to create awareness of Philippine culture among our American sisters and brothers; (3) to raise funds for charity projects in the United States and the Philippines. Nowhere does the consulate suggest ambivalence or ambiguity in its effusive rhetoric, which inscribes a parochial conception of "Filipino-Americans: One People, One Heritage." Notably, the celebration is sponsored by several large American corporations, including AIG, Costco, Western Union, Verizon, and Wachovia; www.philippineindependence.com/index.html.

41. The Sangandaan International Conference stated its objectives as such: "To commemorate one hundred years of Philippine-American relations, the conference will confront, understand, and come to terms with the fact of American colonization in order to hasten the processes of decolonization and nation building in the Philippines, on the one hand; and the creation of a strong identity and galvanization of all Filipino-Americans into a dynamic force in the United States, on the other" (Sangandaan 2003 International Conference call for papers).

42. Fanon, *The Wretched of the Earth*, 103.

43. Ibid., 100.

44. Constantino, "The Mis-Education of the Filipino," 24.

45. "Love–Hate Relationship," *Philippine Daily Inquirer,* July 4, 2006, 10.

46. While the meaning and legitimacy of "postcolonial" as a historical modifier, political naming, and intellectual pursuit is, of course, hotly contested and often dismissed, I find it useful to deploy the term here, with some intended irony. Since the Philippines (as I will discuss later in the essay) never formally underwent the process of "decolonization," its formal political status as an independent nation (having been "granted" by the United States in 1945) is, arguably, a ruse. Thus, I use the term "postcolonial" in accordance with Ania Loomba's critical summation in *Colonialism/Postcolonialism* (New York: Routledge, 1998). Loomba, quoting Hulme's essay "Including America" (*Ariel* 26, no. 1 [1995]), writes, "the word 'postcolonial' is useful as a generalization to the extent that 'it refers to a *process* of disengagement from the whole colonial syndrome, which takes many forms and is probably inescapable for all those whose worlds have been marked by that set of phenomena: "postcolonial" is (or should be) a descriptive not an evaluative term.' " She continues, in her own words, "postcoloniality . . . is articulated alongside other economic, social, cultural and historical factors, and therefore, in practice, it works quite differently in various parts of the world" (18–19).

47. "National Quotas for Immigration to End," *Congressional Quarterly Almanac: 89th Congress, First Session* (Washington, D.C.: Congressional Quarterly Service, 1965), 459, 461.

48. Public Law 89–236 (HR 2580), "An Act to amend the Immigration and Nationality Act, and for other purposes," *United States Statutes at Large,* 89th Congress, First Session (1965), vol. 79 (Washington, D.C.: United States Government Printing Office, 1966), 912–13.

49. For a spectrum of examples, see Richard Alba and Victor Nee, *Remaking the American Mainstream: Assimilation and Contemporary Immigration* (Cambridge, Mass.: Harvard University Press, 2003); Edward J. W. Park and John S. W. Park, *Probationary Americans: Contemporary Immigration Policies and the Shaping of Asian American Communities* (New York: Routledge, 2005); Charles B. Keely, "Effects of the Immigration Act of 1965 on Selected Population Characteristics of Immigrants to the United States," *Demography* 8, no. 2 (1971): 157–69; Paul Y. Watanabe, "Global Forces, Foreign Policy, and Asian Pacific Americans," *PS: Political Science and Politics* 34, no. 3 (2001): 639–44; John M. Liu, "The Contours of Asian Professional, Technical and Kindred Work Immigration, 1965–1988," *Sociological Perspectives* 35, no. 4 (1992): 673–704; and Takaki, *Strangers from a Different Shore.*

50. Bill Ong Hing, *Making and Remaking Asian America through Immigration Policy, 1850–1990* (Stanford, Calif.: Stanford University Press, 1993), 30–31.

51. Ibid., 14.

52. Lowe, *Immigrant Acts*, 7–8.

53. Lumbera, "From Colonizer to Liberator," 195. Lumbera also discusses the circulation of American cultural forms during the 1950s and 1960s vis-à-vis the proliferation of television programming, "glossy magazines and fashion and mail-order catalogues," popular film, and music (from Perry Como to Elvis Presley) (200–202).

54. Lowe makes these gestures most pointedly on pages 8, 16, and 17 of *Immigrant Acts*.

55. Ibid., 7–8.

56. San Juan, Jr., "One Hundred Years of Producing and Reproducing the 'Filipino,' " 20.

57. Cordova, *Filipinos, Forgotten Asian Americans*, 221.

58. *Oxford English Dictionary*, 2nd ed. (1989), s.v. "Apocalypse." See also "Apocalypse" entry, *The Barnhart Dictionary of Etymology* (Bronxville, N.Y.: H. W. Wilson Company, 1988), s.v. "Apocalypse."

5. "Death Was Swiftly Running after Us"

1. An earlier rendition of this chapter appeared under the title "The Meaning of 'Disaster' under the Dominance of White Life," in the collection *What Lies Beneath: Katrina, Race, and the State of the Nation*, edited by the South End Press Collective (Cambridge, Mass.: South End Press, 2007), 133–56.

2. This contention can be made only in the context of recent, engaging critical work by scholars examining gender, sexuality, and queer formations as they have constituted Filipino socialities in different historical moments and political geographies. Martin Manalansan, Lucy Burns, Vernadette Gonzales, Antonio Tiongson Jr., Allan Isaac, Martin Joseph Ponce, Nerissa Balce, and others have successfully resituated this field of inquiry such that, at the very least, it cannot be asserted that these axes of analysis are either inadequately conceptualized or undertheorized.

3. Stuart Hall, "Introduction: Who Needs Identity?" in *Questions of Cultural Identity*, ed. Stuart Hall and Paul du Gay (London: Sage Publications, 1996), 2–3.

4. Invoking the biblical story of Job, Graham told *Newsweek* managing editor Jon Meacham, "The Devil might have had nothing to do with this; I don't know. But God has allowed it, and there is a purpose that we won't

know maybe for years to come." See "Newsweek Interview: Rev. Billy Graham," *Newsweek,* March 12, 2006. Around the time of this interview, Graham's son Franklin preached to an audience of over thirteen thousand in the New Orleans Arena, "I don't believe the hurricane was God's judgment, but I believe it's an honest question.... People are quick to blame God, but you know there is a devil. The Bible says he's the liar. He's the one who wants to destroy each and every one of us." See Gwen Filosa, "Graham Brings a Message of Hope," *New Orleans Times-Picayune,* March 12, 2006, Metro section, 1.

5. White enjoyment of both mundane and spectacular black suffering is a historical staple of American national and racial formation and has been the subject of both critical black intellectual work and traditional academic investigation for over a century. Four works that particularly shaped the ideas in this part of the essay are Ida B. Wells-Barnett, *On Lynchings* (1892) (Amherst, N.Y.: Humanity Books, 2002); Malcolm X, *The End of White World Supremacy: Four Speeches* (New York: Arcade Publishing, 1971); Stewart E. Tolnay and E. M. Beck, *A Festival of Violence: An Analysis of Southern Lynchings, 1882–1930* (Urbana: University of Illinois Press, 1995); and Saidiya V. Hartman, *Scenes of Subjection: Terror, Slavery, and Self-Making in Nineteenth-Century America* (New York: Oxford University Press, 1997).

6. See Orlando Patterson's extended comparative anthropology of social death in his classic text *Slavery and Social Death.* Here I have chosen to emphasize the specificity of the genealogy of a racially articulated and juridically encoded social death in the history of U.S. racial chattel slavery.

7. In addition to a wealth of investigative journalism and public editorial commentary (highlighted in many ways by the writings of Azibuike Akaba), the recent work of Clyde Woods (University of California, Santa Barbara), Cheryl Harris (UCLA), Ruth Wilson Gilmore (University of Southern California), and other scholars has thoroughly visited on this condition of black life during and in an orchestrated civil disaster. See also the collection in which a different rendition of this chapter appears: *What Lies Beneath.*

8. See Giovanni Rantucci, *Geological Disasters in the Philippines: The July 1990 Earthquake and the June 1991 Eruption of Mount Pinatubo* (Rome: Italian Ministry of Foreign Affairs, Directorate General for Development Cooperation, 1994), 107–8; Maria Cynthia Rose Banzon Bautista, ed., *In the Shadow of the Lingering Mt. Pinatubo Disaster* (Quezon City, Philippines: University of the Philippines, 1993); and Eddee RH. Castro, "Global Effects," chapter 2 in *Pinatubo: The Eruption of the Century* (Quezon City, Philippines: Phoenix Publishing House, 1991), 78–83. For other useful references to the immediate context of the Mt. Pinatubo eruption,

see Lee Davis, *Natural Disasters: From the Black Plague to the Eruption of Mt. Pinatubo* (New York: Facts on File, 1992); and *Report of the Task Force on the Damage Caused by the Eruption of Mt. Pinatubo and Proposed Rehabilitation/Restoration Measures,* Asian Development Bank Agriculture Department, August 1991.

9. Vernadette Vicuña Gonzalez (University of Hawai'i) has written of this intersection between militarization, tourism, and war in the Philippines in the essays "Touring Military Masculinities: U.S.–Philippines Circuits of Sacrifice and Gratitude in Corregidor and Bataan," in *Militarized Currents: Decolonizing Futures in Asia and the Pacific,* ed. Setsu Shigematsu and Keith Camacho (Minneapolis: University of Minnesota Press, 2010) and "Military Bases, 'Royalty Trips' and Imperial Modernities: Gendered and Racialized Labor in the Postcolonial Philippines," under review by the journal *Frontiers.*

10. Castro, *Pinatubo,* 2.

11. Frantz Fanon's well-known meditation on "The Fact of Blackness" best articulates the notion of race as a formation of power that condenses at the sight of the racialized body, more specifically the overdetermined site of the epidermis. In one famous passage from this essay, he reflects on his experience with a white child on a public train, whose exclamation "Look, a Negro!" instantly invoked the alienation of the black body/subject from human history, displaced by a racist "historicity" of blackness: "Then, assailed at various points, the corporeal schema crumbled, its place taken by a racial epidermal schema. In the train it was no longer a question of being aware of my body in the third person but in a triple person. In the train I was given not one but two, three places. I had already stopped being amused. It was not that I was finding febrile coordinates in the world. I existed triply: I occupied space. I moved toward the other ... and the evanescent other, hostile but not opaque, transparent, not there, disappeared. Nausea ... [all ellipses in the original]" (Fanon, "The Fact of Blackness," in *Black Skin, White Masks* [New York: Grove Press, 1967], 112).

12. Victor Villa, "ADA Chairman's Personal History and Ayta Consciousness," translated in Hiromu Shimizu, *The Orphans of Pinatubo: The Ayta Struggle for Existence* (Manila: Solidaridad Publishing House, 2001), 263.

13. Elvie Devillena, "Activities of PINATUBO and Ayta Consciousness," translated in Shimizu, *The Orphans of Pinatubo,* 288.

14. Castro, *Pinatubo,* 109.

15. Stefan Seitz, *The Aeta at the Mt. Pinatubo, Philippines: A Minority Group Coping with Disaster* (Quezon City, Philippines: New Day Publishers, 2004), 1–2.

16. Ibid., 19–20.

17. San Guillermo Parish Church was built by Augustinian Friars in 1576 at the time of Bacolor's founding. On September 3, 1995, more than four years after Mt. Pinatubo's eruption, lahar flow from the volcano buried the town. The church, previously twelve meters high, was buried to half its height, and the town's fifty thousand residents were forced to flee to surrounding areas. (Account paraphrased from English language signage posted at San Guillermo Parish Church.)

18. Tagalog interview with Eck, Bacolor (Pampanga province), Philippines, December 18, 2006. Interpretation and translation by the author.

19. Tagalog interview with Michael, Bacolor (Pampanga province), Philippines, December 18, 2006. Interpretation and translation by the author.

20. Tagalog interview with Mercy, Bacolor (Pampanga province), Philippines, December 18, 2006. Interpretation and translation by the author.

21. Fanon writes of racist colonial domination that it is a constitution of "history" itself: "The colonist makes history and he knows it. And because he refers constantly to the history of his metropolis, he plainly indicates that here he is the extension of this metropolis. The history he writes is therefore not the history of the country he is despoiling, but the history of his own nation's looting, raping, and starving to death. The immobility to which the colonized subject is condemned can be challenged only if he decides to put an end to the history of colonization and the history of despoliation in order to bring to life the history of the nation, the history of decolonization" (Fanon, *The Wretched of the Earth*, 15).

22. See Mike Davis, "Gentrifying Disaster: In New Orleans, Ethnic-Cleansing, GOP-Style," *Mother Jones*, October 25, 2005; Jesse Jackson, "Eased Out of the Big Easy," *Chicago Sun-Times*, October 4, 2005, 39; Gary Younge, "Big Business Sees a Chance for Ethnic and Class Cleansing," *Guardian* (London), April 20, 2006, 33; Nadra Enzi, "Katrina: the Aftermath," *Atlanta Journal-Constitution*, September 15, 2005, 21A.

23. Ruth Wilson Gilmore, "Race and Globalization," in *Geographies of Global Change: Remapping the World*, ed. Peter J. Taylor, R. J. Johnston, and Michael J. Watts (Oxford: Blackwell Publishing, 2002), 261.

24. Bienvenido Capuno, "Historical Consciousness of the Aytas," translated in Shimizu, *The Orphans of Pinatubo*, 105.

25. Aurelio Lahut, "PNOC Triggered Eruption and the Hard Life in Iram Resettlement Site," translated in Shimizu, *The Orphans of Pinatubo*, 142.

26. Barbara Mae Dacanay, *Mt. Pinatubo 500 Years After* (Quezon City, Philippines: Mass Media Publishing Corporation, 1991), 72–73.

27. Victor Villa, "Suffering Caused by the Eruption and Memories of Old Days," translated in Shimizu, *The Orphans of Pinatubo,* 152.

28. Emelito Melicia, "A Man Went Back to Higala Near Kakilingan," translated in Shimizu, *The Orphans of Pinatubo,* 181.

29. Victor Villa, "ADA Chairman's Personal History and Ayta Consciousness," translated in Shimizu, *The Orphans of Pinatubo,* 262.

30. Ric Guiao, "Organization and Activities of CLAA for Sociopolitical Empowerment," translated in Shimizu, *The Orphans of Pinatubo,* 310.

31. This notion is concisely and brilliantly elaborated by native Hawai'ian scholar-activist Haunani-Kay Trask in "The New World Order," *From a Native Daughter: Colonialism and Sovereignty in Hawai'i* (Monroe, Maine: Common Courage Press, 1993), 79–84.

32. Jerry Cabalic, "Eruption and Ayta Consciousness," translated in Shimizu, *The Orphans of Pinatubo,* 216.

33. Statement of the Central Luzon Ayta Association issued on June 15, 1992. Quoted in Shimizu, *The Orphans of Pinatubo,* 36.

34. Antonio Negri and Michael Hardt, *Empire* (Cambridge, Mass.: Harvard University Press, 2000), 20.

Index

References to photos are in **bold face type.**

Aetas (Aytas) (indigenous Philippine group): as noble savages, 210; interpretations of Mt. Pinatubo eruption, 210; as racialized subjects, 202–4; *see also* Negritos; Pinatubo, Mount

affirmative action, post-Proposition 209, 14, 77–78; *see also* Connerly, Ward

African Americanism, 197

African Americans: and genocide, 116–19, 197; legacy of slavery, 197; and model minority myth, 72, 92

Agoncillo, Teodoro, 153–54, 173

Aguilar-San Juan, Karin, 223n

Akaba, Azibuike, 242n

Alamar, Estrella Ravelo, 224n

Alcantara, Margarita, 223n

Althusser, Louis, 36, 222n

Alvarez, Heherson, 52

Anderson, Benedict, 27, 38–39

Anderson, Warwick, 151, 152

Aquino, Benigno "Ninoy," Jr., 52, 201

Aquino, Corazon, 101, 167

Asian Americanism: assimilation, role of, 28, 54, 73; erasure of Philippine history by, 156, 178; as multicultural project, 180; panethnicity of, 156, 179, 229n; post-1965 Immigration Act, 155, 178; racial formation of, 155; *see also* Filipino American subjectivity; Filipino Americanism

Bacolor, Philippines, 1995 lahars in, 205–8, 244n

Balce, Nerissa, 104–5, 236n, 241n

balikbayan: defined, 226; as ideological structure, 57; Philippine law regarding, revisions in, 56–57; Philippine tourism of, 55–56

Bayanihan Dance Company, 20

Barrows Hall (UC Berkeley), takeover of, 12–23, **16**, **17**, **22**; *see also* Filipino American college students; Pilipino Cultural Nights (PCNs); Proposition 209 (California); student activism among Filipino Americans; Third World Liberation Front (twLF); University of California, Berkeley; University of California Police Department

Barrows, David P., 17, 221n

Bartov, Omer, 106

Bascara, Victor, 152

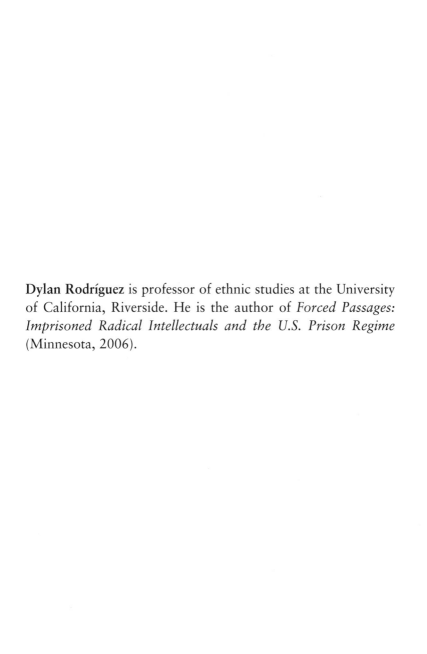

Dylan Rodríguez is professor of ethnic studies at the University of California, Riverside. He is the author of *Forced Passages: Imprisoned Radical Intellectuals and the U.S. Prison Regime* (Minnesota, 2006).